The Parents' Guide *to* Teaching Kids *with* Asperger Syndrome and Similar ASDs Real-Life Skills *for* Independence

Patricia Romanowski Bashe,
MSEd, BCBA

foreword by
Peter Gerhardt, EdD

Three Rivers Press / New York

Excerpt from *Mozart and the Whale: An Asperger's Love Story,* by
Jerry and Mary Newport, with Johnny Dodd, Touchstone Books,
2007. Copyright © 2007 Jerry Newport, Mary Newport, and
Johnny Dodd.

Library of Congress Cataloging-in-Publication Data
Bashe, Patricia Romanowski, 1949–
The parents' guide to teaching kids with Asperger syndrome and
similar ASDS real-life skills for independence /
Patricia Romanowski Bashe. — 1st ed.
p. cm.
Includes bibliographical references and index.
1. Asperger's syndrome in children. 2. Life skills.
3. Parents of autistic children. I. Title.
RJ506.A9B3335 2011
618.92'858832—dc23
2011026126

ISBN 978-0-307-58895-1
eISBN 978-0-307-58896-8

Printed in the United States of America

Book design by Donna Sinisgalli
Cover design by Jessie Bright
Cover photograph © by Susan Barr/Getty Images

1 3 5 7 9 10 8 6 4 2

First Edition

*For my amazing husband, Phil, who is the answer
to the question, "How do you do it?"*

*For my wonderful son, Justin, who is the answer to
the question, "Why?"*

*Thank you both for being the right answers to
everything.*

*And to my agent, friend, mentor Sarah Lazin,
who opened a golden door for me many years ago.
Thank you. Again and always.*

Author's Note

No book, including this one, can ever substitute for the care and expert guidance of a fully qualified health or education professional who knows and works with your child. All opinions and views expressed herein are those of the author, her interview subjects, or sources cited. Nothing in this book should be construed as having the endorsement of any organization with which the author is or has been affiliated.

Although the strategies in this book are based on the principles of applied behavior analysis (ABA), the purpose of this book is not to teach ABA, only to increase readers' awareness and understanding of a powerful science that is, in my opinion, too often overlooked for children with the AS/HFA/PDD-NOS learning profile. All children and parents described herein, with the exception of the author and her family, are fictional composites; they are not based on real persons or real cases. Any resemblance to persons living or dead is coincidental.

Contents

Foreword

Peter Gerhardt, EdD

While reading *The Parents' Guide to Teaching Kids with Asperger Syndrome and Similar ASDs Real-Life Skills for Independence*, I began thinking about how far we have come in our understanding of people on the autism spectrum, particularly those with Asperger syndrome, who were not always recognized, even in the autism community. We live in a time of unprecedented awareness and understanding of those with AS and similar profiles. We have made great strides in our ability to teach effectively in the classroom, and we have a fuller understanding of the causes of their social challenges. We have truly come a long way.

Individuals with autism spectrum disorders (ASDs) have a come a long way, but too often not as far as we had hoped and certainly not as far as they wish. As the first generation of children identified as having Asperger syndrome reached adulthood, we began to see that despite our progress—and theirs—for too many adulthood was more a chronological distinction than anything resembling what the world-at-large would recognize as a "competent adulthood." It seems we have succeeded masterfully at teaching kids to sit at their desks, factor binomial equations, and behave "appropriately" at lunch, but we have failed to give them the basic adaptive living and social skills they need to enter adulthood with access to the myriad choices life presents, exert reasonable control over factors that impact their lives, and experience actual adult competence.

What do I mean by choice, control, and competence? Think for a moment about the movie *Home Alone*. Imagine that you go on a trip to Europe and you have someone staying at your house helping your son. Something incredibly bad happens, like a volcano in Iceland, and now you can't get back, and the person who is staying with your child can't get back to your house, for whatever reason. What does your son do? Does he make a phone call for help? Does he cook? Does he know how to go out and buy food? What does he actually do as an independent adult? Does he do his laundry, does he make his bed—all those things that define your life, that make you safer, more comfortable, happier? Think about your own child for a moment. What *would* she do? What *could* she do? What *should* she do? Helping you to teach your child the skills that would correctly answer that last question is what this book is all about.

Every person I know on the autism spectrum who is sufficiently verbal tells me that we neurotypicals put more limits on them than their disability does. We're the ones saying, "That's too hard, that's too far, that's too difficult, that's too challenging." And while it may simply be human nature to want to protect our children and our students, what we are really doing is making them more dependent, less capable, and less safe. If we really are concerned with their future happiness, we need to focus on "How do I give you as many skills as possible so that dignity, competence, and quality become the defining characteristics of your life?" The less we are able to do that, the more narrow we make somebody's world and the fewer opportunities they will have to lead happy, fulfilling adult lives. It's that simple.

Educationally, for students with AS and similar disabilities we are operating with a basic misunderstanding. While we may congratulate ourselves when these students attend regular schools, get As and Bs, and seem to be "doing well" (i.e., no overtly disruptive behaviors), we're overlooking the fact that the classroom (and the school in general) is the simplest environment he or she will ever again be in. While adult life is complex, challenging, unpredictable, and demanding, few school curricula ever tackle teaching these kids the skills they need to navigate life. After all, for many kids with Asperger syndrome, theirs is not an academic disability; it's a social/behavioral one.

Transitions, however, can and do occur at any age. Some transitions are large and may involve such challenges as moving from one classroom to another, from one school to another, or from one town to another. Conversely, many transitions are small and may involve such challenges as changing from one shirt to another, from one DVD to another, or from taking a bath in the evening to taking a shower in morning. Most transitions are difficult for most people. Adaptive behavior, in the form of a repertoire of relevant life skills, reduces the challenges presented by the multiple transitions faced every day by your son or daughter. Whether your child is six years of age or sixty years of age, their ability to manage their world relies on the depth and breadth of their adaptive behavior—their repertoire of real-life skills.

I believe that parents are uniquely qualified to help their children grow up with the skills for independence. Too often in our approach to addressing the needs of individuals with autism spectrum disorder, we professionals resemble the seven blind men sharing their wisdom about an elephant. At team meetings each discipline naturally focuses only on its part: the speech pathologist talks about speech, the occupational therapist about fine-motor development, the special educator about reading, the behavior analyst about appropriate behavior, and so on. Each can tell you what areas of instruction need attention and how they can be addressed, yet rarely does anyone but the parent ask, "But what does all of this mean?" While we professionals all talk about person-centered transition planning, it is parents who are often the only ones thinking about the child beyond this semester or, more critically, graduation. The questions and concerns parents have about who their children will be and how their adulthood will be defined need to become everyone's questions and concerns.

The Parents' Guide moves the discussion forward, from "What does it mean to grow up with Asperger's or autism?" to "What does it mean to grow up?" Because despite all the differences between these youngsters and most of their peers, we know that their definition of a satisfying, happy, and secure adulthood is really no different from anyone else's.

We need to have a vision of life that is about more than successfully transitioning from elementary school to middle school, from middle school to high school, or from high school to college or a job. We need to have a vision of life that has challenge, growth, interest, happiness, failure, dignity, risk, and joy at its core every day, starting today. It's time we gave everyone the chance to embrace life as it is.

Dr. Gerhardt is the Director of Education—Upper School for the McCarton School in New York City.

Mission Statement

At every age, at every level, people with Asperger syndrome and similar autism spectrum disorders too often fail to gain access to or sustain participation in social, emotional, educational, vocational, and recreational situations they consider meaningful or desirable.

The skills that they need for independence are often mistakenly considered "simple" and "easy" enough to be learned without intensive intervention, direct teaching, and guided practice. However, we now know that having Asperger syndrome and other forms of autism spectrum disorders complicates the learning—and the teaching—of these "basic" skills.

There are specific, research-based, and data-driven strategies and techniques for teaching these skills. Most of them are based on applied behavior analysis, or ABA. While we can do little to change how someone with Asperger syndrome learns, we can do much to change how we teach.

For many of these skills, the best place to learn is at home, and the best-qualified teachers are parents and others who care.

PART I

Simple Skills *for* Complex Learners: *The* Overlooked Curriculum

Chapter 1

IS THIS YOUR HOME?
IS THIS YOUR CHILD?

Nine-year-old Sally's friend Beth just knocked on the door. Beth is the ideal buddy for Sally: kind, understanding, and tolerant of Sally's Asperger/autism quirks and odd phobias. This is a perfect—and all too rare—social opportunity.

"Come on, Sally," Beth says. "Let's go!"

"Wait for me! Mom has to tie my shoes."

While Beth waits at the screen door, Sally roams through the house whining "Mooooommmmmm!" until she finds Mom halfway through infant brother Nick's diaper change. A typical five-year-old would read her mother's tone of voice and follow her request to wait. But Sally can't do that, so she melts down, crying and stomping her feet. Overhearing the commotion through the screen door, Beth looks around nervously. She knows that Sally is "different," and she's witnessed some of these tantrums before, in class, right before Sally's special teacher takes her out of the room. Maybe, Beth thinks, Sally doesn't really want to play after all. Two minutes later, when Mom finally can tie Sally's shoes, Sally is in such a state of emotional upset that she can't go out to play. And it doesn't matter anyway, since Beth has taken what she assumes is the hint and gone off in search of another playmate, someone who is not such a "baby."

Ten-year-old Tommy has just received his first invitation to a sleepover with a group of boys at his church. Though Tommy has Asperger syndrome, he attends his neighborhood school, has been successful implementing his new repertoire of social skills during specially structured group activities led by the school psychologist, and has recently started talking about wanting to "be like the other kids." He's even made a couple of friends who share his interest in all things Pokémon.

Tommy's father, Craig, stares blankly at the colorful flyer announcing the sleepover, listing drop-off and pickup times, a night full of activities, and a supplies list. As Tommy anxiously pulls at Craig's arm, begging, "Can I go, Dad? Can I go?" his father wonders what the adult group leaders will say if he asks them if it's okay for him or his wife to drop by around bedtime. Despite years of occupational therapy and countless attempts to teach him his bedtime routine, Tommy still needs help brushing his teeth, washing his face, and attending to the finer details of toileting hygiene. Already a veteran of teasing from older bullies at school, Tommy can't go it alone, and Craig knows it. What will the other ten-year-olds think when Mommy or Daddy shows up at the sleepover? He's overheard some of the kids at the bus stop calling his son a "weirdo" because Craig or his wife waits with him until the bus comes. Either way, it is a risk. Craig starts racking his brain for a way to tell Tommy that the family has "other plans."

Sixteen-year-old Adam scowls as his older brother, Aidan, sits staring at the flat screen and furiously kicking his ninja opponent by clicking the buttons on his Wii controller. "It's not fair!" Adam whispers just loudly enough to ensure that his mother hears. "Every night, it's 'Adam, set the table'"—the dull thud of stoneware plate against the woven cotton placemat—"'Adam, fold the towels'"—a louder thud—"'Adam, load the dishwasher.'"

After a long day reviewing briefs on her next case, Christine is beat. But, as she often says, nothing that crosses her desk at work is ever as hard as what she does at home. Adam has a valid complaint—

one she's heard a thousand times. And what can she do about it? Aidan is Aidan; he will always be Aidan. It isn't fair, but life isn't fair.

"You know why!" she hisses, crossing the kitchen to stand close enough to Adam to stop him from thunking down the next plate. With her hand on his, Christine looks into Adam's eyes as she says, "You know Aidan can't do these things. You know—"

"It's the Asperger's. Right, Mom, I *do* know. How could I not? It's the reason he can't do anything around here, and the reason I can't hang out with my friends, because I have to do everything he can't."

Christine pats her son's shoulder. "I know, honey, but it's just his fine-motor skills—"

"Like what he's using right now, playing with his video game?"

Do these scenarios sound familiar?

They may if you are one of the millions—parents, grandparents, family members, friends, or teachers—who know and care about a child with Asperger syndrome, a child like Sally, Tommy, or Aidan. These are the kids who have come a long way in growing through an early diagnosis of autism spectrum disorder (ASD), kids for whom we all share high hopes and in whom we sense uncharted potential. Yet despite years of special education, intervention, social skills, and other therapies, we find these kids stuck, stranded, and left behind academically, socially, or emotionally.

Is this your child?

At every age, at every level, individuals with Asperger syndrome (AS) and similar ASD learning profiles too often fail to get access to or sustain participation in social, emotional, educational, vocational, and recreational situations they consider meaningful or desirable. Dr. Ami Klin, chief of the Division of Autism and Developmental Disabilities at Emory University School of Medicine, and director of the Marcus Autism Center, in Atlanta, says, "There is an enormous discrepancy between their cognitive power and their ability to negotiate everyday life." One reason is that they often have failed to acquire skills or learn behaviors needed to pursue socially relevant, personally fulfilling goals with no assistance or with the least amount of assistance possible. Many of these skills are often mistakenly considered simple and easy enough to be learned without intensive intervention, direct teaching, or practice.

HOW DID WE GET HERE? FROM OVERLOOKED TO OVERQUALIFIED FOR HELP

Interestingly, the need for intensive, structured, and data-based instruction and practice in these areas is well recognized and addressed for children with other forms of autism and types of learning and cognitive disorders. Little ones with autistic disorder or pervasive developmental disorder—not otherwise specified (PDD-NOS) tend to be identified while still babies or toddlers. They typically receive between ten and thirty hours a week of highly specialized one-on-one teaching—applied behavior analysis, or ABA—either in their homes or in special schools and programs.

In contrast, most kids with Asperger syndrome follow a strikingly different course. Most often, they are not identified while still young enough to receive special education services prior to kindergarten, or else their ability to speak, combined with higher scores on evaluations that favor verbal performance, places them above the cutoff to qualify for services. This means that these families lose the opportunity to have specialist teachers and therapists in the home teaching not only the child but also the parents, so that they can learn how to incorporate these strategies into their parenting repertoire.

Once kids have been identified as having AS, many education professionals view teaching the needed skills as the parents' responsibility. (Interestingly, this is not the view when it comes to children who are less cognitively able.) By the time most children enter kindergarten, the spotlight of special education has shifted from early intervention's mission to foster development of the "whole child"—encompassing not only language and cognitive skills but also self-help, daily living, and social skills—to the student. In the world of the school, if a child's particular deficit does not adversely affect the acquisition of academic skills—reading, writing, and arithmetic, in addition to the factoids kids need to survive the avalanche of standardized testing—odds are it will not be addressed. The take-home here: Mom and Dad are on their own.

Too often, the result is bright kids who make a confusing and sometimes unfortunate impression on adults and peers. These are children who can speak knowledgeably and in detail on complex topics yet leave the restroom with their clothing askew or fail to grasp simple table manners. They may have done the hard work of developing social skills yet be cruelly rejected by their classmates because they lack basic dressing, toileting, hygiene, and eating skills. They may experience anxiety unnecessarily or be at risk both at home and in the community because of their lack of basic safety skills. Most important, because these children struggle with a gamut of social challenges daily, deficits in basic skills take an even greater toll by adding to an impression of difference, immaturity, and dependence. And this is not to mention how readily these skill deficits invite teasing and bullying from peers.

WHY THIS BOOK

This book evolved over many years of experiencing as a parent and witnessing as a special educator what happens when kids have problems because they lack basic independence skills. Via internet message boards, telephone calls, conference questions, emails, online surveys, and individual interviews, parents shared their frustration and fear that the lack of what most of us would consider a simple, basic, everyday skill would be their child's Achilles' heel—the one thing about her that would push out of reach something she desired, deserved, or needed now or later in life. Certainly for any young person with Asperger syndrome, there is plenty to do and much to work on—academics, emotional understanding, social skills, and so on—and every area is important. For some children with Asperger syndrome, however, the basic independence skills that support and provide access to a wider world, or at least to the world of their choosing, are missing or incomplete. Think back a moment to Sally and Tommy. Their wanting to be with their friends, and their having found friends who want them there, too, are the really big accomplishments. How sad and unfair that both miss a chance to do what they want to do for lack of a simple, teachable skill. That's the goal of this book: to instruct parents and other teachers how to teach age-appropriate skills for independence.

WHY PARENTS?

Why not? One of the interesting side effects, if you will, of living with a child with a lifelong disability or other serious problem is a changed sense of ourselves as parents. Parents who do not find themselves having to rely on the opinions of experts to make important decisions are safe to go it alone or do just fine, thank you, with the advice of family and friends. Familiarity with the basics of child care and development and a faith that children's abilities unfold in a familiar, predictable developmental progression give these parents confidence in their decisions. For those parenting a child with something such as Asperger syndrome, the experience can be strikingly different. Even the most experienced, sure-footed mom or dad becomes a beginner when a disability is determined. More than parents of children who do not face serious problems, parents like us are more afraid of making a mistake. We research (and research and research) our choices; we talk to anyone we believe might know something. We network, we share, we commiserate. But one other thing that some of us do—and that most of us never admit—is lose a little faith in our own judgment of what our priorities and expectations as parents should be. While we might have a finely tuned idea of what constitutes good table manners or a neat appearance, or what independence looks like, the awareness of our children's disabilities and resulting challenges sometimes causes us to edge back a bit. Should we hold our children to the same standards we would expect if there were no AS? My personal thoughts ran along the lines of "So many things are so much harder for him. Can't I just give him a break on [fill in the blank]?" I know I'm not alone. Is this desire to protect my child, to spare him stress or frustration, understandable? Of course it is. But does it always lead to decisions that are in the best interest of a child with a condition such as AS? Probably not.

Having a child with a disability requires us to accept certain facts and, sadly, usually some limitations. However, it does not mean that we or our children have to settle for less than what is realistically possible.

ABOUT THIS BOOK

This book is written specifically for parents and other teachers of young people who have been diagnosed with Asperger syndrome; those with high-functioning autism (HFA), atypical autism, or PDD-NOS who, based on professional evaluation, may seem to have grown into the Asperger category; or those who have academic, social, recreational, or vocational goals that acquiring these skills would help them meet. Throughout the book, when I write "AS and other ASDs," I'm referring to Asperger syndrome, so-called high-functioning autism, and PDD-NOS accompanied by verbal skills and average-range (or higher) cognitive abilities.

Why not write a book for everyone under the autism spectrum? First, as we will see later, children with forms of ASD whose history or learning profile resulted in their receiving special education and related services through early intervention or preschool services may have had or currently have access to teachers and programs that provide instruction in these skills. Second, there exists a handful of books written specifically to address the needs of parents with children who are nonverbal, whose speech did not emerge until after age three, and/or who have continuing delays in language or cognitive skills. The best are listed under "Bibliography and Sources" in the back of the book. Third, because of Asperger syndrome's unique learning profile, parents of children with AS must prepare them to function comfortably in a wider range of current and future academic, social, recreational, and vocational settings. Further, they should also prepare them to do so with very little supervision or even none.

The book is written with the following assumptions about the young person you will be teaching, regardless of his or her current diagnosis. He or she:

- Has no history of language or speech delay at age three, or if there was such a history, the child is now considered verbal (meaning he speaks in full sentences and engages in reciprocal conversation even if it is unusual in terms of topic, level of detail, appropriate response to listeners, and so on)
- Can understand oral explanations of the skills and why they are worth learning
- Has a full-scale minimum IQ of 70, even with learning disabilities
- Follows one-step and two-step spoken directions
- Does not engage in any behaviors harmful to himself or others related to the activities we will be covering

It is important to note that while most of the strategies presented here are based on the science of applied behavior analysis (ABA), following these strategies does not necessarily mean that you are "doing" ABA, nor will reading this book make you competent in the science. Once parents and teachers learn about and understand ABA, one of the first things they say is, "That just makes sense," and it often does. However, behavior analysts bring a lot more technical training, practice, and judgment to a problem, even when the solution looks like common sense. If your child is having serious learning or behavior issues, do seek the assistance of a Board Certified Behavior Analyst (BCBA) (see box on page 110).

OUR JOURNEY

When my son was diagnosed at the age of five, my response was like most parents': confusion, shock, sadness, anger, fear. It was as if there existed right alongside my everyday reality a parallel universe, like Superman's Bizarro World, that I didn't know existed until I woke up to find my family, my home, and the life I knew suddenly moved there.

Everything around me looked the same, but everything had changed. My son's pediatric psychiatrist had said the nine words that divided our lives between "before" and "after" like a knife: "You will have to change your expectations for Justin." Looking back, I realize that was probably the kindest way to put it, and the most realistic. He did not say, "Congratulations, your son has Asperger syndrome." He did not talk about "special abilities" or which famous person with AS had done which remarkable thing. He did not tell us everything would be all right, nor did he present us with a litany of all the things that would go wrong. He didn't tell us what our expectations could or should be, only that they would change. And so they did.

At that moment, I would have been speechless had someone told me how fortunate we were. After more than a dozen years in the world of autism spectrum disorders and getting to meet, talk with, or correspond with hundreds of parents whose stories were different, I can fully appreciate the gifts of clarity and purpose we received then. For one thing, we did not waste valuable years chasing one incomplete diagnosis after another. The first doctor Justin saw diagnosed him almost immediately. We found someone whose expertise and care we trusted enough to allow us the luxury of having honest, helpful discussions about interventions and therapies, discussions untainted by emotion or pseudoscience. Early on, we made the decision to treat Justin's extreme anxiety with medication.

We also took off our blinders long enough to realize that he needed real special education, provided by professionals who understood what ASDs are about, not the generous, loving (and so very much appreciated) coddling of the private preschool he'd been attending. We lived in a good school district, where Justin's teachers and therapists had adequate resources and training opportunities. We lived in a state, New York, that had a long history of being at the forefront in special education and that officially recognized applied behavior analysis as the recommended treatment for ASDs. We lived in an area (Long Island) that boasted several universities and colleges recognized for outstanding teacher education and applied behavior analysis programs and which would soon be home to two internationally recognized centers for autism (the Matthew and Debra Cody Center, at Stony Brook University Children's Hospital, and the Fay J. Lindner Center for Autism, at North Shore–Long Island Jewish Health System). Only when I began corresponding with other parents on the Online Asperger Syndrome Information and Support (OASIS) message board did I realize how little was available to families touched by ASD around the country and how fortunate we were. Everyone we encountered in those early days offered support and encouragement. It was easy to take the big steps, face the big truths, and—most important—make the big decisions. I wish that could be the case for everyone.

WHERE ARE YOU?

Not all families are so lucky, though. When children are diagnosed, parents may get mixed messages about what AS means and what to expect. Of course, we all dream for our children a life of independence, meaning, acceptance, and love. We wish for them, as we would wish for any child, the abilities and the opportunities to realize their dreams. But if we are honest, we admit that Asperger syndrome presents challenges and imposes limitations that cannot be ignored or wished away. Despite all the research and the collective years of experience with ASDs, the ability to predict long-range outcomes for children with AS is surprisingly poor. Between best-case and worst-case scenario predictions lies an infinite spectrum shaded in grays. Though they share enough in common that we can safely draw the general outline of what it means to have AS, it is also true that people with AS are as different from one another as they are different from those of us without the diagnosis. Not surprisingly, professionals offer a similarly wide range of forecasts. For now, though, let's take a look at the two extremes.

On one hand, there are professionals who regard having AS as not that big a deal. They stress the idea of it being a "difference" as opposed to a "problem." In their eyes, the sky's the limit for your child, especially if he claims an intensive, encyclopedic, all-consuming special interest (or two or ten of them) that quickly emerges as his favorite topic to read, talk, and write about and which can surely be the raw material for a fabulous career. (This presumes, of course, that there is a job somewhere for someone whose special interest is manhole covers, the history of the typewriter, or Swedish Elvis impersonators.) You may find yourself walking out of these appointments oddly inspired and perhaps a bit envious of the patients he alludes to who all seem to hold amazingly creative jobs or big scholarships to top universities. On the other hand are the professionals who view the diagnosis as a loss and the gateway to lingering disappointment over what your child could have become were it not for Asperger syndrome. These are the professionals who greet every report of a troubling behavior, every anxious moment, with a shrug, a sigh, and a story about another patient who's got it even worse. They may also be the same people who view your pushing away the Kleenex box and vowing to move ahead toward something better for your own child as a symptom of your "denial."

Somewhere between the two, you will forge your own path. Choose your guides and your companions wisely. There is no cure for AS, or for any form of autism. While there may be a small subgroup of children who seem to have responded favorably to any number of non-teaching-based interventions, with the exception of psychotropic medication, none of these has been found effective for a significant percentage of kids with ASDs. Nor have any of them been subjected to rigorous testing or peer-reviewed studies. While it may be fashionable to disregard the experts, the fact is that the most important advances in autism diagnosis, education, and treatment are based on their work. Yes, parents and other caring civilians get all the credit for raising awareness, increasing research funding, changing laws, and improving schools. But the interventions that have proven the most effective for the greatest percentage of learners with ASDs come from science, from labs and clinics, from universities and schools, from dedicated, disciplined, trained professionals—not from Jenny McCarthy's "University of Google."

TAKE BACK YOUR CHILD'S FUTURE

Even from the start, when I felt myself caught in an undertow of opinions, options, acronyms, horror stories, mysteries, and doubts, something pushed me forward. One day recently while talking to a family member who wondered, "How do you do it?" I replied, "I think it's simple: Either the disorder raises your kid or you do."

I don't believe it's anthropomorphizing to say that ASDs come with a preset developmental agenda that, if allowed to proceed unhampered, would take you and your child places no one really needs to go. Yes, kids with ASDs have differences that make it more likely that they will say something that is perceived as rude or that they will struggle more than others to learn to tie their shoes. I get that. But it doesn't always have to be that way. We all grow, learn, and change. If every life has a plan, a fate, a destiny, how much of my son's will be written by this diagnosis? How much by him? How much by me? While it is true that I cannot and should not attempt to change who he is, I do not believe he would have gotten to be who he is—and get to who he might be tomorrow—if we had let the delays, deficits, frustrations, fears, and worries this diagnosis bestowed upon him to remain unchallenged.

Although we cannot predict any child's future, we do know some things about kids growing up with AS and similar ASDs. First, we should plan for their independence. Prognoses are probably less reliable for individuals with AS than for those with other forms of ASDs. One factor may be the high rate of co-occurring, or co-morbid, psychological disorders, specifically anxiety and depression. How any of these might develop over time—whether symptoms will intensify or diminish, how well they will respond to treatment, and what impact they may have—is unpredictable. Another variable we cannot predict is how a child will respond to growing up. Generally, those with AS are more dependent on their parents at later ages for help in a wide range of areas. Yet unlike children with other forms of ASDs that have greater impact on a wider range of abilities, we cannot assume that someone with AS will either need or want to live at home with Mom and Dad forever. Once these children reach school age, their strong showing in certain skill areas places them perpetually at risk of falling through the cracks, and this becomes a greater problem once they reach their teens and young adulthood, when services are significantly reduced. Finally, many of our kids tend to be late bloomers in one or several developmental domains. The good news is that just because something is difficult to do today does not mean that it will be that way tomorrow. As we learned in our informal online survey of adults with AS for *The OASIS Guide to Asperger Syndrome,* a surprisingly large percentage of respondents claimed to have outgrown a number of issues that were troublesome for them in childhood.

REAL-LIFE SKILLS REALLY MATTER

There is a rich literature created by adults who have grown up with and continue to cope with Asperger syndrome. We are blessed with a growing number of adults with AS who have generously shared their stories, including Temple Grandin, Stephen Shore, Jerry Newport, John Elder Robison, Liane Holliday Willey, Michael John Carley, Tim Page, and others.

Jerry Newport is an adult with Asperger syndrome who is well known in the community for, among other books, *Mozart and the Whale*, an account co-written with his wife, Mary Newport, and Johnny Dodd of his and Mary's relationship. Early in the book, Jerry recounts growing up on suburban Long Island in the 1950s as a profoundly self-conscious misfit and math whiz "who dreaded attending math class." He describes a repertoire of visual self-stimulatory behaviors, including an unusual use for his bike: "In the afternoons after school let out, I went to the garage and turned my bicycle upside down on the concrete floor. I'd crank the pedals with my hands and watch the back wheel spin itself into a blur in front of my face." Like many kids with ASDs, Jerry not only found his own idiosyncratic use for a common object, but it also caught the attention of neighborhood kids and his brothers. Jerry writes:

For me, a new chapter started one afternoon toward the end of third grade when a group of neighborhood kids, along with my brothers, discovered my upside-down bike in the garage and wheeled it out into the driveway. Up until that point, my bicycle had always served as a powerful symbol in my life. All the other kids knew how to ride, but not me. Years before, I learned to dread that moment when we'd all be goofing around in somebody's yard and everyone began hopping on their bikes. It meant that whatever time I had with those few kids who would tolerate me was now officially over.

Jerry, like Temple Grandin, grew up in the 1950s, a time when children spent much of their daily social and play time free from constant direct adult supervision. On the day Jerry describes, Alfred, Jerry's "hell-raising Eddie Haskell sort" of neighbor, decides that Jerry's going to ride his bike—now. With trepidation, Jerry climbs on the bike and listens as Alfred outlines the "intervention" as five kids support the bike with their hands:

> "Okay, Newport, we're going to walk with you and you're going to go faster and faster," explained Alfred, as he pushed and pulled my legs up and down on the pedals. "When we get going fast enough, we're going to let go and you're going to keep going all by yourself."
>
> For once, I didn't have time to consult my brain. Everything was unfolding far too quickly. I was petrified. But the farther we journeyed down Oak Tree Lane, the more I began to enjoy the rhythm of my legs pushing the pedals. Then, before I realized it, the hands clutching the bike let go and I continued sailing down the street, free as a bird, perfectly balanced. I could hear cheering behind me. I never wanted to stop moving, but at the end of the block, I pushed on the brakes and turned the bike around. My heart nearly beat itself out of my chest. Sir Edmund Hillary must have felt like this that day he stood on top of Mount Everest. Nothing was ever the same

again. Once I learned how to ride a bike, my universe immediately changed.

This passage says so much about having AS. For all the attention we lavish on special intellectual abilities, Jerry is dissatisfied with his life as a math prodigy. Dazzling feats of computation provoke his peers' attention and awe, but that fades, and some of them regard him as a "nut job" to boot. Although he often feels uncomfortable and misunderstood, Jerry still longs to be with his brothers and friends. Their unplanned, unsupervised "intervention" changed his life. Of course, Jerry knew that he was as awkward as a "drunken elephant"; he also knew that he was afraid. But this was in the 1950s, not the 1990s or 2000s. Jerry's friends and brothers were just kids. They knew nothing of the unnamed condition Jerry struggled with; they knew only that being a kid meant being included with your gang. Unburdened by the knowledge of why this skill had eluded Jerry until then, they understood that he needed it. Why? Just because.

What struck me about this story is the underlying message: Even though a skill does not come naturally does not mean that it can't be taught. But someone has to take it upon him- or herself to assume the responsibility for really teaching it. Jerry's friends had a plan—a program, I guess you could say. They had broken down the task; they saw the start point and the end point. And they went for it. They used some direct physical prompting; five of them supported the bike and then shadowed him a bit before they finally let him go. The other quality they shared with concerned parents and good teachers everywhere is that they did not let Jerry's past learning history, reluctance, or lack of physical grace stand in the way. Most important, it never occurred to them that his having some unusual behaviors or difficulty learning automatically meant that he could not or should not learn. By teaching Jerry this one skill, they changed his life. What more motivation could you possibly want to work with and teach your own child?

FROM "LET ME HELP YOU" TO "YOU CAN DO IT YOURSELF!": A HOME-BASED, PARENT-TAUGHT CURRICULUM FOR INDEPENDENCE

No one—no matter how intelligent he may be—feels very bright when he cannot negotiate the skills he recognizes as easy for others. Kids with Asperger syndrome often pride themselves on their intelligence, and, for them, praise that specifically tells them they are smart, bright, brilliant, clever, sharp, et cetera, is more effective for them than "great job" or "good work." By giving a child with an ASD the "basics" he may be missing, you are helping ensure that he will feel—and be viewed by others—as being as smart and as capable as he truly is.

You may be surprised to see some of the skills I've listed in the synopsis in chapter 3. I'll bet you consider most of them as "so simple," and you cannot recall having to actually learn them. They are classic examples of Rick Lavoie's zero-order skills, which we'll explore more in chapter 2. Think for a moment what your life would be like if you suddenly found yourself unable to button your jacket, brush your teeth well, use a can opener, or fold laundry correctly. How capable, smart, and grown-up would you feel? Welcome to Asperger's.

In preparation for a conference presentation on this topic, I conducted an informal survey of parents through the OASIS website's general message board. These preliminary surveys (approximately one hundred) yielded a glimpse of the problem's extent. It is important to note that all of these children performed at or above average academically. None of the respondents' children was diagnosed with cognitive delays.

Skill	Age Typically Acquired	% with AS Who Acquired by 9.5 yrs.	Average Age at Which Children with AS Acquire
Dressing, undressing	4 to 6 yrs.	63%	7 yrs., 3 mos.
Tying shoes	6 yrs.	45%	8 yrs., 5 mos.
Buttoning, unbuttoning	5 yrs.	88%	7 yrs., 5 mos.
Brushing, combing hair	5 yrs.	69%	8 yrs., 6 mos.
Showering, bathing	5 yrs.	48%	7 yrs., 9 mos.

As you can see from the informal survey results above, children with AS, as a group, were significantly later than their typical peers in developing some basic self-help skills.

THE BIGGER PICTURE

Imagine being ten years old, bright, and less than socially successful. Then imagine not being able to brush or comb your own hair adequately. Imagine your classmates seeing your teacher or your dad doing it for you. Nearly one-third of ten-year-olds with AS and exceptional academic ability still required adult assistance to brush their hair. Similarly, by age nine and half, more than half the kids still were not able to tie their own shoes, in contrast to the majority of typically developing kids who had mastered it by age six. Such a seemingly minor skill deficit can ruin a child's self-esteem, independence, and social standing. Kids with AS are already prime targets for bullying and social ridicule. Statistically, even a brief history of being bullied is associated with lifelong anxiety, depression, and post-traumatic stress disorder in children with AS. Dr. Tony Attwood, renowned psychologist, lecturer, and author of *The Complete Guide to Asperger Syndrome*, observes, "It becomes conspicuous to the peer group, and once they spot it, they

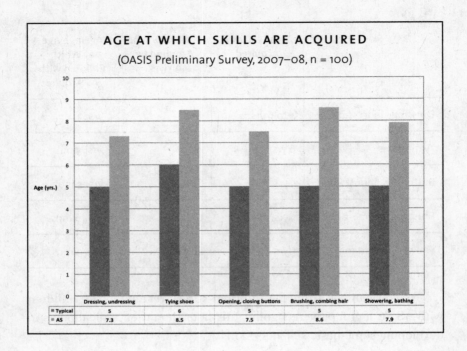

AGE AT WHICH SKILLS ARE ACQUIRED
(OASIS Preliminary Survey, 2007–08, n = 100)

Age (yrs.)

	Dressing, undressing	Tying shoes	Opening, closing buttons	Brushing, combing hair	Showering, bathing
Typical	5	6	5	5	5
AS	7.3	8.5	7.5	8.6	7.9

see it as a wonderful target to make that person feel alienated. . . . It becomes another one of the reasons why that child feels a failure, and especially in the adolescent years, when they are grappling with the concept of self and 'who am I?'. . . It also means I can't get my act together to do the things that my intellect knows I could do, and I'm not functioning at a level that my brain says that I should be able to." Clearly, a strong repertoire of basic independence skills also contributes to emotional well-being, both today and in the future.

Like all kids, those with AS grow up, but to varying degrees they will probably remain more dependent on parents and family than their typical peers. Most parents recognize that they will continue being involved in and responsible for their kids with AS all their lives. Studies have demonstrated conclusively that, as a group, parents of disabled children experience more stress than parents whose children are not disabled. Of interest here is the further finding that parents of children with ASDs experience stress that is both unique and measurably greater than that of parents of children with other disabilities. Parents raising kids with Asperger syndrome typically feel that they are actually parenting three kids in one, because an eleven-year-old with AS may sound twentysomething when talking about his special interest, eight years old when relating socially to his peers, and perhaps five when it's time to log off the internet and get ready for bed.

Parents look forward to helping a child learn to dress, make a sandwich, or ride a bike. The development of typical children is a constant, predictable, and usually smooth progression toward independence and mastery. Regardless of the task, we can expect that within a few days or a week or so, we will be boasting to family and friends about the latest accomplishment and feeling pretty good about ourselves, too. Everybody feels like a winner. Things can be very different for parents of kids with AS after they—and their kids—fail repeatedly at learning something that most kids don't even need to be formally taught. Many parents feel the stress of teaching, reteaching, and ultimately just doing for their kids the things they can't do themselves. As they grow older, kids resent being "babied," and parents get tired of being needed (and adding another layer of stress is how little support most would receive if they ever voiced that admission). However, as the child grows older and the stakes of failure rise, parents often feel that they have no choice. Having a clear plan for teaching independence skills not only benefits kids but also helps parents by allowing them to interact with their children in ways that are more age-appropriate, more positive, and more rewarding emotionally for everyone.

INDEPENDENCE FOR KIDS = INDEPENDENCE FOR EVERYONE

Another bonus: when independence skills help to organize the daily lives of kids, there is a positive ripple effect for parents and the household as a whole. Families of children with AS face a range of challenges. Parents, siblings, and extended family tend to fall into routines of accommodation and compromise that can breed dependence and resentment. Adam's reaction to having to do more around the house than his brother, Aidan, is an example. Raising a child with Asperger syndrome amply fills any parent's or family's plate. There are a number of AS-related issues that parents and families may be powerless to do much about: co-occurring psychiatric conditions, learning disorders, and difficulties in social, language, and emotional development. It seems only logical, then, that parents do all that they can to give their kids skills that will increase personal independence, allow for fuller participation in family life, and help parents conserve their time, energy, and attention for more pressing, less remediable issues.

Finally, people learn to be independent by doing things independently. By the time most children with AS are diagnosed—between ages five and seven—they have become victims of what's called prompt dependence (see chapter 8). Parents conclude—correctly in that moment and in the absence of a real fix on what's going on—that their kids need their help, that it's "just easier to do it myself," that they will somehow, someday outgrow this "stage" and one day just *know* what to do. Part of this is a natural, protective impulse, and completely understandable. But part of it is simply not knowing what to do.

This book will help you gain the essential tools to teach these skills and strategies, making them part of your child's repertoire forever.

The SurveyMonkey Results

In March 2009, I launched the first of three informal, online surveys for parents and others who care about or teach kids with Asperger syndrome and similar ASDs: the 2009 Asperger and Self-Help Skills Survey. Participants were invited to fill out three surveys, which they could answer anonymously through the SurveyMonkey website. SurveyMonkey is an online service that provides templates for designing surveys and the tools needed to create links, collect, sort, graph, and analyze data.*

*You can learn more at www.surveymonkey.com.

Participants in this convenience survey came from four groups: the original group that had responded to a request to answer an even more informal survey through the OASIS message board in 2007–8, a group who responded to a general invitation that was relayed through Long Island–based autism and Asperger syndrome email newsgroups, a group that responded to a description of the surveys and a link posted on Dr. Tony Attwood's webpage (www.tonyattwood.com), and a group that responded to a description of the survey and the book in progress posted on the home page of my own website (www.pattyrbashe.com).

As of September 2010, the first survey had received 312 responses from parents all over the world. A slight majority (57.4 percent) were from the United States; 26.6 percent were from Australia, 4.5 percent from Canada, 3.8 percent from the United Kingdom, 1 percent from the Netherlands, and the remaining 6.7 percent representing one or two responses each from Brazil, China, Colombia, Ecuador, Estonia, France, Germany, Greece, Hong Kong, India, Ireland, Portugal, Russia, Slovenia, Sweden, and Uruguay. (One respondent did not indicate country of residence.) The majority of respondents were mothers (87.5 percent), followed by fathers (4.2 percent), grandmothers, stepmothers, and stepfathers (1.3 percent each), and sisters and brothers (less than 0.1 percent each). Another 7.7 percent identified themselves as "other."

In terms of diagnosis, 87.5 percent of the individuals who respondents were reporting about had Asperger syndrome; 8 percent had pervasive developmental disorder—not otherwise specified; and 4.5 percent had autistic disorder.

The individuals respondents answered the survey about were divided by gender at a male-female ratio of a bit more than 4:1 (259 males, 83 percent, to 53 females, 17 percent).

The majority of respondents (72.4 percent) reported on children between the ages of six and fourteen—prime learning years for independence skills. More specifically, 33.7 percent represented children age eight, nine, or ten. Only 5.4 percent reported on children age three to five, and

5.1 percent on individuals twenty-two and older. The low percentage representing teens from fifteen to twenty-one is probably not so much a reflection of the need for these skills in that age group as it is of the relationship between age of children, time from diagnosis, and the likelihood that their parents or other adults will be actively seeking new information and contact with organizations and websites that would have led them to this survey.

Chapter 2

THE VERY SHORT COURSE
ON ASPERGER SYNDROME

If you are reading this, I assume you already know a lot about Asperger syndrome or PDD-NOS. For a more in-depth look at AS, see *The OASIS Guide to Asperger Syndrome*. While current statistics suggest that 1 in 110 children in the United States has some form of autism spectrum disorder, there has yet to be a head count of those diagnosed with Asperger syndrome. One 2005 study estimated a prevalence of 9.5 per 10,000, or a bit less than 1 in 1,000. However, other experts assume that Asperger syndrome affects as many as 1 in every 250. We do know that it is four times more common in boys than in girls.

A form of autism without the speech delay or severe cognitive impairments that are the hallmarks of autistic disorder and occur in some instances with PDD-NOS, Asperger syndrome commonly confers upon children marked differences in play, social interaction, and use of language. In the mass media version, Asperger syndrome is a mild form of autism typified by social awkwardness, quirky behaviors, encyclopedic knowledge of esoteric subjects, and intellectual brilliance. Unfortunately, the types of the absentminded professor and the tech geek are overrepresented in the media. Certainly they exist, but each person with AS has a unique array of skills and difficulties. Officially, AS is one of five pervasive developmental disorders; the important word in this diagnostic category is *pervasive,* for there is no aspect of daily living—from understanding interpersonal relationships to using a can opener—that may not be affected.*

Professionals arrive at a diagnosis not only by determining what symptoms or behavior someone has but also by considering those the person does not have. Since AS was the last ASD to become an official diagnosis, it can be helpful to understand how it differs from the other PDDs. Remember, however, that regardless of what diagnosis your child receives, appropriate educational placement and intervention is determined by the needs of the individual, not by the diagnosis. We do not have an "autistic disorder curriculum" or "PDD-NOS therapy."

WHAT MAKES ASPERGER SYNDROME DIFFERENT . . . OR NOT?

Autistic disorder is sometimes referred to informally as "classic autism" or "Kanner's autism." Dr. Leo Kanner (the last name is pronounced like "Conner"), a child psychiatrist at Johns Hopkins Hospital in Baltimore, coined the term *autistic disorder* in 1943 to describe eleven children whose behavior was characterized by severe deficits and abnormalities in verbal and nonverbal communication and social interaction. Perseverative, stereotypic, and repetitive behaviors are common. While some may have average IQs, a substantial percentage—as high as 80 percent—have IQs that are substantially below normal (mental retardation). In addition, these children may have unusual responses to sensory stimuli, a seeming lack of interest in other people, an abnormally intense insistence on routine and sameness, and an unusual attraction to specific objects or parts of objects. Autistic disorder can range from mild (so-called high-functioning) autism to severe mental

---

*The other two PDDs are Rett syndrome and childhood disintegrative disorder (CDD). When we refer to autism spectrum disorders, Rett syndrome and CDD are usually excuded because they are exceedingly rare and their symptoms include developmental regression that is more severe and often permanent. Generally, children with these disorders develop normally, and then experience dramatic regression; in the case of Rett syndrome, it also includes physical and neurological degeneration, and in both cases can result in death due to complications or seizure.

retardation. No two individuals have the same profile in terms of symptoms, onset, or prognosis.

Pervasive developmental disorder—not otherwise specified is widely considered a "subthreshold diagnosis" and is sometimes referred to as "atypical autism." This diagnosis is given when an individual does not meet the diagnostic criteria for another pervasive developmental disorder, or if the symptoms are felt to be less severe than autistic disorder. Although it is often said that the PDD-NOS diagnosis is given to children who present with symptoms after thirty months of age, many younger children with any ASD presentation will receive this diagnosis. A child with a language delay may be given a diagnosis of PDD-NOS rather than Asperger syndrome. This does not mean that a child with PDD-NOS is any more or less impaired than a child with AS or autism; rather, it means simply that his or her behaviors and symptoms don't fit neatly into current diagnostic criteria.

Unfortunately, parents (and some professionals whose area of expertise is not autism) fall prey to the misconception that because PDD-NOS does not include the word *autism* or *autistic*, this diagnosis is "not really" autism. They may also be under the false impression that mental retardation does not occur with PDD-NOS (it sometimes does). Professionals making the diagnosis who may be less experienced or who are simply less comfortable delivering a serious diagnosis have been known to use PDD-NOS rather than the more accurate autistic disorder because they believe they are making it easier on parents by offering something that does not include the dreaded "A-word." How often does this diagnostic substitution occur? That depends on where you live, your access to specialists, and countless other factors. I can tell you that in the decade I've been working in this field, with individuals spanning the entire spectrum, I have not encountered a single child diagnosed with autistic disorder. Some professionals believe that since the interventions will be essentially the same regardless of diagnosis and that effective intervention has the potential to dramatically shape future development, there's nothing wrong with "offering a little more hope," as one psychologist told me, by giving a diagnosis of PDD-NOS instead of autistic disorder. A more recent development along these lines is assigning Asperger syndrome as a diagnosis for autistic children with any degree of expressive language at any age, even in the absence of a special interest or in the presence of IQ scores far below the threshold for mental retardation.

High-functioning autism is not an official diagnosis in the *Diagnostic and Statistical Manual of Mental Disorders*, 4th edition (DSM-IV*), but it is a term that is frequently used throughout the community and in research. Those described as having HFA run the gamut in terms of the range of their skills and their areas of strength. Individuals with HFA may be verbal or not. For example, someone with HFA may have limited verbal skills yet be highly skilled at using numbers, figuring out how to assemble complex machinery, or spotting errors in computer code. Similarly, someone with HFA may be able to travel independently within the community, hold a job, and display social behavior that is appropriate though somewhat atypical. Sometimes HFA is used to describe someone whose symptoms, behaviors, and limitations in language, speech, and cognition were more severe before but who has made substantial, sometimes even dramatic, progress through effective intervention.

Prior to AS becoming a diagnosis in the United States, many individuals with Asperger syndrome were described as having HFA. Defining the line between AS and HFA remains a goal for some; however, practically speaking, most interventions appropriate for one are appropriate for the other. That said, a broad description of the differences usually places those who do not express a special interest, who experienced expressive language delay, and who may be more ambivalent about social relationships under the HFA umbrella. Generally, the presence of the special interest, the absence of expressive language delay at age three, and the desire for social relationships are considered distinguishing characteristics of AS. That said, there are always

---

*The Diagnostic and Statistical Manual of Mental Disorders is published by the American Psychiatric Association. Professionals in the United States who work in the fields of medicine, psychology, education, research, and others consider the *DSM* the definitive source for setting diagnostic criteria.

exceptions. It is not unusual for someone who at a younger age perfectly fit the diagnostic criteria of autistic disorder or PDD-NOS or fit the looser description of HFA to emerge at an older age with one or all the characteristics of AS (minus, of course, typical early language development). For example, someone diagnosed with PDD-NOS and severe speech delay at three may become a teenager who attends a regular high school, takes advanced placement courses in favorite subjects, and enjoys interacting with peers. Another with the same history might find a more appropriate education on a life skills track, express little interest in relationships outside her family, yet be much more advanced in terms of personal independence, moving about the community and using marketable job skills, than someone with stronger language and cognitive skills. Temple Grandin is a famous example of someone whose early childhood history is a classic presentation of autistic disorder but is today a woman whose profile better aligns with AS.

The Asperger Syndrome Profile

Unique Strengths
- Average IQ (higher or lower)
- No deviation in speech development at age three (verbal, expressive language largely typical)
- Strong rote memory
- Strong systemizing, "the drive to analyze and construct systems"
- Awareness of the social world, desire to have social relationships
- Potential to learn
- Desire to pursue opportunities (education, career, social, independent living)

Unique Challenges
- Presence of ASD symptoms such as perseverative, repetitive, or ritualistic behaviors, poor eye contact, difficulties with transitions, et cetera

- Social impairment
- Poor nonverbal communication
- Poor empathy
- Failure to develop friendships
- Language/communication problems
- Poor prosody (rhythm, pace, pitch, and emphasis of spoken language) and pragmatics (aspects of language used in a social context, aspects of communication that are not literal: tone, body language, expression, word choice, and so on)
- Idiosyncratic language (the creation of new words, or using words to convey meanings not generally accepted within the community; for example, saying "Toby ran off the track" instead of "I hurt myself")
- Very limited imaginative play (e.g., same topics, same toys, same scenarios repeated)

Other Characteristics

Over time, researchers have noted a number of other characteristics rarely listed in most diagnostic descriptions but still commonly seen with AS:

- Academic difficulties
- Atypical sensory responses
- Emotional problems
- Poor adaptive behavior
- Motor clumsiness

If there is anything typical about Asperger syndrome, it would probably be how atypical those with the diagnosis can be, both when compared to their average peers and when they are compared to one another. Of course, each of us is a unique individual, but having Asperger's commonly turns up that uniqueness and individuality a few notches. While there are some commonly accepted rules (as reflected in the diagnostic criteria), in a large enough group of kids with AS you will find exceptions and variations galore. There are people with Asperger syndrome who have no problem with self-help skills or who do not struggle with fine- or gross-motor skills or coordination. Some are exceptionally gifted athletes; others may struggle less with social skills than you might expect. Others function in the world in a way that would strike most as quite typical. As you read this book, remember that being able to do something that is described here as frequently difficult for someone with AS, or not being able to do something that is frequently easy for someone with AS, means nothing in terms of a person's diagnosis.

AS: SOMETHING TO "HAVE" OR SOMEONE TO BE?

My *OASIS Guide* co-author Barbara Kirby and I touched upon this in that book, and it's a thought that bears repeating for a couple of reasons. First, every mature person with Asperger syndrome should be free to determine for himself what part having AS will play in his life, what to embrace and what to change, what to disclose and what to keep private. For professionals in the field, it is easy to agree to support the basic right of someone to have his own feelings about having a disorder such as Asperger syndrome and to decide, for example, not to pursue interventions, even ones that could have a positive impact. For parents, however, it is much harder to grant someone you love the space to have and express his own thoughts and feelings—not all of which always support the positive self-image you try so hard to bolster. Even young people who are generally doing well may yearn for more friends or see their AS as a flaw or a problem. Someone with AS can have both positive and negative feelings about that fact, just as any of us can express the pros and cons of any aspect of our own lives (including being a parent).

So to be clear: Asperger syndrome is not "the enemy" or something that must be vanquished or remediated. This book is not about changing people; it's about increasing their opportunities in life and giving them the skills to exercise *their* choices in life as *they* see fit, when and where appropriate.*

For most of our kids, the mushrooming understanding of AS has been a positive development, fostering the creation of a more thoroughly integrated, open, and accepting society, from the playground to the office suite. The political philosophy guiding American special education and disability rights legislation also reflects the idea that it's our society's job to build the bridges to equal access in education, jobs, housing, and overall quality of life. Most parents, educators, and professionals agree that the optimal outcome for someone with an ASD involves learning new skills and new behaviors that reduce or eliminate ASD-related skill deficits and behaviors that impede a person's access to the opportunities *he* or *she* deems worth seeking.

One interesting development is a countermovement that promotes the concept of Asperger syndrome (and to some extent autism generally) as simply neurological "differences" that should not be changed but rather tolerated and accommodated in every way, to every degree possible. Clearly, there is much about AS that cannot be changed and that we all must learn to live with. At the same time, there is much that can be improved simply by learning. Some advocates for people with AS believe that even teaching basic, necessary skills is forcing someone to be who he is not. The result is a philosophy that deems it okay for a child with AS to be dependent on others for help with the most basic skills that a child half his age would have, because "That's the way he is" or "That's just Asperger's."

Under the guise of acceptance, you can find educators who cannot or will not provide the type of individualized, nonacademic training these children need and experts who suggest that your efforts toward independence are a waste of time. Well-intended but ignorant reassurances that it doesn't really matter whether Jason ever learns to catch a ball or Jessica ever learns to button her own jacket are not acceptance

---

*While this seems clear enough to many who work with or care for people with ASDs, not everyone in the AS/ASD community agrees. That discussion, however, is beyond the scope of this book.

of Asperger syndrome but capitulation to every deficit and obstacle it presents. Accepting your child's Asperger syndrome is not the same as accepting every limitation, every potentially excluding or stigmatizing difference. Accepting your child with AS is recognizing what needs to happen to support her in becoming as independent as she can, because it is only in being independent that people are free to pursue paths in life reflective of who they truly believe they are.

ASPERGER SYNDROME, STILL

If your child has received this diagnosis, you are probably aware that there is some controversy surrounding it. As I write this, the American Psychological Association is in the process of rewriting the diagnostic criteria for all five autism spectrum diagnoses (officially, pervasive developmental disorders). There is some talk that the term *Asperger's disorder* may be removed from the next edition of the DSM entirely. The arguments for and against that are beyond our scope here. Whatever the outcome, I'm using the term *Asperger syndrome* because I believe that when it is applied correctly, it does describe a particular type of autism spectrum disorder. After a lot of thought, I also believe that given the vast number of people—children and adults—who have found in the diagnosis a sense of community, a feeling of hope, and direction, the use of the term will not fade anytime soon.

That said, there is not as much difference between AS, HFA, and some forms of PDD-NOS as one would think. In addition, research demonstrates that as children reach late adolescence and young adulthood, the differences between those "officially" diagnosed with AS and those with HFA are not as marked as they might have appeared in childhood.

QUICK HISTORY LESSON

Asperger syndrome is named for Dr. Hans Asperger, a Viennese pediatrician who observed and wrote about four boys who came under his care during World War II. While Asperger syndrome was known throughout

Europe to readers of his seminal 1944 paper "'Autistic Psychopathy' in Childhood," few English-speaking experts were aware of his work until Dr. Lorna Wing first used the term in 1981 and Dr. Uta Frith translated Asperger's original paper in 1994. Even those not academically inclined will find Asperger's paper interesting. Not only does he describe four boys who would be familiar to anyone who knows the diagnosis, but his compassion and willingness to learn from them are touching and serve as a reminder that behind the jargon and technical language that we associate with scientific research, there is often a person who cares.

Experts in autism compared Asperger syndrome to the established profiles then labeled "autistic" and seem to have begun defining AS not by how it resembled other forms of autism but instead by how it appeared to be different. Suddenly professionals encountered a group who shared criteria with other forms of autism but who appeared to have bypassed the most challenging hurdles to learning and independence: severe deficits in language acquisition and use and cognition. They could tell you— though, granted, sometimes in unusual ways—what they thought and what they felt, what they wanted, what they didn't. Later, experts would realize that advanced ability in expressive speech (talking, writing) often camouflaged confounding deficits in receptive language (understanding). In the meantime, though, seemingly age-appropriate language skills coupled with an apparent absence of cognitive impairment grew into a concept of Asperger syndrome as a disorder of primarily social deficits. Since those with AS appeared to have escaped the most perplexing, disabling deficits of learners with other ASDs, in some quarters the idea of AS as "autism lite" took hold. Even when deficits in self-help and independence skills emerged, the unspoken assumption prevailed that AS made learners "smart enough" to acquire those skills on their own.

Because sound language skills and early academic skills helped these children appear different from others with autism, they were labeled "high-functioning."* Parents who hear their children so de-

---

*Though *high-functioning* and *low-functioning* are terms commonly used by professionals as descriptive shorthand, I side with the late Dr. Ivar Lovaas and others who argue that these terms are discriminatory.

scribed may wonder why someone considered "high-functioning" has a hard time learning apparently simple things such as folding clothes or brushing teeth. The truth is, no one with *any* ASD diagnosis is high-functioning in every developmental domain. At the risk of sounding flip, if they were truly high-functioning across the board, they would not have an ASD. It's important to keep in mind, then, that when you hear the term *high-functioning*, the speaker is probably referring to expressive speech and perhaps academic skills, but not all of the skills required to go through the day independently and successfully.

YES, WE NEED SOCIAL SKILLS, BUT SOCIAL SKILLS ARE BUILT ON INDEPENDENCE SKILLS

In the absence of evidence-based research, well-meaning professionals charged onto the field of social skills training as if it were the only game in town. Never mind that it would be a while before anyone accurately defined what constituted the behaviors that define having social skills, identified the particular AS characteristics that made new behaviors so difficult to learn, or created anything resembling a curriculum to be applied. Teachers, psychologists, speech pathologists, occupational therapists, pediatricians, coaches, karate instructors, dance teachers—everyone was offering social skills training to kids with AS. Most of the time, these programs adapted social skills curricula designed to address issues related to other disorders (ADHD, for example) or life issues. One elementary school placed a student with AS in his elementary school's Banana Splits group, a program designed for children of divorce, for "socialization." Sometimes program leaders simply made it up as they went along. Parents anxious to see their children doing something—anything—outside home or school, among their peers, and with a social dimension welcomed these opportunities. How well kids with AS actually acquired social skills through them varied widely, however.

Even families that succeed in getting the social and emotional problems under a degree of control find that deficits in basic self-help and daily living skills remain stubbornly impervious to change. Repeated teaching, patient demonstrations, helping, prompting, rewarding, punishing—sometimes nothing seems to work. Parents, teachers, coaches, family members, and friends—in fact, just about anyone who knows someone with AS—sooner or later will wonder, "If Eric can tell me everything there is to know about the history of military aircraft [or ants or pylons or anime or *Futurama* or rocketry or US presidents or collectable Troll dolls], why can't he just . . . ?" Fill in the blank: tie his shoes, take a shower without supervision, catch a ball, organize his backpack, set the table, do his homework, place a greeting card inside an envelope without leaving it in tatters like one of Harry Potter's self-shredding "Howler" letters.

When children do not acquire these skills, we seem to always cycle back to the "If he knows . . . "/"If she can . . ." chorus. After all, these kids have language and show a great capacity to handle certain kinds of information. Many parents and professionals seem baffled, as if the skills needed to learn and recite the name of every US battleship in the order it was commissioned were the same as those needed to make a bed. Certainly, if your child or student is struggling to learn some of these simple things, it has crossed your mind that such tasks may not be so simple after all.

In *The OASIS Guide to Asperger Syndrome,* Barb Kirby and I wrote of our own personal shifts in how we viewed our children having AS. I share it here again because once parents and others stop focusing on the mystery of these incongruities in abilities, a clearer path to solving the problem (as opposed to endlessly feeling perplexed by it) emerges.

> It is only natural and right to count a child's outstanding characteristics and talents as pluses. Doing this with AS, however, can be misleading. . . . Be realistic about your child's having AS. The first step is learning to see deficits and problem areas for what they truly are, not what you wish they would be. It helps to learn not to say, "My child talks only about earthquakes and has no relationships with peers, *but* he is very bright," but rather, "My child talks only about earthquakes and has no relationships with peers, *and* he is very bright."

THE FIRST ASPERGER GENERATION GROWS UP

In recent years, there's been an important shift in thinking, and it is reflected in such seminal federal education legislation as No Child Left Behind and the most recent reauthorization of the Individuals with Disabilities Education Act (IDEA): that effective interventions are data-driven and evidence-based. What does that mean? It means that researchers investigate a question or problem and determine what works and what does not, what is true and what is not, based on what they observe objectively—not on what they believe they already know or what they think should be so. For those working in the field of autism using applied behavior analysis, this is not news; it's been a given of the practice since the late 1960s. This explains why teaching strategies based on ABA are by far the most consistently effective and the most extensively documented of any autism-related intervention. But elsewhere in Education Land and Therapy-Ville, different customs have prevailed. The history of education, and the history of autism intervention in particular, reads like a laundry list of concepts and therapies derived from unproven theories, scientific crackpotism, and misguided, uninformed idealism. While researchers exploring other forms of autism have had decades to document prognosis and development, that opportunity did not exist here in the United States for Asperger's until the first generation that was identified as having AS entered its teens in large numbers, around 2000. Despite the tens of thousands of kids with AS around the world who transition to adulthood, the number of well-conducted research studies on outcomes for adults with AS is shockingly small. And when you realize that most of those studies look at a mere handful of participants (and then that a percentage of those included will have a diagnosis of high-functioning autism, not AS), it's easy to see why it's been difficult to get a clear picture on prognosis.

WHAT DOES THE RESEARCH TELL US?

A few years ago, several studies examining outcomes for older teens and adults with AS presented a puzzling picture. For example, in the field of developmental disabilities, historically there has always been thought to be a strong relationship between IQ and the development of adaptive daily living skills. In other words, it has been thought that the higher someone's IQ, the more easily he or she could learn and apply what I am calling independence skills. This may explain why, when AS arrived on the scene with all those shiny IQ scores, experts simply assumed that these children would follow the pattern they had seen in others with developmental disabilities. If high IQ was predictive of strong adaptive daily living skills, then surely there was nothing to worry about. Once the data came in, researchers were surprised to discover that in fact there seemed to be no correlation between IQ and adaptive daily living skills for people with Asperger's. In fact, individuals with Asperger syndrome often scored surprisingly low in the realm of adaptive behavior when compared to a control groups matched for age and IQ.

In an important study published in 2007, Dr. Ami Klin and his co-authors summarized earlier research on adaptive behavior functioning by saying, "Quite often, standardized instruments testing cognitive and language functioning and attainment are used to measure outcome, and yet, outcome studies of individuals in the higher end of the cognitive spectrum of autism . . . seem to indicate that higher intellectual potential and academic achievement cannot be seen as an assurance of better outcome in adulthood."

Asperger Syndrome Adult Outcome Studies

Outcome studies attempt to answer the question "What happens when people with Asperger syndrome and similar ASDs near or reach adulthood?" Unlike the type of study where researchers compare results between one group that receives an intervention and another that does not, outcome studies serve more of a descriptive function. Usually these studies compare participants with Asperger syndrome and/or high-functioning autism with one or more groups who are similar in age, IQ, and other characteristics but may be neurotypical, or have another type of psychiatric diagnosis (mental retardation, autistic disorder, et cetera). They typically explore questions about employment, emotional health, education, independence, psychiatric issues, and social engagement.

When early outcome studies through the 1990s revealed low rates of employment and independence among those with AS, it was logical to wonder if the real problem was not just that these individuals had grown up before awareness and treatment of AS, or that they had been misdiagnosed and ineffectively treated, or that opportunities to live more independent lives simply did not exist for them. For example, one of the first studies, by Digby Tantam, in 1991, found more than half of the forty-six adults studied were living in residential care, 41 percent were living with their parents, and only 3 percent were living on their own. But, you are probably thinking, what about now? Don't awareness, intervention, earlier and more accurate diagnosis make a difference? The answer seems to be a cautious "Yes, but . . ."

In a well-regarded 2008 study, Mats Cederlund and colleagues followed seventy males with Asperger syndrome (mean age 21.5) and seventy males with autism (mean age 24 years) over a period of five years after diagnosis. In the Asperger group, 26 percent had what the researchers defined as a "poor" or "restricted" outcome in terms of employment, independence, and acceptance by peers, despite 92 percent of them having an average or above-average IQ. The authors' conclusion: "Given their good intellectual capacity, the outcomes must be regarded as suboptimal."

Contrary to popular belief—and a big surprise to many professionals and parents alike—is that many aspects of adaptive daily living skills, play skills, and other skills needed for independence do not necessarily depend on intelligence. In fact, while IQ is usually associated with greater adaptive skills in children with other ASD diagnoses, in children with AS, average or high IQ were not associated with even average adaptive daily living skills.

Another interesting (and somewhat alarming) finding is that the regular school curriculum, which many kids with AS can handle intellectually, may not be meeting other important needs. In fact, according to Susan Williams White, et al, "Placement in regular education may inadvertently widen the gap in higher-functioning children if the teaching focus on traditional academics overshadows teaching other social and self-care skills these children need." Dr. Ami Klin points out that as such children grow older, instruction in adaptive skills should in fact be intensified. This was among the conclusions of a 2007 study that explored the adaptive skills of higher-functioning individuals between the ages of seven and eighteen with autism spectrum disorders. Despite a mean full-scale IQ of 99.4, age-equivalent scores on the Vineland Adaptive Behavior Scales in the areas of play/leisure, daily living, personal, and domestic ranged from 5.1 years to 6.9 years, a finding Klin and colleagues describe as "worrisome." They also call attention to "the need to prioritize adaptive skill instruction as its own goal in intervention."

As kids with AS grew older, it became abundantly clear that something in how people with AS learn made what we consider higher-order skills easy for them and what we consider zero-order or lower-order skills harder. As special education expert Rick Lavoie explains in *It's So Much Work to Be Your Friend*, zero-order skills are essential. These are skills that Lavoie defines as "only significant if they fail to exist." Lavoie cites basic hygiene as one such skill, noting, "It is unlikely you would say, 'I really like Ron; he never smells bad.'" However, everyone would notice if hygiene skills were lacking. Some zero-order skill deficits result from neurological "soft signs": problems with balance, coordination, directionality, and so on. Competent people are expected to possess all of these zero-order skills, but of particular interest are those that I have also called "independence skills," such as basic hygiene and unprompted completion of household chores.

Lavoie also makes an interesting point about why some of these skills are not as easily learned by children with learning disabilities:

Zero Order Skills are generally performed automatically with minimal forethought or planning. They are learned quite naturally from childhood interactions with and observations of adults and peers in social settings. Children learn these behaviors by trial and error. Impromptu "lessons" in Zero Order Skills occur on a daily basis. Children soon learn how to adapt their verbal and nonverbal behavior in a way that makes them socially acceptable to others. . . . Zero Order Skills are particularly important in regard to the routines and rituals of everyday life.

Later, in chapters 5 and 6, we will explore further how and why kids with ASDs learn and why they don't. But for the moment, keep in mind Rick Lavoie's description of how these behaviors are typically learned: through "interactions with and observations of adults and peers."

Experts initially identified social skills as the must-have intervention, usually while downplaying the need for basic play skills and independence skills. We are now realizing that in order to fully participate in the social realm, kids need to bring a lot more to the playground, the classroom, and the sleepover than a well-rehearsed repertoire of conversation skills and an ability to decode the nonverbal elements of communication. I believe we have done kids with AS a disservice by drawing an imaginary line between so-called higher-order social skills and the allegedly lower-order play and adaptive daily living skills. The fact is, it's not enough to recognize when your friend is inviting you to join the basketball game; you also need to know how to pass the ball while you talk and how to shoot a basket.* It's not enough to

---

*No one's saying your child has to grow up to play for the Los Angeles Lakers. And please, let's retire the threadbare rationalization that unless your child is going to turn pro someday, fitness and sports are a waste of time. Ignoring physical fitness is a luxury our kids really cannot afford, given that childhood obesity has increased dramatically, from a 1971 average of 5 percent for youngsters between two and nineteen years of age to 17 percent for the same age group in 2008, and that kids with ASDs tend toward sedentary recreational activities and many have dietary preferences and/or take prescribed medications that increase the tendency to gain weight.

want to be with your girlfriends at the sleepover; you also need the age-appropriate skills for each unique situation in which you may find yourself at the sleepover, including mealtime, bedtime, dressing, and cleaning up. There are many reasons why our kids do not acquire these skills on a typical developmental schedule, and I'll go into those later. For now, let's focus on how we parents may look at the problem.

Chapter 3

INDEPENDENCE: SKILLS FOR A LIFETIME

What do you think of when you hear the word *independence*? If your child was considered "independent" for his age, what do you think that would look like? What could he do for himself? Where could she go by herself? What kinds of decisions would he be ready to make? What activities could be part of her everyday life?

There are many textbook definitions of independence, but what they all share is the idea that a person is fully prepared with the skills, experience, and judgment to be an agent in his own life. In other words, he is free to make things happen without an inappropriate or limiting amount of assistance from others. While it would not be unusual for someone with AS to benefit from some degree of support in a range of situations, and there may be areas in which it would be too difficult or unsafe for her go it alone completely, the focus here is on situations where independence is both desirable and possible.

All parents want their children to grow up to be independent, but it is not always clear how we get there. Especially in American culture, we associate independence with thinking for ourselves, holding fast to our values, and other personality traits that look a lot like some characteristics of AS. So to be clear, we are not talking about independence as a set of values or a personality profile. Nor are we talking about viewing the acquisition of these skills as a sink-or-swim proposition. And we are certainly not suggesting that the ability to acquire these skills is a reflection of character. For our purposes, we will be talking about independence as a state of being: the daily condition of someone who has mastered a repertoire of skills that enable him to accomplish his personal goals and meet his personal responsibilities in safety and in comfort without relying on the help of others to a degree that is age-inappropriate or that interferes with social, emotional, academic, or vocational development.

The capacity to be independent depends on your child's repertoire of adaptive behaviors. Adaptive behaviors include social and communication skills, too, but here we'll be focusing on skills your child needs to take care of his health, grooming, and domestic responsibilities. These are the basic skills we use around the house, in school, and in the community every day.

Also, keep your eye on the word *adaptive*. What does it mean? It means that a person will be able to apply his skills and adapt them to unforeseen or changed circumstances he may encounter. Why is this so important? Dr. Peter Gerhardt sums it up nicely: "Because the world does not always play by the rules." Things happen, and plan B (or C or D or E) goes into effect without notice. *C'est la vie.*

What Is Adaptive Behavior?

Adaptive behavior is the term used to describe a constellation of skills people need for "personal and social self-sufficiency in real-life situations." Another definition to consider is the "ability to translate cognitive potential into real-life skills." Adaptive behavior includes not only the independence and self-help skills we focus on in this book, but also abilities in the realms of social skills and relationships, communication, and physical activity. The most widely used standard assessment is the Vineland Adaptive Behavior Scales, which additionally asks a number of questions about problem behaviors. Which adaptive behavior skills a person should have is determined by comparison to what is typical for someone of the same age who is functioning normally according to accepted standards. Other considerations in determining what is adequate or appropriate adaptive behavior include the demands and expectations of an environment (school, work, community, et cetera) or a social community.

It would be impossible to cover the entire repertoire of adaptive behaviors—probably thousands of discrete, individual skills—in one book. Our focus here is the skills that parents can teach comfortably at home and that serve to help kids with organization, time management, self-monitoring, and other executive function skills that might generalize to other adaptive behaviors.

WHERE IS YOUR CHILD TODAY?

You probably have some idea—either vague or uncomfortably firm—about where your child is right now in her development of these skills. If you feel you would like a more concrete measure of where she stands in relation to her peers, a good place to start might be to have your child assessed with the Vineland Adaptive Behavior Scales. This is one of the most frequently cited assessment instruments for measuring adaptive behavior, and it is often recommended for children with AS in particular, because it identifies deficits in these areas that may not be picked up as readily by other types of assessments.

Adaptive behavior is behavior demonstrating that someone not only has a skill—say, knowing how to make a call—but also has a high-level understanding of related considerations, such as when to make a call, whom to call and under what circumstances, what to say or not to say, the tone of voice to use, what to do if there is no dial tone, what to do if the phone rings, what to do if the caller asks, "Are your parents home?" or "Are you there alone?" and so on. Now, some of this might sound strikingly similar to what we think of as social skills, and that makes sense, since social skills are encompassed under the term *adaptive behavior*. The word *adaptive* describes one's ability to adapt to daily demands, to recognize the signs that a different response is the better choice, and to be able to change course and do whatever it takes to accomplish the task at hand.

BASIC SKILLS FOR COMPLEX LEARNERS

Interestingly, the role of independence skills in the lives of kids with AS has received scant attention. Dr. Gerhardt cites as one of the problems the incredibly small number of published studies on interventions for older individuals with all autism spectrum diagnoses and Asperger syndrome in particular. A search of a major online professional database revealed that while the number of published, peer-reviewed journal articles with the word *autism* in the title increased nearly ninefold—from 126 in 1990 to 1,133 in 2008—the number with the terms *employment, adolescent* or *adult, quality of life,* or *adaptive behavior* made up a mere 0.04 percent. So while from a parent's perspective the universe appears to have exploded with books, articles, websites, seminars, media coverage, and greater general awareness of ASDs, in the places where the hard research gets done and an evidence-based, data-driven understanding of what really works gets hatched, the explosion is closer in scale to what happens when you drop a few Mentos in a bottle of Pepsi. This is especially baffling when you realize that independence skills are considered among the top priorities for people with other forms of ASDs. So the good news is that there is a strong technological base, in terms of basic principles and strategies, for teaching these skills. The bad news is that not nearly enough work has been done in this area on kids like ours.

New discoveries about how minds shaped by autism perceive and respond to the world force us to reevaluate what we mean when we describe someone as "high-functioning," as kids with AS often are. Recent research confirms not only that people with autism spectrum disorders learn differently but also that many of the reasons for those differences are neurological—hardwired, so to speak, into the brain. (More about this in chapter 5.) We know that these neurological differences can have a direct impact on how independence skills must be learned—and, even more important, how they must be taught. How easily someone learns these skills has virtually *nothing* to do with how smart they are but *everything* to do with the skill and perseverance of their teachers (and by "teachers" here, I include parents). In our aca-

demically driven culture, where intellectual prowess is so highly val-
ued, it is difficult to imagine how someone who demonstrates normal
to above-average cognitive ability or who masters massive amounts of
highly detailed information cannot seem to learn "the simplest things"
or "just use common sense." The first conceptual hurdle many of us
have to clear is the idea that these skills are easy to learn or easy to
teach. They simply are not. A second conceptual hazard is the idea that
cognitive ability will save the day and compensate for a lack of exposure to the work, a lack of practice in the skill, or a lack of fluency in a
skill once it is learned. There is no shortcut. While these children find
it "much easier . . . to learn about the world," Dr. Ami Klin, chief of
the Division of Autism and Developmental Disabilities at Emory University School of Medicine and director of the Marcus Autism Center,
explains, "the problem is that they don't learn how to function in it."
For them, it's "learning by action, learning by doing," that leads to them
learning to "competently perform a task."

INDEPENDENCE: WHAT'S IN THE WAY?

While you probably could say, "If Joey didn't have AS, he'd probably be
able to ride a bike," that's not the same as saying that AS is the reason
he cannot ride a bike. A more constructive approach runs something
like this: "So far we have failed to teach Joey to ride a bike in a way that
he is able to learn." Because of AS, Joey may need to learn a different
way, but that does not mean that he can't learn.

My friend and teacher Dr. Bobby Newman believes that it is more
helpful to view ASDs as conditions resulting in an excess of behaviors
that do not serve an individual's best interests coupled with a deficit of
behaviors that do. Or, to put it another way, there's too much behavior
that is inappropriate or undesirable in a given situation and too little of
behavior that is appropriate and desirable in a given situation.

And what are these situations? Environments and circumstances
that provide access to the good things in life we all want: acceptance,
praise, friendship, tolerance, welcome, and satisfaction across a range
of settings—school, work, recreation, or social situations—over the

course of a lifetime. Changing behavior by teaching skills is not about "changing" someone; it is about removing impediments to a child growing to become everything he may wish to be.

No one seems to worry that sending a child to school will change him. But the truth is, if your child goes to a school that does its job, he will be changed: he will emerge knowing more. Little Joey is not a different person or suddenly a "normal" person because he's learned to do his homework without help or eat nicely at the table. Remember who you were at, say, age twelve. About how many of your favorite activities, foods, toys, videos, songs, or clothes are exactly the same today as they were back then? Few, probably. And if you are determined to work toward the most independent outcome for your child, think ahead. The child you first came to know the day of his diagnosis was one whose behaviors, challenges, and even skills you may not have understood. Your child that day—let's call him version 1.0—was someone whose developmental course was largely dictated by ASD. Simply by knowing about AS, you have already helped alter your child's environment, relationships, and learning in ways that probably would not have occurred otherwise. Kids with AS grow and change like everyone else.

When it comes to all but the most severely impaired individuals, experts' ability to accurately predict their adult outcomes is uneven. While some parents find that troubling, others find it a reason for hope.

When professionals talk about increasing someone's skills, often the rationale seems to be more about improving things for other people: family members who don't have to do her chores, classmates and teachers who don't have to put up with disruptions caused by her lack of organizational skills, and so on. Certainly we cannot pretend that our kids with AS do not have some effect on the people around them. That said, though, the most important reason to teach skills is to give your child choices. And do think ahead: your seven-year-old son may be ambivalent about softball, helping around the house, or dressing himself today. Your thirteen-year-old daughter may think makeup is "irrational" and friends "unnecessary." There's no guarantee it will be that way tomorrow, though. As your child matures and her world broadens, many things will change. Our job as parents is to prepare our kids for whichever path they eventually choose, even if we cannot see them there from where we stand today.

"It pays to have one's eyes on the future," Dr. Ami Klin observes. "The three things that we want our children to do in life are the things that adults [with ADSs] tell us that they want to do in life. They want to live independently. They want to have a vocation, a profession that can give meaning to their lives. And they want to have meaningful relationships."

The Benefits of Having Independence Skills

- Bolsters self-esteem, confidence, and the willingness to try new things
- Provides natural reinforcement (it feels good to feel good about yourself and what you do)
- Reduces the need for assistance and the involvement of others (parents, teachers)
- Increases opportunities to focus on more complex, difficult concerns such as socialization, school or job responsibilities, handling the unexpected, and so on
- Increases chances for future success in all aspects of life

BUILDING REAL SELF-ESTEEM

We base our self-esteem on what we can do, not on how wonderful others tell us we are. The data are in: the well-intentioned but terrifically misguided emphasis on self-esteem in child rearing flopped, even for typical children without developmental challenges. When applied to children with disabilities, who actually need to learn more and need to do so more quickly than typical peers, it is disastrous.

The Self-Esteem Debates:
What to Praise and How

Dr. Tony Attwood and other leaders in the field point out that for praise to be meaningful to a person with ASD, it must address what that person values within himself. Not surprisingly, compliments that play to a typical child's longing for social conformity, maturity, and greater responsibility—"You'll be just like your friends," "Oh, what a big boy you are!" and "You can do it by yourself"—simply do not carry the same weight for kids with AS and similar profiles. Most of them do not start out naturally seeking that kind of goal. Kids with AS value the compliment that acknowledges what many of them value highly about themselves: their intellect, their curiosity, their knowledge, their smarts.

Interestingly, about the time I began researching this book, I heard authors Po Bronson and Ashley Merryman speaking on NPR about their book *NurtureShock: New Thinking About Children.* In their eye-opening, common-wisdom-debunking bestseller, Bronson and Merryman devote a chapter to the pitfalls of a focus on self-esteem. They report that research on typical children who underperformed despite being showered with compliments for their brilliance found that rather than building self-esteem, indiscriminate praise actually had the opposite effect: it made children less confident and more averse to risk.

Where does this leave our kids? First, because of their unique learning styles, they're an exception to the rules that apply to typically developing kids in this regard. While I still encourage praising your child for being smart, don't just stop there. Be sure to include in your praise what they have actually done. Say: "That's really smart of you to remember to turn off the light when you're done," "You were brilliant coming to breakfast on time," or "You are the genius of sorting laundry." (Yes, the last one might be stretching it a bit, but you will be handing out so many compliments, you're going to have to get creative.)

Second, kids with ASDs do not always feel that they have the power to influence outcomes in their own lives, and they do not always recognize the true factors that brought about their success. Behavior-specific praise is praise that directly identifies what the person did to achieve the result: "You took your time and did a fantastic job folding the towels neatly." "The way you arranged your bookshelves is so logical; I can see a lot of planning went into it." "It's obvious that you really focused and remembered where to put all the groceries. Yay!"

Third—and here's one great tidbit from the research on self-esteem— when we praise effort, we praise something most children believe they can control. In studies of typical schoolchildren, those who were praised for effort actually put more effort forth in future tasks, whereas those who were praised only for their intelligence gave up easily—very likely to save face and protect their self-image as smart by not risking failure. So be sure to praise the effort, and be sure to acknowledge that you notice when your child tries a little harder, sticks to it a little longer, asks for help appropriately, and gives it her best shot. These are all skills, too.

Why does it matter? From baby's first steps to our great-grandparents' golden years, we value individual independence: the ability to meet one's own needs without the help of others. As children grow, we anxiously await and celebrate every independence "milestone," from the insistent two-year-old's "I did it!" to a teen's first job. If later, because of illness, disability, or age, we find ourselves less able to do things for ourselves and others, we mourn that loss deeply. We may even feel that we are not the same person we were before. Most would agree that independence is more than the sum of the countless acquired skills; it is, in fact, an important aspect of *who we are*. The irrational sense of failure and even shame expressed by those who consider themselves dependent on others is a sobering reminder of the value we place on independence and what we believe being—or not being—independent says about us.

Because of the neurological differences that define AS, these children struggle mightily to learn to do things that neurotypicals seem to learn as if by osmosis. Even if kids with AS can be taught these skills—and we're talking about everything from putting on their shoes and toileting independently to managing a checkbook and handling the basics of dorm life—they are often plagued by what appears to be inertia, disorganization, or ambivalence. It's easy to see why these children are denied social, academic, and recreational opportunities that could change their lives.

We are also concerned about how others—parents, teachers, peers, strangers—respond to kids who have these skill deficits. Despite the familiar socialization challenges many with ASDs face, most value and desperately wish to have friends. Adults with AS identify having a friend as an extremely important factor in their satisfaction. Anything you can do to help your child put his best foot forward with his peers will be worth the effort. Another reason these skills matter is that peers react negatively to children who are dependent on adults for basic help. This presents another challenge to developing strong self-esteem and socially appropriate, satisfying peer relationships. We know that while kids with AS are socially awkward and require specialized, explicit training to understand the social world, they crave friendship and acceptance from their peers. Several studies have demonstrated some of the factors that make young people perceive another child as "different": frequent removal from class, the presence of a one-on-one adult assistant, and extreme or disruptive behaviors. Although there may be academic reasons for separate teaching, adult aides, and other situations that set a child apart, many times the need for these can be traced back to problems with independence skills.

When our children need more help than they should, parent-child relationships can also suffer. When kids have trouble doing the things they need to do—in school, around the house, in their communities, with friends, at work—the fallout is rarely positive. This is especially true as they grow older and the gap between what is developmentally appropriate and what a child can do widens. When your child is always late getting ready, sloppy in table manners or cleaning his room, and disorganized to a degree that is no longer age-appropriate, patience can wear thin. Too often parents, teachers, and others get sucked into a perpetual cycle of explaining, nagging, pestering, reminding, threatening, and punishing. Proof that just telling your child to do something is a losing strategy is clearly headlined in the universal lament, "How many times I have told you . . . ?" that's served up in these moments like ketchup with fries. Worse, though, the words we do offer in these moments are not always positive or patient. Or if our words are okay, our tone and body language give our frustration and disappointment away.

You should also prepare for the day when your child demands more independence, even if right now it is difficult to imagine. For example, your child may be prone to meltdowns or need some extra support and is assigned a paraeducator or aide to assist her in school. At some point, this was no doubt a good idea; often, in the younger grades, such support is necessary to maintain a child in the regular classroom, where he "fits" in terms of cognitive ability. In the world of school, we are good at putting supports, prompts, and all manner of assistance in place. However, we are not always as quick to spot when a student is ready for more independence or for a plan to fade those supports in an organized, systematic fashion. This same pattern often plays out at home, too. Unlike typically developing children, ours are far less likely to initiate the move away from adult assistance and toward independence on their own.

THE REFLECTION IN YOUR EYES

Children derive a sense of well-being and self-esteem from how they are treated by others, and they are especially sensitive to how those they are closest to see them. As Hans Asperger brilliantly observed in his original 1944 paper:

> These children often show a surprising sensitivity to the personality of the teacher. However difficult they are even under optimal conditions, they can be guided and taught, but only by those who give them true understanding and genuine affection, people who show kindness towards them and, yes, humor. The teacher's underlying emotional attitude influ-

ences, involuntarily and unconsciously, the mood and behavior of the child. Of course, the management and guidance of such children essentially requires a proper knowledge of their peculiarities as well as genuine pedagogic talent and experience. Mere teaching is not enough.

This is perhaps the most widely quoted passage of Asperger's paper, and with good reason. Yes, socially speaking, kids with AS might tend to miss a lot, but they are acutely attuned to the behavior of people they care about and what they perceive your behavior says about them. For these children, already at greater risk for anxiety, depression, and suicide, unhealthy, esteem-eroding interactions are a threat not only to their self-image but also to their relationships with us.

Let's be honest: your decision to actively teach skills to your child puts you right on the front line for incoming frustration, disappointment, and maybe even a classic "difficult moment" meltdown or two. While it's tempting to skip ahead and start working on your big to-teach list, remember that teaching with positive behavior strategies means that everybody wins. And if you are to teach in that way, usually some aspect of your behavior will need to change, too.

Chances are you're reading this book because you have tried teaching some of these skills before. Today we're starting with a clean slate, and your contribution is believing that your child can do it.

SOCIALLY AWKWARD YET PAINFULLY AWARE

Unlike children with other forms of ASDs, kids with AS are acutely aware of themselves and of others. They may not always accurately interpret the social information they take in, but they are attuned to how others treat them. Parents we polled for *The OASIS Guide to Asperger Syndrome* were asked when they had shared the diagnosis with their child. Of 258 parents responding, 64 percent told their child within a year of diagnosis, while 28 percent waited anywhere from one to three years. Many parents wrote comments to the effect that they had not shared the diagnosis because they did not think that their child realized that he or she was "different." Interestingly, though, when we asked adults with AS, "Was there a specific age when you realized that you were struggling and didn't understand why, and when knowing you had AS might have helped?" we got a very different view. Granted, this was a much smaller sample—only thirty respondents. However, what they said reflects what many memoirists with AS have confirmed: they knew something was up at a very early age. In this sample, more than half detected a difference by age nine, and nearly 20 percent by age five. For a population for whom genuine self-esteem is so desperately needed, for whom so many challenges lie ahead, the realization that you're different and not as capable as others can be devastating.

WHAT DOES THE DIAGNOSIS HAVE TO DO WITH IT?

Why? Why does Joey or Amber or Zak or Emily do that? "That" could be anything, since our kids' behavioral repertoires are as unique as they are. Does someone with an ASD do something because her brain is configured, programmed, designed, or working in a way that is different? Or is that just who she is? How we view AS-related behaviors and challenges depends a lot on how we think of AS. Again, an accurate diagnosis is important for many reasons. It can be a gateway to a better understanding of behavior and learning; it can also point the way to the most appropriate treatments and interventions. However, a diagnosis does not always provide the best explanation for why someone does or doesn't do something.

When I asked more than two hundred parents what condition or diagnosis explained why their children struggled to learn skills in six basic areas—dressing, personal hygiene, mealtime, household, organization, and time management—from 51 percent to 73 percent said it was because their child has Asperger syndrome. Interestingly, when I asked what the professionals they had consulted believed was the cause, the percentages were nearly the same (53 percent to 71 percent) for AS. To what degree any specific condition was viewed as a factor depended on the type of skill. For example, despite all the attention that sensory integration disorder receives, it was one of the least often identified causes in three of the skill areas, but it was considered a major factor in the other three areas (personal hygiene, 31 percent; mealtime, 19 percent; dressing, 18 percent). Interestingly, parents cited deficits in fine- and gross-motor skills as important obstacles in the same skill areas (personal hygiene, 22 percent; mealtime, 27 percent; dressing, 42 percent).* Among the other conditions cited as contributing to problems acquiring independence skills were executive function deficit, attention deficit disorder, perseverative behaviors, self-reinforcing behaviors ("stims"), anxiety, low frustration tolerance, and inattention to detail.

Clearly, parents quickly learn that having AS automatically means having deficits in these skills. Again, this is good information if it helps you take a look at your child's learning profile, interests, and strengths and extract from them a positive way to teach. But too often this information sets up a perpetual cycle of using the cause of the problem to explain the failure to fix the problem. For example, we may say that Sammy does not have good table manners because he has AS. If we try to teach Sammy this skill and he does not learn it, many would also conclude that he cannot learn to have good table manners because he has AS. It's this kind of no-win, circular thinking that holds back many of our kids by leaving us with the impression that there is nothing we can do.

While it would be incorrect and unproductive to conclude that your child cannot hold scissors properly "because he has Asperger syndrome," it can be helpful to approach the problem by acknowledging the neurological differences that may be part of having Asperger syndrome and then using that information to develop both an effective way to teach and a realistic, attainable idea of what we call success, independence, or mastery.

Having any ASD usually means having a lot of other things, too. As you will read throughout this book, executive function deficits (EFDs) are very common in ASDs. One study found that 90 percent of adults

---

*Because parents could choose from ten different possible conditions and they could pick more than one for each skill area, the totals for some of these exceed 100 percent.

with Asperger syndrome experienced significant problems with executive function. Unlike some other facets of ASDs, executive function has a hand in virtually every activity of our waking lives. In the survey of parents cited above, however, executive function deficits were not recognized as a factor as often as that 90 percent figure would suggest. EFDs were only the third most often cited explanation, and were mentioned in only three areas (housekeeping, 21 percent; and organization and time management, both 32 percent). Given this, setting a goal of, say, having your ten-year-old—or even your twenty-year-old—get through an entire day without using prompts or reminders would not only be unrealistic but also set him up for failure. Similarly, it is safe to say that for many with Asperger syndrome, it would be a waste of time to devote endless hours to developing exemplary penmanship. That time could be better spent improving skills that could be improved.*

Now back to scissors. First, we reject the "because" explanation for any skill deficit. Why? Because the fact that Sally has Asperger syndrome—or fine- and gross-motor problems, sensory issues, ADHD, or any of the other possible conditions—does not really explain why she can't use scissors. Intuitively, of course, it makes sense on some level, and you have probably heard professionals who know your child say the same thing. But let's look at it a bit more critically. If we believe Sally can't use scissors because she has Asperger syndrome (or fine-motor issues, or motor planning problems, et cetera), we're really stuck—because, barring some unforeseen medical advance or a miracle, Sally will always have Asperger syndrome. If we accept the "because" premise, we're stuck, done, finished. There's nowhere left to go.

The other problem with this perspective is that it assumes there is a limit on what Sally can accomplish. As mentioned before, we may have to temper our expectations and our concept of what the best we can do looks like, but that is not something we should do at the outset. In fact, you can't ever determine an acceptable stopping point—the

---

*This is not to say that handwriting is a dead issue, either. Your child should be able to write somewhat legibly and be fluent in writing the important basics, such as his signature, address, shopping lists, phone messages, and essential correspondence.

point at which you can safely say that a skill has gotten as fluent, complete, independent, or good as it's going to get—at the start. It will evolve as you and your child move forward with teaching and learning. In other words, until your experience tells you otherwise, the sky is the limit.

Those of us who approach learning from a behavioral perspective offer what I find a more realistic and a more hopeful explanation of Sally's scissors problem: it's not because she has Asperger syndrome, it's because she has not been taught in a way that recognizes and addresses how having Asperger syndrome shapes learning and doing. At first glance, this may not seem like a big difference in perspective, but give it a moment. What we are doing is shifting the responsibility for learning from the child to the teacher and looking at a skill deficit as a teaching problem as opposed to a problem with your child.

First, when you understand some of the Asperger- or ASD-specific characteristics of learning, you can relax and be more patient. When the first approach doesn't work, or it takes days, weeks, or months to get there, at least you have an idea why. Most important, that reason has nothing to do with your child's "personality," "attitude," "motivation," "will," or some "character flaw."

Second, such understanding can help you choose the most effective strategy the first time. (Or, to be honest, the second or third or fourth time.) When you picture that laundry list of skills you hope your child will acquire, spending days or weeks going down the wrong road not only wastes time but also represents time away from success and the reinforcement—the compliments, the self-esteem boost—that go with it.

Everyone Can Learn

My first teaching job was at a small private school that is recognized nationally as a model for children with autism. This school used the only intervention proven effective to treat autism, applied behavior analysis

(ABA); had the highest student-teacher ratio possible (one teacher per student); offered intensive supervision of both students and teachers; and provided in-home and in-class parent training run by teachers from the school.

Thanks to individualized curricula, applied behavior analysis, positive reinforcement (the word *no* was prohibited in the school), and a more structured, consistent, and systematic approach to teaching than anything my son had ever received in regular public school special ed, these children were surprisingly independent. Many dressed themselves, brushed their teeth, handled age-appropriate household chores (putting away toys, setting the table, folding laundry)—all things my son either could not do at the same age or did inconsistently or with a lot of frustration and, at times, anger. As I learned to teach children to do things that most of us take for granted, I realized that my blind, albeit loving, acceptance of Justin's limitations was holding him back. My well-intended, protective love—evidenced daily by my doing for him instead of teaching him to do for himself—dovetailed with the AS to make my son less able than he could have been when he was younger.

Like most parents of kids with AS, I had read and heard the "expert opinion" that ABA is not for children with Asperger syndrome because they're too "high-functioning." I squeezed out perhaps too much comfort from the doctor's or teacher's veiled reassurance that our child was "too smart" to benefit from techniques whose principles were developed with the help of small lab animals pushing levers for food pellets. But now I know what I did not know then: that many parents encounter professionals whose understanding of ABA is outdated, limited, or just plain wrong; that daily living skills are the key; that diagnosis is not destiny. And, most important, that no one is "too smart" to be taught something he doesn't know.

Chapter 4

WHAT SHOULD YOUR CHILD
BE DOING RIGHT NOW?

From birth to about age seven, parents and pediatricians monitor children's developmental progress by tracking when they reach specific established milestones for walking, talking, and so on. After first grade or so, the milestones are less clearly defined. While we know that autism can affect the rate at which development progresses, no one has yet come up with a set of norms for children with ASDs. It would probably be impossible. Generally, though, do not be surprised or alarmed to find that your child seems to be "running late." As we will see, there are numerous reasons why this may be the case.

The skills chart that follows is a mere sampling of the hundreds, probably thousands of little skills children need to learn. Each of these is a component, a distinct stand-alone skill that combines with a sequence of other individual skills in a routine or behavior chain of more complex behaviors. The responses of the more than three hundred parents who kindly answered our surveys confirmed an important point. First, while a larger-than-average percentage did experience varying degrees of difficulty in acquiring a component skill—even after a number of building-block skills were safely on board—things seemed to fall apart when they tried to put those basic skills together in a routine or behavior chain. For example, ten-year-old Denise can wash her face independently, brush her teeth independently, and comb her hair independently. However, when she attempts to apply each of these skills in a more complex behavior sequence—getting ready for bed—it becomes clear that there is a lot more to doing things than just the physical movements that are involved. When we engage in complex behaviors, we have to plan, monitor ourselves, self-correct, keep track of time, and use countless abstract, invisible processes to make it all work.

It can be tempting to decide not to waste precious time on the little things and instead move ahead to the more complex tasks. No question about it: being able to get ready for bed fully independently is a more useful and more age-appropriate ability than being able to wash your hands. But back to the difference between components and composites.* The component skills are the building blocks of a more complex behavior sequence. So in Denise's case, the basic skills—washing her face, brushing her teeth, combing her hair—are independent. In other words, she can complete each task without anyone else's help. The composite behavior sequence, however, presents challenges. Because Denise has mastered the little skills, the next step is teaching her how to bring it all together in a smoothly flowing sequence. Learning these skills is about much more than just going through the motions. It's also knowing when, where, how, and how much. Unless a routine is built upon a solid foundation of mastered components, it will be harder to teach and learn, and the need for ongoing adult involvement and supervision will continue. Remember our ultimate goal: true independence.

Another point to bear in mind is that typically developing children move quickly from picking up a collection of discrete skills to putting them together in routines. In fact, they do this so readily that research concerning acquisition of specific skills after the age of six or seven is rare. For that reason, I've chosen to focus on complex behavior chains that link a series of different discrete, little skills in daily routines and household chores.

---

*The terms *component* and *composite* have different meanings in the study of precision teaching and fluency training than they do here.

Age by Which Most Children Acquire This Skill	Dressing	Eating	Play	Household	Safety	School	Self-Care	General
2 years	Removes pants, socks, and shoes.	Drinks from an open cup.		Imitates doing housework and other adult activities with realistic "toy" versions (e.g., toy broom, appliances, tools, etc.).	Responds to the word "No."		Begins to brush teeth with help.	
3 years	Puts on undershirt or T-shirt. Pulls on elastic-waist pants.	Eats with a fork. Pours liquid from a pitcher to a glass or cup.	Takes turns when playing games with others; kicks a ball.	Screws and unscrews a jar lid. Puts away toys. Feeds family pet. "Dusts" with a sock or mitten on hands.		Roughly imitates another person folding a piece of paper.	Washes and dries hands.	

4 years	Unties shoelaces; puts on socks correctly. Dresses but still needs help with some fasteners.		Throws a ball overhand; catches a bounced ball most of the time.	Puts soiled clothing in hamper.		Folds a piece of paper in half, more or less accurately.	Washes and dries face.	Follows basic two-step oral/verbal direction that contains prepositions.
5 years	Dresses and undresses independently. Buttons clothing that opens in front.	Can prepare own bowl of cold cereal.	Bounces a ball twice or more; does somersaults and skips.	Puts clean clothes in drawers. Makes own bed (not perfectly). Helps put away groceries in cabinets or refrigerator within reach.	Knows and can say name and address when asked.	Copies basic geometric patterns.	Totally independent in meeting toileting needs; brushes teeth thoroughly. Blows and wipes nose independently. Dries whole body with a towel.	Follows three-part oral/verbal direction that contains prepositions.

Age by Which Most Children Acquire This Skill	Dressing	Eating	Play	Household	Safety	School	Self-Care	General
6 years	Ties shoelaces. Does not need reminders about getting dressed. Prepares backpack for next day of school.	Cuts most food with a knife. Spreads with a knife.		Clears and/or sets table.			Brushes hair so that it looks brushed, if not perfect.	
7 years			Most ride a bike.					
8 years	Can choose clothing based on activities or occasions.			Helps care for pets; vacuums, mops floors.				Starts helping with shopping.

11 years	Helps prepare simple meals.		Helps wash car, dishes; organizes shelves and collections, toys, etc. Uses washer and dryer.		Files papers; organizes schoolwork.
14 years	Prepares a meal.		Replaces lightbulbs; does laundry; makes a grocery list; does basic yardwork.		

Component and Composite Skills

Examples of Component Skills

Eating

- Cut with knife
- Cut with edge of fork
- Spread butter or jelly on bread
- Pour liquid from one container to another
- Use napkin
- Order from a menu

Dressing

- Use buttons, zippers, snaps, buckles, hooks and eyes
- Tuck in shirt or blouse
- Fasten shoes (with Velcro closure, with shoestrings)
- Put shoes on correct feet
- Put on socks
- Turn inside-out clothing right side out
- Fold clothing
- Hang up clothing on hanger

Personal Care

- Brush teeth
- Wash hair
- Brush, style hair
- Use Q-tips
- Clean glasses
- Use toilet paper appropriately
- Use deodorant
- Clip fingernails, toenails

Daily Living Skills

- Make a phone call in an emergency
- Discriminate clean clothing from soiled clothing

- Find items in supermarket
- Open doors for others in public
- Make own bed
- Put away dishes
- Run a vacuum

Examples of Composite Skills
- Set table
- Make a sandwich
- Fix snacks
- Bathe, shower independently
- Follow skin care routine
- Know what to do if alone at home for a short period
- Carry a wallet, money, cell phone
- Unpack, repack bag for school

THE IMPORTANCE OF ROUTINES

All children require a certain level of structure and predictable routines in their days. For children with AS, predictability can be a wonderful support to foster developing independence. As Dr. Tony Attwood says, "Structure is crucial, because without it, people with AS either get distracted by imagination or their special interests or can't get started, and it just seems totally chaotic. When I look at successes with adults, one of the greatest criteria of successful outcome is a good job that matches their intellect, not only for the money, but because it provides structure and purpose: time to get up, someplace to go, something to do."

To improve structure in your home, use routines as much as possible. When routines are reasonably predictable:

- **They are easier to learn and easier to remember.** For children who have problems with attention or executive function, a set order of "what comes next" when they come home from school or get ready in the morning reduces the chances of mistakes due to distraction.

• **They help your child notice what he has missed and what the next step should be.** The ability to monitor his own behavior is one of the most important aspects of developing executive function and independence.

• **They remove the guesswork.** Eliminating the "what if?" and the "what next?" can be crucial for youngsters who have a history of failure at such tasks or who are anxious at the prospect of making mistakes. Predictability and consistency reduce anxiety. Children approach the task with a cushion of confidence knowing what to expect.

• **They make it easier for everyone to stick with the program.** There is a time for packing your backpack for tomorrow, a time for unloading the dishwasher, and a time for helping Mario rescue that princess.

If you and your family are comfortable with less structure, perhaps consider embracing routines in those areas where your child with AS is either struggling or you are actively trying to teach new skills. Learning independence skills can tax the patience and concentration of people with AS. Sticking to a predictable routine is one of the most important ways you can set up your child to succeed.

Of course, some of you are thinking, "We don't have a lot of routines at our house and my child with AS does just fine." If that's the case, write down everything you did every day for a week. You probably will see what behaviorists see: most of your activity consists of doing pretty much what you did the day before at about the same time and in roughly the same order. We tend not to think about these activities much, not because they are boring or we don't care about them or they are not important, but basically because *we don't have to*. Getting ready for school or work, making everyone breakfast, straightening the house, doing the dishes, taking care of daily chores—each of these is a behavior chain, a "strand" of discrete skills, like so many beads of action strung on a length of time. Granted, you may not do the *exact* same things in *exactly* the same order every day, but generally speaking, your day runs smoothly because, once mastered, routine behavior chains do not demand your full attention to complete, freeing you to focus on other less predictable, more challenging tasks.

For now, however, make a two-column list. In the left column, write down everything your child does at home over the course of the day. On the right, make a checkmark next to any of the activities that at some point require your involvement:

Initiation. Does your child know where, when, and how to start?

Planning. Does your child think ahead about the materials and time required to complete an activity?

Organization. Does your child know where to find the materials needed and can he have them at hand when needed? Does he do the work in a logical, efficient order?

Attention and prioritizing. Is your child distracted or sidetracked easily? Does your child pay too much attention or spend too much time on a task that is less important than another?

Accuracy/fluency. Does your child have the skills to execute the task in a reasonable period with a reasonable level of accuracy?

If your presence, attention, direction, or damage-control services are needed at any point in the chain, things may not be going as swimmingly as you think.

THE LIFELONG VALUE OF DOING CHORES

The idea that children participated in the care and running of the household used to be a fact of life. We of a "certain age" all grew up performing household chores, and our parents assigned them with confidence. Our parents knew that doing chores was a valuable learning experience, and they didn't have to consult the experts to determine if, when, and what kinds of tasks we would be doing, whether or how much we might be paid for them, or how to design a fancy chore chart for the refrigerator. Working together as a family to keep the household running was just what we did.

Times have changed. Interestingly, even though more mothers are holding down jobs outside the home and many parents are putting in longer hours at their workplaces, leaving less time for housekeeping, the number of hours children spend doing chores has *decreased*. According to a recent study, children between the ages of six and twelve spend only about 24 minutes per day helping around the house. That's 12 percent less than 1997 and 25 percent less than in 1981. Among the explanations for this trend: parents who don't have time for housekeeping don't have time to supervise children helping out (the old "It's easier/faster/done better if I just do it myself"); they hire help to do it; or some parents believe that their children's time is better spent on studying, extracurricular activities, or being with friends.

Of course, for parents of children with ASDs, there are other valid reasons why many miss out on learning these valuable skills. Our kids may need to spend more time on homework and studying, and their extracurricular activities may not be exactly optional (appointments with doctors and therapists, involvement in social-skills or other therapeutic groups, having time to relax and unwind from the day). And as for being with friends—priceless! In many homes, a chance to spend time with peers trumps just about everything else on the family calendar. Now stir in the basic problems with learning the skills needed to perform even a very short list of chores, and it's easy to see how too many eighteen-year-olds with AS step into adulthood unable to handle the basics of daily living. (For the record, some experts are not convinced young people without disabilities are always adequately prepared, either. Or as writer Sue Shellenberger observed in the *Wall Street Journal*: "One consequence [of children not learning housekeeping] is never more obvious than [in the fall], when hundreds of thousands of college freshman move into their dorms and promptly begin destroying their laundry.")

How do kids with AS fall so far behind? As with many other independence skills, learning for neurotypical children occurs seemingly on its own. Children as young as two typically are very enthusiastic about the idea of helping out, being a "big boy" or a "big girl," and getting to "do it myself." Starting at about that age and continuing all through early childhood, little ones watch and—crucially important, as we'll see—imitate the adults around them: sweeping with toy brooms and vacuums, washing toy dishes, wiping down the Cozy Coupe, dressing dolls, "fixing" things with little plastic screwdrivers and wrenches. As with so many other skills, neurotypical children observe, record, and rehearse dozens if not hundreds of times before they ever actually perform a task for real. Now think back to how your child spent her playtime while a toddler or a preschooler. Chances are most of her play was self-directed, idiosyncratic, and limited to a select number of toys or activities, so the "observe, record, rehearse" part of learning daily skills was lost.

Another difference is initiation. The typical toddler or preschooler is often an enthusiastic helper who can't wait to get in on the action. Up through about age six, children have a natural eagerness to learn and derive a lot of social reinforcement from being included and praised. Experts advise parents to capitalize on this enthusiasm—which seems to have an expiration date sometime in early elementary school—to teach children that helping others, having responsibilities, and being part of the family team is expected and rewarding.

To contrast again, think about your own child. Preschoolers and younger kids with AS tend not to venture beyond their comfort zones if they can help it. I have always found it interesting (and worth a study, perhaps) how many parents say that they never worried about their child because he or she "never got into things." Whereas children with other types of ASDs can be so adventurous that it threatens their personal safety, many little ones with AS are different. This is not to say that they cannot show determination and perseverance when it comes to obtaining something they want. Generally speaking, however, there's a missing curiosity about things outside a limited range of personal interest. These children also tend not to initiate—that is, ask to help, spontaneously imitate another person doing a chore, or insist on joining in.

Whether you have a few skills you want to tackle or a full day's routines, write them all down on the blank "Wish List" sheet here. Leave the first column—Priority—blank; you can go back later and prioritize your choices. In the second column, list the skill or routine. Next, check all the items that apply when you think about the impact of your child not having the skill, the impact of his having the skill, and what generally happens in situations where a missing skill is needed. Here are some factors to consider:

- **Is there a serious safety issue?** When a skill deficit leads to unsafe behavior or dangerous conditions, the answer is obvious: this one goes to the top of the list. Most parents are aware of the usual dangers, but kids with ASDs—through skill deficits, sensory input seeking, or stumbling upon a more efficient way to do something—can come up with amazingly creative but risky behaviors, such as unscrewing a plastic bottle cap with their teeth; overstuffing their mouths; eating too quickly; using sharp implements such as scissors, knives, or nail clippers incorrectly; and giving too much information to strangers. For kids with ASDs in this department, the list is endless— and not in a good way.
- **Is there a health issue?** Poor self-care and hygiene can lead to health problems ranging from skin breakouts to major infections, serious dental problems, and so on. And one child's health issues can impact everyone else in the household or classroom (through neglecting to wash hands, cover sneezes and coughs, wipe the nose, clean fingernails, and so on), not to mention create negative social repercussions.
- **Is this skill necessary for acquiring another skill or building a more complex or lengthy daily routine?** There are two types of skills: components and composites. Components are

It is a skill you can teach								
Support for teaching the skill from others								
You are ready to teach								
Age-appropriate								
Starting point for interfering behaviors								
Prerequisite for improved opportunities								
Child considers it a problem								
Prerequisite for another skill								
Health								
Safety								
Skills or Routines "Wish List"								
Priority (fill in last)								

Use this sheet to identify and prioritize the skills you want to teach.

the parts, the little skills or skill units you need to build a more complex advanced skill or behavior chain. A composite is this longer behavior chain. For example, buttoning is a component skill of getting dressed, whereas getting dressed is a composite skill made of the components of putting on undergarments, buttoning, zippering, and so on. It is critical to have each component mastered before you begin working on the larger composite routine.

• **Does your child consider it a problem?** If your child gets teased for not wiping her nose or because she cannot button her blouse correctly after gym, and this upsets her, then it is a serious issue. *If it bothers your child, it is a priority.* As you will read further in chapter 10, capturing that motivation to learn and using it to your—and your child's—advantage is the key to making this work. Being troubled by a skill deficit can serve as a powerful motivator, just as being relieved of the unpleasant consequences of not having the skill can be a strong reinforcer.

• **Does lacking this skill lead to social problems?** Or does not having the skill limit access to social, educational, recreational, or vocational opportunities and acceptance? Falling under this category are missing self-care skills or skills at a level below what is age-appropriate; difficulties with completely routine independence activities or taking too long to complete them; and lack of basic safety awareness.

• **Does the current state of this skill function as a starting point for interfering behaviors or problematic emotional responses?** Many parents are reluctant to admit that sometimes our children's reactions to daily obligations are simply overwhelming—for us. Procrastinating, getting distracted and doing something else, whining, questioning, negotiating, crying, arguing (sometimes very logically), protesting, shouting, tossing items, slamming doors—the list of kids' responses to the prospect of doing something they don't wish to do is endless, and the result can be power struggles, unsupportive verbal exchanges, or emotional outbursts (yours or theirs). Later we'll go into more detail about reinforcement, but for now, realize that whatever behavior your child offers occurs because it has a history of reinforcement. In other words, if procrastinating, crying, or arguing happens on Tuesday, it's a good bet that the same behavior was immediately followed by something your child considered worth his while Monday or before. It's not that our kids are being "manipulative." Let's accept the premise that doing these tasks can be extremely hard work mentally, physically, and emotionally for some of our children. What is the consequence of acting out? Usually it's to be relieved of the task, given lots of extra help doing it, or allowed to stop after making a substandard or incomplete effort. Your kid is not being a bad person in trying to avoid something he finds frustrating and taxing; he's being human. If nothing else, these types of reactions should highlight again how important it is to teach these skills so that they are, if not easy, at least much easier for kids to carry out.

If emotional reactions disrupt your home, you will have an extra to-do on your teaching list: learning not to engage. Chapter 5 delves into that in more detail. For now, just remember that you really can change your child's behavior by changing your own. When you're facing what Brenda Smith Myles tactfully terms "difficult moments" and you feel hopeless or powerless, don't give up. There is a way around it: giving your child the skills, then making it worth his while to use them.

• **Is it age-appropriate to have this skill?** In other words, compared to the recognized developmental timetables for these skills, or simply by comparison to siblings and peers, where is your child? Granted, just being behind should not in and of itself be cause for alarm. However, how far behind is *too* far behind? This depends on several factors: the type of skill, how it impacts your child's daily life, and how acquiring this skill would improve daily living. For example, an eleven-year-old's lackadaisical attempts to dust her room are easier to let slide for now than her poor personal hygiene.

Also consider age-appropriateness from another angle. Sometimes when a child with a disability has trouble mastering the basics—the things that most others his age do easily—parents focus instead on teaching a more advanced skill in an unrelated domain. For example, a nine-year-old girl with AS has the self-care skills of a toddler but a precocious ability in math. Rather than devote intensive intervention to eliminating the self-care deficits, parents and others concerned choose to focus on pushing the math envelope because "it will get her into college someday." Or teachers decide that instead of addressing the fact that a bright, verbal six-year-old boy eats everything with his fingers, they will further encourage his professorish special interest in advanced rocketry because "it makes him happy and keeps him from having outbursts."

News flash from the land of rude awakenings: *no one* lacking age-appropriate self-care or eating skills will last long anywhere, regardless of their impressive intellectual gifts or other skills. Is focusing on the skills or talents a child already has a way to make up for things the child cannot do? I'm not sure; I know only that I've seen this happen too many times to chalk it up to coincidence. Sure, it feels great to point to things your child can do, especially when what he can't do is so often the focus of family members, friends, teachers, and sometimes even strangers. But my advice? Don't do it. If your child happens to pick up a more advanced skill on her own, that's great. There's nothing you can do to prevent it and no way she can unlearn it, anyway.

Remember that we all acquire skills in a particular order; complex skills usually build upon simpler, previously mastered skills. An obvious example is the crawl-stand-walk-run sequence. Another is the order in which a child's grasp develops from grabbing a crayon in his fist to the "tripod" grasp that is the most functional for handwriting. When it comes to skills that involve physical movement and coordination, it is futile to try teaching something that developmentally your child simply will not be able to do easily, no matter how much practice. Sometimes the brain and body simply are not ready to do certain things.

• **Are you ready to teach the skill?** Chapters 7 and 8 outline the tools parents need to become great teachers. For now, however, ask yourself if you are ready to set aside time consistently every day for the next week or more to teach this skill to mastery. Remember, we are setting up our kids to succeed. In the process of teaching, we should also be modeling a degree of persistence, frustration tolerance, and patience. Stop-and-start teaching is ineffective and frustrating. Consider for a moment: if you give up, or if you merely tackle the problem in fits and starts, what message does that send to your child? For kids with low frustration tolerance, little patience, and an unhappy history with these skills, *you need to teach more than the skill to truly teach the skill.* You can do that by making the time to work on the skill together, persevering when the going gets bumpy or progress is inconsistent, and letting your child know that you recognize and applaud her effort.

• **Whom else can you count on for support in teaching this skill?** In an ideal world, everyone involved with your child would follow your lead and use appropriate opportunities to teach or reinforce the skill your child is working on. Alas, while you're out enjoying date night, Grandma may not be so firm with Alex on the rule about clearing the dishes from the table before he turns on the Xbox. Though consistency is extremely important (more on that in chapter 7), slips are inevitable. Better to plan for them than to delay teaching a skill because you're waiting for the perfect time. What you do want to avoid wherever possible is teaching a skill when or where your teaching will be seriously undermined. For example, if you are teaching your ten-year-old daughter to wash and dry her hands thoroughly after using the restroom, you do not want her teacher at school inviting her to use the classroom Purell dispenser instead. In chapter 5, we'll talk more about ways to bring others in your child's life on board.

• **Is teaching this skill something that can be presented like a recipe?** One of the best examples of a blueprint for teaching something new is a good recipe. So ask yourself: is this skill or routine something you can break down and describe in a list like a recipe (see box)?

The Recipe for Teaching an Independence Skill

A good recipe reflects a great understanding of what people need to learn and how they learn it—how to bake that cake. The organization of a good recipe is also a fantastic template for any task that requires executive function skills.

Think for a moment about a recipe. What does it tell you?

- The environmental conditions required
- Approximately how long it should take
- The equipment, ingredients, and techniques that you will use
- What to do with each and in what order
- When to begin and when to complete each step
- What to expect at the end of each step
- What the final result will be and how you will know that you are done

---

Thinking of a skill or a routine you would like to teach in these terms not only helps you to conceptualize the challenge—and, ideally, some solutions—but also prevents you from viewing a child's emotional responses or attitudes as "skills" that need improving. Someone who doesn't understand ASDs might attribute a child's alleged bad attitude, laziness, inattention, and so on to something he hasn't learned to do yet: self-regulate, appropriately express his emotions, and so on.

Granted, those are valid developmental milestones all kids need to reach. However, when we're talking about teaching concrete skills, we need to dig a little deeper.

I can't stress it enough: for some of our kids, learning can be extremely hard, probably harder than you or I can even imagine. For them, a so-called bad attitude is a logical response, a symptom of the real problem: *lack of skill*. The job, then, is to improve the skill. If the skill that is lacking cannot be broken down recipe-style, you may be facing an emotional issue or more serious problem with learning, not a simple skill deficit. (For more on possible associated psychiatric conditions and learning disabilities you may need to consider, see chapters 5 and 6.)

ONWARD

Sure, it looks like a big job. It *is* a big job. With the tools and the know-how, though, you can do it. No matter how daunting the task ahead seems, remember that no one works harder than our kids! Remind yourself that the reason you're embarking on this teaching journey is not simply to teach your child but also to make some aspects of his day easier, less frustrating, and more within the realm of his personal control. This is the beginning of the gift of independence. Let's go.

Chapter 5

"THE USUAL SUSPECTS": COMMON ROADBLOCKS AND HOW TO WORK WITH THEM—OR AROUND THEM

Kids with Asperger syndrome and other ASDs do learn differently, but I propose that instead of viewing them as challenged in terms of how they learn, we focus on the real problem: how challenged most of us—even professionals—too often are when it comes to teaching them.

This chapter focuses on the specific neurological differences or anomalies that may contribute to many skill deficits. While there is no direct treatment or cure for any of these problems, recognizing which of them is interfering with or adversely affecting a child's ability to execute a movement, task, or skill can help you identify which approach may be most effective—hand-over-hand prompting, a visual list or schedule, or video modeling of the skill, for example.

By now, surely, you have amassed a trove of suggestions from professionals and others. Being a conscientious parent, you give several a try, only to discover that sometimes one works, and sometimes none do. Or the "surefire" approach touted by a teacher or therapist or savvy parent does nothing for you. As you move forward with teaching your child, keep in mind that every strategy discussed here, like most of those that professionals offer you, has been effective somewhere, sometime, for someone. What we often encounter when dealing with a child with an ASD is that *what works for most does not always work for all*. Not only is every child different, but the underlying contributors to the problem may be different, too, and those factors may even change, depending on the time or the situation.

Let's say we have three kids learning to brush their teeth and, co-incidentally, they all do the same thing: put the toothpaste-covered toothbrushes in their mouths, "brush" for three seconds, then rinse the toothbrush and announce that they're done. What's happening? By now, you probably have a good idea of what types of deficits your child has in areas such as attention, fine- and gross-motor skills, executive function, and so on. But that doesn't mean you should always pin the tail on the same donkey.

Yes, Arielle does have fine-motor issues, but she also has a sensory problem with the toothpaste.

Kevin is fine with the toothpaste—he just gets very easily distracted looking at himself in the bathroom mirror.

Maria has none of those problems, but she says she's through brushing because no one has taught her to recognize when she really is done.

Clearly, there is no one-size-fits-all answer that will support teaching the skill equally well to all three kids.

RETHINKING THE LEARNING MOST OF US FORGET, OR TEACHING SOMETHING YOU THINK YOU "JUST KNOW"

While the individual skills that combine to maintain independence seem simple, basic, and easy, it is only because the learning processes and neurological powers involved are extremely complex and—when they function normally—allow us to learn passively, seemingly by osmosis. These are the zero-order skills that we learned about in chapter 1. People who don't have ASDs are not even aware of these processes operating seamlessly in the mind's background, leaving them free to accomplish most daily tasks without consciously thinking about them. This keeps the simple things simple and makes our higher cognitive tools available to apply to tasks that are new, complex, or unexpected.

What makes some stuff easy compared to, say, learning to file your own tax return or decorate the perfect wedding cake is that a typical brain comes hardwired in a certain way, ready to learn everything from smiling that first time at a loving face to using higher-order language to fib about the missing cookies. Typically, this is some of the built-in programming that does not come as standard equipment for many of our friends with ASDs.

People with any form of autism not only learn differently but also often experience extreme difficulty *especially* when learning the basics. And—in what has proved the big surprise for those of us concerned with kids with Asperger syndrome—cognitive ability has little or no effect on how easily these skills are acquired. Until recently, most professionals and parents assumed these skills would develop over time, but the evidence is indisputable: for many with AS, daily living skills do not take root and grow on their own. Therefore, people with AS often need to learn these skills actively (as opposed to passively), and they need to be taught these skills in ways that replace, mimic, prompt, override, or impose missing order on the learning processes that do not work sufficiently well at the neurological level.

Simply having an ASD diagnosis is associated with difficulties in learning a wide range of skills across several domains. Further, as you can see in chapter 6, we know that ASDs commonly are associated with psychiatric conditions and learning disabilities that throw up their own roadblocks to successful teaching and learning. In this section, however, we're going to look at several areas in which deficits, delays, or differences exert an outsized impact on independence skills.

This chapter will introduce you to a cast of diagnoses, conditions, disorders, and dysfunctions that can complicate learning. I like to refer to them as "the usual suspects." Note that none of these is called "Asperger syndrome" or "nonverbal learning disability" or "ADHD." What we are exploring here is what may be going on in the brain and in the communication between brain and body that seems to get in the way of easy learning and fluid performance. (The strategies that we'll be looking at may also help you work around other co-occurring disorders.)

I think of the usual suspects as disorders related to invisible "helpers" we all depend on without being aware most of the time that they even exist. They transform "what we know" into "things we can do" with little or no conscious input from us. In fact, these helpers tend to be noticed only when they are not present or don't run correctly. There's no single part of the brain responsible for any of these, and even the world's leading experts continue to debate which are most responsible for specific skill deficits. For example, in the past few years, mirror neurons have become a hot topic in the science sections of newspapers and magazines. Some articles have even gone so far as to report that mirror neuron deficits may be the key to understanding autism. But, as Dr. Ami Klin points out, these findings are not accepted everywhere. While some research suggests that such deficits are found among people with ASDs and gives us some idea of how they impact daily living, none of these explains it all. If anything, the more we learn about the neurological complexity of autism in all its forms, the more likely it seems that no single explanation will ever suffice for everyone.

When it comes to trying to develop interventions, I've always been drawn to the scientific research over the anecdotal report because, in the end, autism is the result of anomalies in the structure and/or function of the brain. Understanding some of these differences, even in the most basic layman's terms, has given me a deeper understanding and appreciation of the struggles our kids face. And when teaching feels daunting, having some insight into why that is so makes it easier to approach the job with patience and understanding. Remember: the presence of any of these will certainly complicate your work teaching your child. The good news is that they do not make it impossible. Assume they will always be present in some form for your child, and remind yourself that in learning to acknowledge and maneuver around these challenges now, you will be teaching your child invaluable self-awareness, self-advocacy, and other important strategies—physical, cognitive, and emotional—he can use forever.

THEORY OF MIND DEFICIT

Theory of mind is but one of several neurological concepts that attempt to explain an important difference between people with ASDs and those without it. Dr. Simon Baron-Cohen, who introduced the concept of "mindblindness" in 1990, further expanded upon it in later papers and in his book *Mindblindness: An Essay on Autism and Theory of Mind*. Baron-Cohen opens his book with one of the clearest descriptions of what it means to lack a strong theory of mind:

> Imagine what your world would be like if you were aware of physical things but were blind to the existence of mental things. I mean, of course, blind to things like thoughts, beliefs, knowledge, desires, and intentions, which for most of us self-evidently underlie behavior.

People with a strong theory of mind automatically understand that others have feelings, thoughts, desires, and needs different from their own and are continually adjusting and fine-tuning their behavior accordingly. In contrast, individuals with AS will tend toward interpreting the words and actions of others from their own limited perspective. That perspective is often based on the literal meaning of words and a basic, sometimes incomplete, interpretation of people's words, actions, gestures, voice tone, and other nonverbal cues. Not surprisingly, kids with AS sometimes misinterpret and misunderstand.

Though intervention for theory of mind deficits lies more in the realm of social skills and somewhat outside the scope of this book, a lack of theory of mind often plays a significant role in reasons why some kids with Asperger syndrome are not motivated to learn certain skills or do not follow through with them once they learn them. A classic example would be a child who resists learning how to brush his teeth properly because he does not recognize how others might respond to his unpleasant breath. It is important to bear in mind that we engage in many self-help and grooming activities in part because of how we expect others will respond to us if we do or don't. Let's face it: few of us brush our teeth because we like the taste of toothpaste or find it a lot of fun. Choices children make due to deficits in theory of mind often result in situations and behaviors that invite teasing and bullying, two major problems for kids with AS.

So what does theory of mind do? Many things, but for our purposes, let's look at some common ways in which a deficit in theory of mind skills might affect independence skills.

Those with theory of mind deficits encounter problems with tasks that require the following:

- **Taking into account what others know.** It is not unusual for someone with an ASD not to ask for help when he needs it. Many people find this baffling, but when you place it in the context of theory of mind, it actually makes sense. To ask for help requires the ability to imagine or at least suspect that someone else has information that you do not. If, like many people with an ASD, you have difficulty understanding that others know things you do not, the logical conclusion would be that they don't have the information you need. In some cases, recognizing the need for help and asking for it are skills that must be explicitly taught.
- **Reading and responding to unspoken intentions and detecting hidden meanings.** We've all experienced the uncomfortable realization that we made a gaffe or wore something unflattering based only on our "getting the message" from the nonverbal responses of others. Habits of grooming, care about appearance, and awareness of one's current state of hygiene are behaviors that feel like they come naturally, but in fact they are probably formed over years and years of trying to avoid unpleasant social consequences. When someone is not skilled in picking up hidden meanings, he misses out on prompts and cues that signal issues she should attend to. A second way in which these can affect learning is that nonverbal cues such as pointing, gesturing, glancing directly at something, and giving meaningful looks do not carry the same load of information for

someone with an ASD as they would for someone without it. If I am setting the table and my mother's eyes narrow as she looks frowningly at the Lego model of the Death Star that I forgot to remove, I would immediately grasp what I needed to do because I read her nonverbal signal and understand what she was thinking.

• **Anticipating others' future reactions.** Kids with AS whose self-help skills or personal skills could use some work often fail to look ahead and adjust their behavior in the present to seek out or avoid a possible reaction in the future. In other words, they don't automatically think ahead along the lines of "I don't feel like washing my hair, but I know it's school picture day, so I will," or "I feel like wearing my favorite distressed vintage denim miniskirt, but I know Grandma will be upset, because this is her anniversary dinner at a nice restaurant." Again, we often use our independence skills to avoid an unpleasant response or ensure a pleasant one.

• **Understanding the "why" of others' words and actions.** From a surprisingly early age, children can understand the why behind instructions, rules, and routines. You may explain to a typical youngster only a couple of times why it's important to wear matching socks or to tolerate those uncomfortable, clunky rain boots. Kids with AS do not always immediately understand why they need to do something, particularly in the realm of social behavior.* Ironically, kids with AS tend to ask a lot of questions about almost everything else, and you may find that giving a good explanation of the whys behind the skills and behaviors you'll be teaching can go a long way.

• **Understanding the unwritten rules, the "hidden curriculum."** Unless you have the opportunity to really know someone who struggles with the unwritten rules, or hidden curriculum, of daily living, it can be difficult to fully appreciate the degree

---

*Interestingly, understanding the meaning of "why" and answering "why" questions are common goals for kids with ASDs, regardless of where they fall on the spectrum.

to which our understanding of these covert expectations influences our behavior. Understanding the hidden curriculum is kind of like trying to hit a target inside a constantly changing kaleidoscope. What we do depends less on hard-and-fast rules than on where we are, who we are with, what we are doing, the time of year, the day of the week, the time of day, and so on. Especially when helping kids understand the social aspects of behavior, it's important to keep the unwritten rules in sight and teach kids how to deal with the exceptions, the surprises.

Anyone working with kids who have AS should know about Carol Gray's Social Stories. Using *The New Social Story Book* and following the 10.1 guidelines for writing a Social Story are good ways to learn how Social Stories work. I also think it's a great idea for parents to consider some of Gray's suggestions about explaining from the learner's perspective and focusing on describing instead of prescribing.

Strategies That Help Address Theory of Mind Deficits

- Social Stories (based on Carol Gray's work, see page 175)
- Comic Strip Conversations (also based on Gray's work; hand-drawn social autopsies in comic-strip format)
- Social autopsies (nonjudgmental, instructive after-the-fact review of what happened in an incident and how a similar situation might be handled with a better outcome in the future)
- Using visual strategies to help children anticipate others' thoughts, actions, and desires (see *Teaching Children with Autism to Mind-Read*, by Patricia Howlin, Simon Baron-Cohen, and Julie Hadwin)

WEAK CENTRAL COHERENCE

Weak central coherence is another one of those neurological anomalies characteristic to all ASDs but perhaps more obvious in people with

AS because of their verbal and cognitive skills. Dr. Francesca Happé of Kings College, London, offers this definition of central coherence: "the everyday tendency to process incoming information in context for the gist—pulling information together for higher-level meaning." Central coherence deficits are what most people unknowingly have noticed whenever someone with AS walks through a room in muddy shoes, dresses for a summer day in a turtleneck, or walks out the door with the backpack unzipped and spilling its contents down the sidewalk. Central coherence is the ability to take in the big picture instantaneously, completely, and unconsciously, and then understanding the context to guide what you say or do. We hear a lot about central coherence and its role in social awareness, but it is also important in the independence curriculum.

Interestingly, when esteemed autism researcher Dr. Uta Frith first introduced the theory of weak coherence as a characteristic of autism in the late 1980s, she described it as more of a difference in cognitive style than a deficit. On the plus side, in some kids with ASD weak central coherence supports the ability to detect and process fine details and patterns. This is an asset if your task is proofreading or spotting errors on complex financial spreadsheets. Early on, theory of mind deficit was considered simply another aspect of weak central coherence, but later studies demonstrated that even people with ASDs who display relatively good theory of mind skills still have weak central coherence.

Strong central coherence makes it possible for us to almost instantaneously understand the gist, the big picture. It allows us to evaluate countless conditions and details, pick out those that really matter, selectively ignore those that do not, and then shift our behavior accordingly. Strong central coherence is at work when we approach a task, determine what is important (the dirty clothes on the floor), and ignore what is not (the pattern of the carpet). It's easy to see how, lacking strong central coherence, someone could become easily distracted. As one team of researchers put it, for a person with weak central coherence, the focus often settles on attending and processing "stimulus details" (anything and everything in the environment: objects, sounds, smells, people, temperature, time of day, et cetera). During a talk I gave for parents on teaching their kids self-help skills, one mother explained how frustrating it was for her to teach her daughter how to hang up clothes; no matter how she tried to set the scene for success, her daughter would become distracted with concerns such as the color of the hanger, the material it was made of, whether it "matched" other hangers in the closet, and so on. If this sounds familiar, it is not your child being difficult; it's your child's brain doing what comes naturally.

Strategies That Help Address Weak Central Coherence

- Social Stories (page 175)
- Prompts (page 139)
- Graduated guidance (page 155)
- Visual supports (page 166)

EXECUTIVE FUNCTION SKILL DEFICITS

Executive function, or EF, provides the organizing force of our lives. EF describes behaviors that are goal-directed and future-oriented. Effective EF requires that we plan, organize, self-monitor, remember, draw on past experience, and initiate and sustain behaviors and attention that support this pursuit while inhibiting our responses to behaviors and attention that do not. Translation: EF makes it possible for you to establish a goal and then do everything you need to do to make it happen. EF was first researched in relation to brain injury; later it was also recognized as a possible contributing factor or co-occurring problem in learning disorders, ADHD, and nonverbal learning disability. Dr. Ami Klin describes the impact of executive function deficits succinctly: "People may fail to do something, not because they cannot do it, but because they can't plan it or they don't know how to begin it."

Executive function deficit is one of those problems that's difficult to conceptualize if you haven't experienced EFD yourself or don't live with someone who does. Simply put, executive function is the ability to recognize the steps that need to be followed to complete a task: to plan what to do, assemble whatever is needed, and follow through. It sounds like a mental to-do list, but it is actually much more. In addition to instructing you on what to do and how to do it, executive function enables you to understand when, why, and where to do it. EF is the decider, the boss. When it works, it gathers all available intelligence about a situation, analyzes it in milliseconds, and generates a workable plan of action. Two major components of executive function are the ability to inhibit one's responses—in other words, to think before acting—and to identify and maintain focus on the relevant details of a task. This latter faculty is notoriously difficult, because one characteristic of ASDs is the inability to differentiate important cues in the environment from those that are not important (see the section on central coherence, above).

What Does Executive Function Help Us Do? (Hint: Everything!)

- Plan
- Organize
- Prioritize
- Shift attention
- Memorize
- Check
- Keep track of time
- Keep track of more than one thing at a time
- Meaningfully include past knowledge in discussions
- Evaluate ideas
- Reflect on our own work
- Change our mind and make corrections while thinking, reading, writing, acting
- Start and finish on time
- Ask for help
- Inhibit our responses (so that, for instance, we wait to be called upon)
- Seek more information when we need it

Executive function plays a special role in independence skills for our kids. Several specific components of executive function tend to be more problematic for persons with ASDs, including the ability to:

- Use language to help address a problem (by talking to yourself about what you're doing, what you need, mistakes you made, how to correct mistakes)
- Initiate and inhibit behavior
- Shift attention
- Learn and apply strategies
- Learn from past experience
- Incorporate an awareness of one's performance in the present situation

Finally, executive function is necessary to generalize knowledge and skills—that is, to apply what you know to a place, situation, person, or activity different from the ones with which you first learned the skill. Difficulties in generalization are perhaps one of the biggest roadblocks to further progress that kids with any form of ASD face, regardless of diagnosis.

Consider a skill such as folding. Sometime, somewhere, someone taught you how to fold something flat: a towel, your father's handkerchief, a dinner napkin. Chances are you got direct instruction on one or two different items, then you took it from there. In other words, once you knew how to fold a hand towel, you didn't need separate lessons on folding a bath towel, folding a beach towel, folding a tablecloth, folding a throw rug, folding a table runner, and so on. You knew how to *fold*. And knowing how to fold meant that you could fold anything foldable. Even when faced with items that seem to never fold easily back into their original shapes—road maps, big round rain ponchos that store easily (they say) in little square plastic pouches, fitted sheets—you could apply what you had learned from a long and varied folding history to give it a go, thanks to your ability to generalize.

When generalization does not come naturally, however, every new object or situation sends you back to square one. Although we recognize generalization deficits in people who have ASDs and weaker cognitive and language skills, and in people with Asperger syndrome with regard to social skills, generalization's role in undermining independence skills for these people is not as widely appreciated. Now that you know about it, though, it's something to look out for and something to be sure to teach to.

Strategies That Help Address Executive Function Deficits

- Modeling (page 145)
- Prompts (page 139)
- Graduated guidance (page 155)
- Shaping (page 163)
- Visual supports (page 166)

Quick Tip: To See Executive Function in Action

Two of the best examples of people applying superb executive function abilities are the television programs *Top Chef* and *Project Runway*. Contestants are required to conceive, plan, and execute a finished product while being forced to change what they do and how they do it in light of time constraints, surprise requirements, and circumstances beyond their control. They are also constantly drawing not only on their experience and knowledge about the task, materials, and equipment but also on how they have performed similar tasks in the past. Experts in executive function tell us that people who apply it most effectively have an accurate idea of their own strengths and weaknesses, constant awareness of how well they are doing, and the ability to adjust their approach instantly if it is not effective. Crucial components of good executive function are recognizing a problem and asking for help. A good example of executive function gone horribly awry is the classic *I Love Lucy* episode where Lucy and Ethel man the assembly line in the chocolate factory—as the conveyor belt speeds up to deliver more chocolates for wrapping, the two of them panic and begin stuffing the candies they can't wrap into their mouths and shirts.

FINE- AND GROSS-MOTOR SKILLS

For reasons researchers are only beginning to discover, Asperger syndrome and other ASDs are typically accompanied by pervasive deficits and delays in fine-motor skills (handwriting, buttoning, tying shoes, using flatware) and gross-motor skills (throwing, catching, sitting comfortably and in a posture that does not impede other movements).

Sometimes the impact of fine- and gross-motor deficits can be addressed through guided practice and prompting, massed practice (a series of back-to-back repetitions of a behavior with little or no time between; for example, drying a plate fifteen times in a row in one session rather than just the two or three plates that need drying each day), and various levels of prompting. If your child struggles with this category of skills, you have probably heard technical terms such as *motor planning*, *apraxia*, and *eye-hand coordination* to describe what happens (or doesn't) when your child's brain tells her body to do something.

Quick Tip: Ask Your Occupational Therapist

If your child receives or has received occupational therapy (OT) services, contact the occupational therapist and ask for a clear description of his strengths and his weaknesses in this area. What was the OT successful in teaching? Which strategies worked, and which did not?

DEVELOPMENTAL COORDINATION DISORDER (DCD)

Developmental coordination disorder (DCD) is not new: it's been in the *DSM* for years. Yet few parents or professionals have heard of it or are aware of its relationship to AS and other ASDs. In other parts of the world, where symptoms such as motor clumsiness are included in the diagnostic criteria for Asperger syndrome or where professionals are more familiar with Dr. Christopher Gillberg's DAMP (disorders of attention, motor control, and perception) disorder, DCD is well known. In the current edition of the *DSM*, the DCD diagnostic criteria are refreshingly brief and clear. Does any of this sound at all like your child?

> A. Performance in daily activities that require motor coordination is substantially below that expected given the person's chronological age and measured intelligence. This may be manifested by marked delays in achieving motor milestones (e.g., walking, crawling, sitting), dropping things, "clumsiness," poor performance in sports, or poor handwriting.
> B. The disturbance in Criterion A significantly interferes with academic achievement or activities of daily living.

So-called motor clumsiness has been described in the literature about Asperger syndrome going all the way back to Dr. Hans Asperger's original 1944 paper. Children with AS often have problems with body awareness, motor planning, balance, fine-motor coordination (especially handwriting and using scissors), bilateral motor integration, gross-motor coordination, and sensory sensitivities. Given how well DCD explains coordination problems often seen in AS, it's surprising that it is not better known.

A 2002 study compared eleven boys with AS to nine boys previously diagnosed with DCD. The groups were matched for full IQ score (100 for those with AS; 101 for those with DCD) and ranged in age from about six and a half to ten and a half years old. The findings? *All* the participants with AS also met the *DSM* criteria for developmental coordination disorder. Noted areas of weakness included ball skills, copying movements, predicting the movements of others, mime, and imitation. Researchers have already established that about 35 percent of those with DCD also have a co-occurring condition, and in most cases it turns out to be an ASD. Not surprisingly, another team of researchers found a high degree of overlap between young people with DCD and those with ASDs. Both have poor gestural abilities, odd or mannered speech and/or language, problems with tasks involving sequencing and timing, social impairment, emotional difficulties, and problems with reading, writing, and spelling.

SENSORY ISSUES

Most of us have some experience with sensory integration disorder (SID). Science has yet to pinpoint the physiological and neurological causes of sensory integration disorder (the subject of Carol Stock Kranowitz's special-needs classic *The Out-of-Sync Child*), and the medical community has resisted classifying it as a bona fide diagnosis. You will not find it in the *DSM*, nor will your health insurance usually cover its treatment. Nevertheless, children with ASDs routinely receive intervention for SID through occupational therapy. Sensory integration disorder is typified by either undersensitivity or oversensitivity to sounds, tastes, smells, sights, and tactile sensations. They may also be affected by abnormal reactions to vestibular and proprioceptive input—essentially, the internal sense of balance and body awareness, or the sense of where you are in space.

Many independence skills involve sensory input that could be distracting, annoying, or highly aversive to your child. Classic examples include the taste of toothpaste, cooking aromas or the harsh smell of cleaning supplies, the texture of tools or implements, or the appearance of specific foods. Kids with poor proprioception might find it difficult to wash dishes without chipping or breaking them, or to maintain their balance while standing on even a low step stool, or to carry an object using the proper grip. For example, Oscar's first response when handed a hot plate is to grasp the plate edges with his palms down instead of up, putting his thumbs and fingers right in the hot food.

If you know that your child has specific problems in any of these areas, consult with her occupational therapist. If your child is not seeing an OT or does not qualify for services, seek an evaluation through his physician. Sometimes, after a certain age, school districts provide OT services to address only motor skill problems that directly affect school performance. Obviously, motor skill deficits can potentially impact most daily activities, in school and out, across the life span.

Be Sure the Problem Really Is "Sensory"

Parents and teachers often assume that the presence of any behavior suggesting reactivity to sensory input automatically means that the whole problem is "sensory." Upon closer investigation, however, it's not uncommon to discover that the presumed sensory reaction is serving another purpose. For example, a little girl receiving hand-over-hand prompting to zip up a zipper may jerk her hand away. Or, in a moment of confusion, she might start rocking, seek deep pressure or input, or engage in other sensory-seeking behaviors. Teachers and parents may interpret this to mean that the zipper or the hand prompt is aversive; their response is to back off teaching the skill. In most cases, however, breaking the task down into smaller "exposures," increasing the reinforcement, or providing more practice diminishes or eliminates the supposed sensory reaction.

While there is evidence that people across the spectrum do have atypical responses to sensory stimulation and may require sensory breaks, special sensory input, or other sensory interventions, try to be objective about when and how these interventions are used when teaching any skill. Remember that sensory interventions—from deep-pressure joint compression activities to playing with therapy doughs, balls, or other sensory toys—are highly reinforcing and designed for fun. It's no surprise, then, that having the sensory intervention may be more pleasant and certainly is easier than addressing the learning task at hand. When children engage in sensory-seeking behavior during learning, most often parents and other adults believe that they need to stop immediately to access the sensory intervention. But when sensory-seeking behavior occurs consistently during learning, another possibility should leap out: that the sensory activity is easier, more pleasant, and more reinforcing than the task at hand. And how would a child access those activities? By displaying sensory-seeking behavior. As Homer Simpson would say, "D'oh!"

Once again, our little pals are not manipulating us or planning this out. They are just following a familiar cause-and-effect relationship between their actions and the adult response they get. They are escaping a task because past experience has taught them that they have a choice between the mild stress of learning and something that is a lot easier and much more fun. All your child is doing is exercising the right to choose.

How do you determine if the sensory-seeking behavior is really just that or if other factors have created a highly reinforced setup for task avoidance and diminished learning?

• **Try to determine if there is a pattern to the sensory-seeking behavior.** It would not be unusual to discover that there is more sensory seeking during less favored activities than during preferred ones.

• **If your child benefits from sensory intervention, offer it before you start to teach.** Of course, you don't want to make the sensory activity unpleasant, but don't make it so reinforcing that anything else pales in comparison. Keep it as short as possible. Your goal is to delink the avoidance behavior and the positive reinforcement of the sensory intervention.

• **Offer a bigger, better reinforcement.** People choose between competing reinforcers all the time. So be sure that whatever reinforcement you offer during teaching moments is bigger, better, and more powerful than what the sensory intervention has to offer. Also, do what you can to make teaching and learning fun.

• **Offer the sensory intervention as the reinforcer for performing the task instead of for avoiding it.** Think about how to turn what's been working *against* learning to work *for* it instead.

> • Review your setting, materials, and other factors that may be triggering sensory issues. If there truly is a sensory sensitivity and some aspect of the materials is aversive to your child, that association will taint the entire process. Try switching to materials or settings that have a different or no texture, scent, taste, or sound before you conclude that the skill cannot be taught.

MIRROR NEURONS

Mirror neuron deficit is the newest neurological complication on the block. These fascinating brain cells, discovered by Italian researchers in the early 1990s, respond both when we perform an action and when we observe someone else doing the same thing. Found in several brain areas, mirror neurons are crucial to our ability to imitate others, not only in performing physical movements but also in understanding other people's thoughts and feelings. While observing and imitating actions, gestures, and expressions may seem simple, it actually involves a complex cascade of processes. Imitation is the very foundation of most learning, not only in how to do something but also in how to understand someone. As Dr. Justin Williams and colleagues state in a 2006 paper on the possible connection between mirror neuron deficits and autism, "Imitation may be a core cognitive process required for the development of social cognitive ability." In other words, mirror neurons make it possible for us to watch someone eating ice cream and imagine what she is tasting or feeling without actually eating ice cream ourselves at that moment. This, some say, is the beginning of social understanding.

Mirror neurons help us learn in several ways. When we are learning independence skills, they may enable us to unconsciously mentally rehearse the movements and actions of others as we see them. For example, real-time brain imaging studies reveal that when you watch someone, say, kneading bread dough, areas of the brain that would be active if you were to actually knead dough light up, even if you

What Do Mirror Neurons Do?

The mirror neuron system is at work when we:

- Imitate the behaviors of others
- "Mentally rehearse" a behavior we observe but do not execute ourselves at that moment
- Observe another person's behavior and "mind-read" what he is thinking or feeling
- Make predictions about someone else's behavior
- Use what we learn through observation of others to form the foundations of empathy, social understanding, and effective communication.

are nowhere near bread dough. It's as if the brain is testing the cells, connections, and pathways between neurons that later will be used to perform the action. Children with ASDs have been shown to exhibit deficits in mirror neuron activity, and some hypothesize that this may shed some light on why they are less adept at imitating other people's actions or executing movements despite repeated demonstrations and models. Or as Dr. Ami Klin explains, "They mimic the movement but not the goals." For example, your child may be able to copy the movements of wiping the table but without ever noticing where you wipe, when you wipe, how much pressure you apply, when you start, and when you stop. Mirror neuron deficits help to explain why "Just watch me" and "Let me show you again" might not always work. It may also explain why our kids—supposedly such strong visual learners—do not seem to pick up as much information from simple observation as we would expect.

Strategies That Can Help Address Mirror Neuron Deficits

- Modeling (page 145)
- Prompts (page 139)

- Graduated guidance (page 155)
- Forward chaining (page 157)
- Backward chaining (page 161)
- Shaping (page 162)
- Visual supports (page 166)

COMMON CHALLENGES:
HOW THEY COMPLICATE THE "RECIPE" FOR TEACHING

Let's go back to the recipe box on page 78 and see where and when the challenges described above wreak havoc.

To successfully perform a task, your child needs to bring along these skills and abilities:

- For knowing the environmental conditions required, you need good executive function skills, focus of attention, and central coherence.
- For knowing approximately how long the task should take, you need executive function.
- For determining which equipment, ingredients, and/or techniques you will use, you need executive function, focus of attention, short-term memory, sensory integration, fine-motor skills, and mirror neuron activity.
- For knowing what to do with the equipment, ingredients, and techniques, and in which order, you rely on executive function, motor planning, sensory integration, and generalization.
- For knowing when to begin and when to end each step, you need executive function, central coherence, sensory integration, the ability to begin and stop activity, and the ability to inhibit the impulse to do something that does not contribute to completing the task.
- For knowing what to expect at each step, you need good

memory, generalization, central coherence, and the ability to imagine.

- For being able to perceive what the final result will be, you need experience with the task, either from having performed it yourself or from having watched someone else do it.

DON'T FORGET ABOUT LANGUAGE

Although we may not think about it, we talk to ourselves most of the time. Thanks to people sporting headgear made of aluminum foil, talking to yourself has gotten a bad rap, but the truth is, it's probably one of the most important strategies we use to move through our daily tasks. In fact, the ability to talk yourself through a problem is a component of executive function. We know that kids with Asperger syndrome have deficits in receptive language (they may appear to understand more than they actually do) and in using language to reflect, self-monitor, and adjust their own behavior to suit the situation. When we talk to ourselves as we carry out tasks, we provide ourselves with a series of near-constant internal prompts. No doubt a number of routines are so completely on automatic pilot that we may not hear the voice anymore. However, when encountering new tasks that require following steps—say, assembling that bookcase from Ikea or troubleshooting some computer glitch—you probably talk to yourself a lot (possibly using some words that we can't print here). Talking to ourselves allows us to organize our thoughts, catch and correct our mistakes, and keep track of where we are.

Also keep in mind that typically developing children go through stages where they audibly talk themselves through tasks that are novel or challenging. A four-year-old might be overheard saying while playing with a dollhouse, "The bed goes here. . . . The chair goes there. . . . Where's the pillow? . . . There it is." Your seventh grader may be heard muttering over his algebra homework, "Okay, parentheses, then exponents, then multiplication and division, then addition and subtraction," or counting aloud as he counts squares while plotting a graph.

Over time, they learn to internalize that "conversation" and think it rather than say it. Still, most of us do talk through problems occasionally—most of the time silently—no matter what our age.

Children with ASDs often engage in behavior that looks similar. They may repeat words they have heard others use immediately (echolalia) or at some earlier time (delayed echolalia). They may also repeat, out of context, the dialogue from TV shows, movies, or video. Because they are not "talking to" anyone, some people assume they are talking to themselves, though that is usually not the case in the sense that they are thinking things aloud. Rather, this kind of self-talk is often random, nonfunctional, and can interfere with attention, social interaction, and learning. Though it's appropriate to discourage perseverative self-talk, we shouldn't discourage kids from talking themselves through tasks (what is called *private speech*). A 2006 study that compared three groups of children, age seven to eighteen—one group with ADHD, one with an ASD (AS or PDD-NOS), and one with typical development—found that about 70 percent of the children with AS did use private speech to help guide themselves through tasks demanding executive function; the main difference between them and participants in the other two groups was they were more likely to speak aloud rather than whisper or mutter inaudibly. Before you or anyone else implements a program to discourage private speech because it looks inappropriate or makes the child stand out, be sure you are not inadvertently discouraging the use of an important tool in developing executive function. In fact, verbal self-prompting might be appropriate or acceptable in some situations. You may decide that it's okay for your child to verbally self-prompt himself aloud when packing his backpack for school. Frankly, that's preferable, and less restrictive, than having someone stand over him to offer the same prompts. Once the skills are on board, you can then work with him on taking the conversation "inside."

Our kids typically demonstrate a weakness in the internal use of language, too. It is often said that everyone with an ASD "thinks in pictures," but that may not be true in every case. People with AS who are particularly gifted at conceptualizing and building things, problem solving, or visual arts no doubt rely heavily on visual input and organization. However, there is no way to know for sure that anyone has a strong visual guide when it comes to tasks such as getting dressed, and it's probably wise to assume that your child doesn't. For example, some children find using a schedule, a list, or pictorial reminders helpful, while others consider them distracting. Every child is different.

Though many of the skills here seem more physical, remember that there is always a language component at work. Even if you are by yourself, some amount of self-talk occurs. And when we are with other people, not only is there usually talking but also some amount of non-verbal language: pointing, gesturing, nodding, or otherwise instructing without words. People with AS are generally less likely to notice or correctly interpret nonverbal language, and on top of that, their ability to process receptive language—that is, what is said to them, such as directions—may lag years behind the level and complexity of language they use in speaking. We know that AS imposes deficits in language processing, and parents can provide dozens of examples of processing glitches in action.

What we often overlook, however, is that our own language-producing skills are far from perfect. We believe that we say what we mean, but most of the time we assume that our listener will have at least some knowledge of what we are talking about. Lots of what we say is shorthand that we trust our listeners to understand, expand, and fill in to get the full picture of our meaning. Kids with AS, however, may not be able to instantly process an incoming message in this way.

Those of us with typical theory of mind and strong central co-herence can gather a lot of information from relatively few words—and sometimes no words at all—because we have the advantage of instantly and accurately reading another person's intention and the big picture of the circumstances. For most typical kids, such a level of detail in instructions would be redundant and unnecessary. For some of our kids, however, it may be essential—at least when they are first learning new skills—to be as clear and explicit as possible. When you realize that most instructions kids receive describe only the outcome or the end product (because they know all the steps required to get there), the problem comes into sharper focus. Telling someone what you want done rarely includes information on how to do it, and it's often these how-to-do-it steps that our kids either do not know or *do* know but cannot act upon in an organized, timely manner.

- Instead of instructing, "Get your stuff," try saying: "Bring your science book, your notebook, and some pencils to the table."
- Instead of instructing, "Get ready for school," try saying, "Shower, wash your hair, wash your face, brush your teeth, put on deodorant, put on your clothes, and come down for breakfast."
- Instead of instructing, "Clean up your room," try saying, "Place your dirty clothes in the hamper and your clean clothes in the drawers, make your bed, and put away your books, toys, and video games."

Each instruction could be further broken down. For example, "Wash your hair" presumes that you know to (1) get your hair wet, (2) open the shampoo bottle, (3) pour some into your hand, (4) rub it into your scalp for about sixty seconds, (5) rinse with water, and (6) repeat. The sheer number of stand-up comedians who get laughs for questioning the necessity of directions on shampoo bottles tells you that most of us don't need them. Well before entering kindergarten, most kids can tell you how exactly to wash your hair, even if it will be a few more years before they can do it well themselves. Yet for some kids with AS—even very bright kids—what would be obvious to someone else is not so obvious, or it's not so well recalled, not so easily motor-planned, or not so efficiently completed.

THE ROADBLOCK:
PERSEVERATIVE AND OTHER INTERFERING BEHAVIORS

Sometimes, as part of any ASD, a child may also display perseverative behaviors—a compulsion to engage in repetitive behaviors—that can interfere with learning, daily living, and social interactions. Perseverative behaviors encompass a range of repetitious movements, sounds, multistep "rituals," and other behaviors that serve no functional purpose. Some people refer to these as *stims*, short for *self-stimulatory behavior*. I prefer the terms *perseverative* or *stereotypal behavior*, and the box below explains why.

If your child tends to like or need routine, order, and a degree of sameness, you know how that can get in the way of life. However,

Stim: What Does It Really Mean? And Can We Please Stop Using It?

The term *stim*—short for *self-stimulatory behavior*—is often used to describe a repetitive or perseverative behavior. Hand flapping, pacing, twirling, spinning, hand wringing, lining up or otherwise arranging items, rocking, bouncing, and turning lights or appliances on and off are but a tiny sample of the virtual universe of so-called stim behaviors. How did they get this name? Well, for one thing, when we see a behavior a lot, we assume that there is some reinforcement for it, because no behavior continues in the absence of reinforcement. With behaviors like these, the reinforcement is assumed to be internal. What does the person with autism spectrum disorder get from stimming? It may be a release of tension, or a physical or sensory input, or a sense of comfort or calm. Sometimes your child can tell you why she engages in a particular stim; sometimes it is automatically reinforcing, or self-reinforcing.

The real term for this is *stereotypal* (not *stereotypical*) behavior. Although *stim* is handy because everyone readily understands what it means, there are several good reasons not to use it in serious discussions about real people. One is that as youngsters approach puberty and adolescence, *stim* or *self-stimulatory* suggests sexual behavior, namely, masturbation. When used around most laypeople and professionals not as versed in ASD culture, these terms can inadvertently paint a very different picture.

Second, when we describe a behavior with a term that suggests that we already know what's reinforcing it and why it occurs, we throw ourselves off the trail that could lead to a better explanation and an effective intervention. Contrary to popular belief, not everyone engages in stereotypal behaviors because they find them enjoyable or comforting. In fact, there are kids who would love nothing better than to *not* feel compelled to "stim" at all.

Third, our reactions to stereotypal behaviors, or behaviors that may look stereotypal, can sometimes introduce other reinforcers into the situation without our realizing it. Sometimes these reinforcers can turn an occasional or one-time behavior into a predictable, perseverative behavior habit—but not always for the reasons we think.

For example, Nate may put his head down on his desk and squeeze his eyes together tightly every time he is asked, or expects to be asked, to solve a math problem on the SMART Board. After several failed attempts to change Nate's mind, his teacher has given up. And he is doing it again today. She looks at the clock—it's only ten minutes to lunch, and there are two more story problems to cover. She decides it isn't worth the five minutes it will take her to interrupt the lesson and give the other students something to do while she tries to persuade Nate to open his eyes and raise his head off the desk. No wonder she stops calling on him.

There's a lot to say about this scenario, but I'll sum up with this: wrong way to go—unless, of course, you want to ensure that he will continue his avoidance routine. Without intending to or even realizing what she's done, Nate's teacher has just provided reinforcement for what appeared to be stim behavior: escape from the SMART Board. (Further investigation reveals that Nate hates the feeling of writing on the board with his finger.) You probably won't be surprised to learn that Nate's teacher also believes that intervening to disrupt Nate's behavior "is not the right thing to do, because he has autism," and "everyone knows these kids have those stim things."

Finally, stereotypal behaviors can interfere with concentration, learning, social interaction, and even safety. While there is no question that for some kids certain atypical behaviors can have a positive impact in the right situation, it would be a mistake to consider all stereotypal behaviors necessary, permanent, or innocuous. Let's say that your child deals with stress by standing and rocking. More often than not, it truly comforts him. That may not seem like a problem up in the privacy of his bedroom or around family members who can overlook it. But picture it occurring when he's crossing a busy intersection just as the light is turning, or if he gets upset at not finding paper towels in the men's room at the mall.

Given the vast amount of literature suggesting that stereotypal behaviors should be ignored, it's easy to understand why parents and teachers are often reluctant to intervene or to try treating such behaviors as a problem. Not all such behaviors are bad, but not all are good, either. If your child has one stereotypal behavior or a repertoire of them, you should consider taking a good look at each of them. Most of the time the problem is not the behavior itself but when, where, how long, and how often it occurs.

while it is possible to help children develop a degree of flexibility and tolerance for change and the unexpected, perseverative behavior isn't necessarily all bad. As science learns more about the brain, it becomes clear that this tendency is somewhat hardwired. In other words, while we can teach a child to develop a more useful repertoire of ways to respond to the need for sameness or order, it is doubtful that we will be able to eliminate a child's neurologically based feeling of needing to do these things. Having worked with children who have these issues, I've found that there may be opportunities for redirecting or channeling some of these disruptive perseverative behaviors to help build or maintain a skill. For instance, a kid's insistence on organizing items by category, like color or size, may get in the way of shopping if she feels compelled to reorganize the contents of the shopping cart according to her color scheme each time a new item is added. However, this drive to organize can be harnessed in a positive way for putting away groceries, sorting laundry, or filing paperwork. In fact, according to Temple Grandin and other authorities on preparing children for higher education and careers, one key is teaching them to draw on their natural tendencies in order to support success in school and beyond.

NOW WHAT?

Once we identify the autism-related differences that may affect learning, we can modify what we teach and how we teach it—sidestepping some of the inherent roadblocks and forging new detours that are easier and more comfortable for our kids. Chapters 7 and 8 will explore those strategies and how they can work for you and your child.

Quick Tip: Don't Confuse Explanations with Causes

If Bruce cannot pack his schoolbooks into his backpack, the problem is not that "Bruce has a disorder," "Bruce has never been good with that," "Bruce just doesn't get it," "Bruce is immature for his age," or "Bruce has OT issues." (Note that none of these problems has a solution.) Rather, the problem is that he lacks the skills necessary to accomplish the task.

Chapter 6

WHEN YOUR CHILD ALSO HAS "ANOTHER DIAGNOSIS" OR LEARNING DISORDER

CO-OCCURRING (CO-MORBID) PSYCHIATRIC DISORDERS

While there certainly are children who are found to have only ASD, with no associated psychiatric disorders or learning disabilities, the majority of people with autism spectrum disorder have one, two, or more co-occurring conditions. Many of these co-morbidities have a genetic component, and certain disorders seem to occur in pairs or groups. For example, anxiety and ADHD are common in people with AS. A discussion of medication and other treatments for these secondary disorders is beyond the scope of this book. For more information, see Dr. Timothy Wilens's excellent *Straight Talk About Psychiatric Medications for Kids*, now in its third edition. Even if medication is not for your child at this point, this is an informative, evenhanded, and helpful resource that describes these conditions clearly.

If it's suspected that there may be more going on with your youngster, seek a professional opinion from a pediatric psychiatrist, pediatric neurologist, pediatric neuropsychologist, or developmental pediatrician. For many kids, the ASD diagnosis comes with language and communication issues that can hamper our ability to really understand what's going on inside them. Further, any observable symptom or behavior can be a possible indicator of more than one condition. And even conditions that have what appear to be a similar symptom may have very different causes that call for very different treatments.

If you know that your child has another diagnosis or LD, it does not mean that he cannot learn the skills discussed in this book or that you cannot teach him. What it does mean, however, is that you will consider these issues when you design your teaching plan. You probably know better than anyone when your child has reached his limit or when an emotional response is more than run-of-the-mill task avoidance or frustration. Remember that if your child's learning experience cannot be positive and reinforcing for him, nothing will be gained. If you suspect you may run into difficulties or if you already have, consult your child's doctor, psychologist, psychiatrist, or other professional. At the same time, keep in mind that having a problem such as anxiety disorder or ADHD probably points to his needing independence skills even more, not less. So a complicating second (or third or fourth) diagnosis or LD is not a reason not to teach, though it may be a reason to teach with some extra help.

Consider a Board Certified Behavior Analyst

A Board Certified Behavior Analyst, or BCBA, is someone who has been deemed qualified by the Behavior Analyst Certification Board (BACB) to practice applied behavior analysis. The BACB is a nonprofit organization that, according to its website (www.bacb.com), serves "to develop, promote, and implement an international certification program for behavior analyst practitioners." The BACB has established uniform content, standards, and criteria for the credentialing process that are designed to meet "the legal standards established through state, federal and case law; the accepted standards for national certification programs; and the 'best practice' and ethical standards of the behavior analysis profession."

What does this mean to you? Applied behavior analysis is a powerful approach to teaching and fostering behavior change. That's the good news. The not-so-good news is that in the hands of individuals who are not trained in the correct and ethical application of ABA, bad things can happen. Some less-than-ethical people who may have attended a few conferences, taken a single course in "behaviorism" or "behavior modification," or worked in the field for a number of years may try to persuade you that their experience and training is the same as the BCBA credential.* It's not. Nor, for that matter, is that of a person who has taken all the BACB-mandated coursework but has not completed supervision and/or passed the exam.

To sit for the international certification examination, one must hold a master's or higher degree in a related field (psychology, education, social work, et cetera), complete a prescribed number of BACB-approved graduate-level courses in applied behavior analysis, and work under the supervision of a BCBA for between 750 and 1,500 hours. Equally important is the BACB's requirements for maintaining certification: ongoing continuing education, with a large percentage devoted to ethics.

Although the majority of BCBAs have backgrounds in psychology and education, corporate human resources professionals, athletic trainers and coaches, health care professionals, speech pathologists, occupational therapists, physical therapists, and school administrators are also joining the ranks. For more information and to access a searchable registry to find a BCBA in your area, go to www.bacb.com and click on "Consumers."

---

*The BACB also offers the credentials BCBA-D (for an individual with a doctorate and a BCBA) and BCaBA (Board Certified Assistant Behavior Analyst). BCaBAs are required to take fewer courses, have fewer hours of supervision, and take a shorter certification exam. They are required to work under the supervision of a BCBA.

ADHD

Attention deficit/hyperactivity disorder, or ADHD, is a neurobiological disorder characterized by a pervasive difficulty or inability to sustain attention or control impulses at a level deemed appropriate for one's age. ADHD affects between 5 percent and 9 percent of school-age children. According to Dr. Wilens, about 70 percent of those diagnosed in childhood will continue to have ADHD through their teens;

for about 50 percent, attention issues may persist, but hyperactivity and impulsivity may decline over time. There are three types of ADHD: (1) ADHD primarily inattentive type, (2) ADHD primarily hyperactive/impulsive type, and (3) ADHD combined type.

ADHD and AS share similar features, especially in younger children, so it's not uncommon for a child to be diagnosed first with ADHD, then have an AS diagnosis confirmed later. Often this occurs after efforts to treat the ADHD symptoms fail to improve the young patient's social skills and behaviors. In addition, children may have a dual diagnosis of AS and a form of ADHD.

Anxiety

According to the National Institute of Mental Health, anxiety disorders are the most common form of mental disorder, affecting more than 19 million individuals yearly. It's hard to say whether the anxiety experienced by kids with AS is a direct result of their neurobiological makeup, a response to the stresses of living with AS, or a combination of both. But we do know that a significant percentage of children and adults with AS experience some form of anxiety disorder at some point in their lives. In fact, a number of experts in the field believe that addressing a child's anxiety should be considered job one, because of its impact on all aspects of learning and behavior. Dr. Ami Klin describes children who "walk on eggshells all day long until they come home exhausted. This makes it more difficult to use their skills."

Childhood anxiety disorders are common. As a matter of fact, most adults who are diagnosed with anxiety disorders can trace the beginnings to childhood or adolescence. The important thing to remember is that symptoms of anxiety tend to intensify in response to stress. There are several types of anxiety disorders.

Generalized anxiety disorder (GAD) is distinguished by chronic and pervasive worry that goes well beyond what would be considered normal responses to daily living. Someone with GAD may worry excessively about everything, often for no apparent reason. He has trouble relaxing and sleeping, and may have physical symptoms such as trembling, twitching, headaches, nausea, sweating, and irritability. What many people regard as the "negativity" of AS—seeing the glass as half empty instead of half full—may be an indication of GAD.

Obsessive-compulsive disorder (OCD) is a term that people in the ASD world tend to toss about. However, self-reinforcing perseverative behaviors are not the same as OCD. Although the behaviors may look the same, they actually have different causes and call for different treatments. Particularly when your child exhibits perseverative behaviors, a medical diagnosis to confirm or rule out true OCD is in order. Not every person with compulsive tendencies, obsessive tendencies, or both has OCD.

According to Dr. Wilens, children with obsessive-compulsive disorder experience "persistent ideas or impulses (obsessions) that may lead to repetitive, purposeful behaviors (compulsions) that they feel they must complete." OCD is thought to affect one in fifty people, or between 1 percent and 2 percent of the population, at some point in their lives. However, studies have found that up to one in four subjects with AS also has OCD. They exhibit ritualistic behaviors and a need for routines that may detrimentally impact their ability to function in the world. OCD may involve behaviors such as cleaning, checking, repeating, counting, arranging, and hoarding and obsessions involving aggression, contamination, sex, religion, symmetry, or how one looks or feels physically.

Social phobia and general phobias can be defined as extreme and irrational fears that disrupt an individual's life. People with AS are often diagnosed with social phobia, an intense fear of social situations that induces anxiety, panic, and avoidance behavior that can be extreme and adversely affect their ability to function in the world. They may feel incapable of performing in certain social arenas and may avoid interacting with groups of people, prefer to stay with people with whom they're familiar, and be unwilling or unable to seek out new social situations. Because people with Asperger syndrome may face profound social difficulties generally, it can be too easy to attribute aversive behaviors to AS and overlook social phobia as a cause or contributing factor.

Post-traumatic stress disorder (PTSD) refers to stress that results from trauma. Some teenagers and adults with AS who as children were either misdiagnosed or undiagnosed grew up misunderstood and, unfortunately, all too often mistreated. Individuals with PTSD often have pervasive and persistent recollections of traumatic incidents; a common one is bullying or abuse from peers and others. They may also suffer from anxiety, depression, sleep loss, and decreased appetite. People with PTSD may feel excited and seem hypervigilant or jumpy, while at the same time appearing to be emotionally removed or numb. Particularly for people with AS, who tend to send mixed signals about their emotional engagement with others, it may be easy for others to falsely attribute a seeming lack of empathy as simply coldness and not a sign of PTSD. The first step in treating and preventing PTSD is to be sure that your child is safe: from harassment, bullying, and any form of physical or verbal abuse.

Seizure Disorders and Epilepsy

Having an ASD diagnosis increases the risk of developing a seizure disorder at some point in life. While only 2 percent to 3 percent of the general population have epilepsy (defined as suffering two or more unprovoked seizures), it is estimated that seizures occur in about one in four of those diagnosed with autism. Generally, epilepsy is more common among children who have mental retardation and/or severe receptive language problems; the prevalence among those with ASDs that do not involve cognitive deficits and severe language problems is about 7 percent.

Depression

Depression is one of the most common conditions affecting children and adults with AS. Teenagers who are coming to the realization that they are different from their peers are particularly susceptible; however, parents need to be aware that depression can occur in an AS child at any age, even in preschoolers. Generally, notes Dr. Timothy Wilens, "The rate of depression increases with age." Major depression— described as depression lasting more than two weeks—is believed to affect up to one in fifty of all children in their elementary school years and one in twenty teens. According to Dr. Simon Baron-Cohen, the prevalence of depression among individuals with AS is at least 50 percent. Dr. Ami Klin attributes depression-related "despondency, lack of motivation, and negativity" to "repeated experiences of failure." Prior to adolescence, depression appears equally among boys and girls. After that, two-thirds of those affected are girls. Like other disorders, other problems often accompany depression, such as ADHD, anxiety disorders, and conduct disorder. Youngsters with depression are also at increased risk for substance abuse.

Parents need to be particularly diligent in looking for clues that a child may be depressed, especially given that some of the warning signs may seem like typical AS behavior and therefore are not easily recognized. Also bear in mind that depression in kids can look very different from the classic signs of adult depression. For example, children with depression are not always sad in the typical sense. They are more likely to be highly irritable. So you need to be on the lookout not just for specific symptoms but also for wider behavior changes. In addition to watching for irritability and physical complaints such as headaches and stomachaches, the American Academy of Child and Adolescent Psychiatry recommends that parents be aware of the following signs of depression:

- Change of appetite with either significant weight loss (when not dieting) or weight gain
- Change in sleeping patterns, such as trouble falling asleep, waking up in the middle of the night, early morning awakening, or sleeping too much
- Loss of interest in activities that they'd previously enjoyed
- Loss of energy, fatigue, feeling slowed down for no reason, being "burned out"
- Feelings of guilt and self-blame for things that are not one's fault
- Inability to concentrate and indecisiveness

- Feelings of hopelessness and helplessness
- Recurring thoughts of death and suicide, wishing to die, or attempting suicide

Bipolar Disorder

Bipolar disorder, also commonly referred to as manic-depressive disorder, involves episodes of mania and depression that are cyclical in nature, with mood swings that may cycle from high to low and back again. It is caused by abnormalities in brain chemistry and brain function. Though it is thought to affect 1 percent to 2 percent of adults worldwide, only recently has attention been given to children with the disorder, and the diagnosis of pediatric bipolar disorder is not accepted by all professionals. The incidence of bipolar disorder in children is estimated at between 1 percent and 5 percent. Since pediatric bipolar disorder often occurs against the backdrop of other psychiatric conditions (mainly anxiety disorders, ADHD, and depression), only a highly trained medical professional should be trusted to make the diagnosis. While adults with bipolar disorder often experience extreme changes in mood, behavior, and energy, children "usually have an ongoing, continuous mood disturbance that is a mix of mania and depression," according to the Child and Adolescent Bipolar Foundation. In the words of Dr. Wilens, they feel "very depressed but at the same time very agitated and out of control."

Symptoms include:

- Poor social abilities
- Overtalkativeness, loudness
- Expansive or irritable moods
- Depression
- Rapidly changing moods lasting a few hours to a few days
- Explosive, lengthy, and often destructive rages
- Separation anxiety
- Defiance of authority
- Hyperactivity, agitation
- Sleep disturbances

- Bed-wetting and night terrors
- Racing thoughts and distractibility
- Impulsivity, poor judgment
- High-risk behaviors, disregard for personal safety
- Inappropriate or precocious sexual behavior
- Delusions and hallucinations, including the belief that he or she can defy the laws of logic (to fly or to run into traffic, for example)

Tourette's Syndrome and Tics

There are several different tic disorders. The best known, Tourette's syndrome (TS), is a neurological disorder characterized by motor tics, involuntary movements, or vocalizations. Movements are repetitive in nature and may vary in location. Symptoms can be mild to severe and range from simple movements such as eye blinking, throat clearing, and coughing to more complex full-body movements or movements accompanied by vocalizations. Contrary to popular belief, the uncontrollable expression of obscene language (coprolalia) is among the rarest of TS symptoms.

About 15 percent of all children under eighteen experience tics at some point—boys more so than girls. For many, the tics will be fleeting and come to an end, almost always by age eighteen. When symptoms persist beyond one year, the tics are termed chronic. About half of children who experience tics will find that they disappear by adulthood.

Although children with Asperger syndrome may have a diagnosis of TS, it is also important that it not be confused with stereotypies (commonly referred to as "stimming"; see page 105) or with OCD. Since TS is believed to be an inherited condition, it is not uncommon to discover that extended family members also have TS or another tic disorder. Tourette's and tic disorders often develop alongside anxiety, OCD, and ADHD.

Oppositional Defiant Disorder (ODD)

Oppositional defiant disorder is a psychiatric disorder that has not yet been widely documented as occurring frequently with AS. We know that children with AS may be incorrectly diagnosed with ODD before their AS is "discovered," and young people with AS can engage in behaviors that to the untrained eye look a lot like ODD.

According to the American Academy of Child and Adolescent Psychiatry, ODD is distinguished from normal childhood arguing, talking back, and disobedience by its persistence and the degree to which it interferes with daily functioning. Most children will outgrow ODD, but some may progress to a more serious psychiatric condition called conduct disorder. Children with ODD often have ADHD or a mood disorder, such as depression or bipolar disorder. Between 5 percent and 15 percent of school-age children have ODD. Symptoms include:

- Frequent temper tantrums
- Excessive arguing with adults
- Active defiance and refusal to comply with adult requests and rules
- Deliberate attempts to annoy or upset people
- Blaming others for his or her mistakes or misbehavior
- Often being touchy or easily annoyed by others
- Frequent anger and resentment
- Mean and hateful talking when upset
- Seeking revenge

LEARNING DISORDERS COMMONLY SEEN WITH AS

While AS certainly bestows its share of rare and impressive cognitive gifts and creative talents, experts estimate the prevalence of learning disorders among our kids to be somewhere between 25 percent and 75 percent. The current academic emphasis on reading and math skills, for which kids with AS typically test as average to above average through their early elementary school years, can lead parents and professionals to overlook learning problems. But beginning around fourth grade, the curriculum starts to become more challenging, introducing material that requires a deeper-than-literal understanding of words and numbers, and, further, a demonstrated ability not only to perform a task—such as solving a story problem in math or answering a question in history—but to reflect on and articulate the processes involved. With its emphasis on more independent work, small-group learning, note taking, essay writing, and homework assignments that many (including educators) consider excessive, the later elementary school years are often when the cracks in learning skills begin to show.

Dyslexia

According to Dr. Sally Shaywitz, author of *Overcoming Dyslexia*, at least 80 percent of all learning disabilities stem from problems with learning to read. What we now recognize as dyslexia was first documented in the *British Medical Journal* in 1896; however, progress in discovering its causes and effective treatments would not come for another eighty years. Dyslexia is a language-based disability in which a person has difficulty understanding both oral and written words, sentences, or paragraphs. Kids with dyslexia find it hard to decode (that is, match the letters on a page to the sounds they represent) and translate printed words into spoken words, and struggle with reading comprehension. While 15 percent to 20 percent of the population has some form of reading disability, dyslexia is the most common cause of reading, writing, and spelling difficulties. Affecting males and females equally, it is thought to be an inherited genetic disorder. According to the Learning Disabilities Association of America, individuals with dyslexia often reverse or improperly sequence letters within words when reading or writing. In addition, they may exhibit difficulties with spelling, handwriting, computing numbers, and understanding and responding appropriately to spoken language.

Hyperlexia

Many parents are understandably thrilled at the idea that their child might be reading early. From late-night infomercials promoting dubious programs guaranteed to help your baby read to playground urban legends of genius early readers, we have come to believe not only that super-early readers are advanced but also that their learning futures are bright. But in truth, hyperlexia—the precocious ability to read words at a level far beyond one's years and/or an intense fascination with numbers and letters—is a learning disability. Hyperlexic children may later exhibit problems with appropriate socialization skills and an inability to understand verbal language. Some may decode extremely well yet be unable to retain or understand the meaning of what they have read. Hyperlexia is often accompanied by a number of characteristics typical of other learning disorders and particularly AS, such as difficulty answering who, what, where, when, and why questions; perseverative behavior and rituals, such as rocking; repeating words (echolalia); sensory integration problems; and difficulty dealing with information that is more abstract (for example, imagining a personality for a variety of fruits rather than answering questions about how they grow).

Dyscalculia

Dyscalculia is defined as difficulty performing and comprehending mathematical calculations. We tend to view math (because it's about numbers) and language (because it's about words) as two very different kinds of information. But in fact, math is a language, albeit one that uses different symbols to represent words. It even has its own rules of grammar: remember PEMDAS and the order of operations? When you view math that way, the problems that kids with ASDs may have with it make a lot more sense. Between 6 percent and 7 percent of all school-age children exhibit difficulties in some area of mathematics. Contrary to the belief that most children who are diagnosed with AS are mathematically gifted, significant numbers of our kids struggle with mathematical computation and problem solving. Other deficits common among kids with Asperger syndrome, such as language processing, visual-spatial processing, memory, and sequencing, can contribute to dyscalculia.

Dysgraphia

Dysgraphia is a complex learning disorder of written language that affects a considerable number of children with AS, although many remain undiagnosed. There are three types: (1) dyslexic dysgraphia,

(2) dysgraphia due to motor clumsiness, and (3) dysgraphia due to a neurological inability to understand space.

Different children experience dysgraphia differently. For example, both the child whose handwriting is indecipherably messy *and* the child whose letters are neatly, perfectly formed can have dysgraphia. Where the first might be rushing without forming the letters carefully, the second is not so much writing letters as he is painstakingly *drawing* each letter, a process so slow that it might take him an hour to finish a one-page assignment.

Handwriting is a skill most of us take for granted, but it is an incredibly complex process that involves the coordination and timing of attention that may shift from, say, the blackboard or book to the page; eye-hand coordination; motor planning; memory; fine- and gross-motor skills (weak upper-body strength can make it difficult for the child to position his body appropriately for the task of writing); language; and the ability to process and perform multiple tasks such as listening, looking at a blackboard, and taking notes simultaneously. Proper writing demands that you be able to recall instantly the answer to a test question while forming letters, a feat that some persons with AS simply cannot accomplish. Dysgraphia can make the writing process mentally and physically exhausting, so it's not surprising that resistance to the task is often viewed as stubbornness, laziness, or perfectionism. Further confusing matters is the fact that a dysgraphic child may be able to render beautiful drawings or do other things that require strong fine-motor skills.

Some of the hallmarks of dysgraphia are resistance to or avoidance of writing; unusual, awkward, or unproductive pencil grip; difficulty with note taking and test taking; problems placing letters and numbers in the right place on the paper; complaints of discomfort, frustration, or tiredness before, during, or after a writing task.

Nonverbal Learning Disability

Nonverbal learning disability (NLD or NVLD) is one of the more confusingly named learning disabilities, because those who have it are often highly verbal; *nonverbal* refers to types of learning that do not depend on language. NLD shares many of its characteristics and behaviors with AS, and so many children with AS also fit the NLD learning profile and respond to NLD strategies. Though many of our kids can also be said to have NLD, it is possible to have NLD without AS and AS without NLD.

The widely used Wechsler Intelligence Scale for Children measures IQ with three different scores: VIQ measures an individual's abilities in terms of expressive and receptive language, while PIQ is a measure of how someone uses reasoning to plan and carry out actions. PIQ is determined through performance tests that assess fine- and gross-motor skills and visual-spatial and visual-motor function. FSIQ (full-scale IQ; the figure we're usually referring to when we say "IQ") is derived from the scores on seven subtests. Typically, there is little discrepancy between VIQ and PIQ; the scores may not be the same, but they fall within a comfortable range. With NLD, however, often VIQ is higher than PIQ, though not in all cases.

Central Auditory Processing Disorder

Central auditory processing disorder (CAPD) is an extremely complex and little recognized inability to listen to or comprehend auditory information despite having normal hearing. A youngster with CAPD has reduced or significantly impaired ability to identify, recognize, discriminate, and understand what he hears. What's more, he may be unusually sensitive to typical noises and/or be unable to discriminate between foreground and background noise and may respond to each simultaneously; in other words, a child may perceive the sound of wind rustling leaves outside a closed window to be as loud as the voice of the teacher standing two feet away. Children with CAPD can become emotionally overwhelmed by certain sounds and noisy environments, sometimes resulting in withdrawal or tantrumming. They may have difficulty following spoken complex sentences and instructions despite having an average or above-average IQ. Children with CAPD often mishear words and sounds; to compensate, they try to fill in the blanks, sometimes resulting in a complete misunderstanding of what they heard. A brain-imaging study of sixty-four children, roughly half of them on the autism spectrum, determined that children with ASD actually perceive and process sounds one-fiftieth of a second (twenty milliseconds) more slowly than their neurotypical peers. According to the lead researcher, Dr. Timothy Roberts of Children's Hospital in Philadelphia, "Although we are only talking about fractions of a second, these can have a catastrophic impact on spoken language." Interestingly, the study included both children with and without language delays. Although there seems to be an association between longer processing delays and more impaired language, even children without language problems were still processing more slowly than typical peers.

Chapter 7

UNDERSTANDING BEHAVIOR

Now that we have taken the grand tour and have a solid understanding of why kids with Asperger syndrome and other ASDs might find learning certain types of skills more challenging, let's open the map and start charting our route to success. As I've said before—and yet somehow feel I can never say enough—one of the biggest roadblocks we confront when teaching is trying to conceptualize how we can show someone how to do something that we ourselves do not recall having ever learned consciously. You know how to do things such as fold a towel or cook an egg; you surely have a crystal-clear image of what getting dressed or cleaning up looks like. Yet when the learner has an autism spectrum disorder and we try teaching in a way that feels natural to us, the gap between knowing how and knowing how to teach comes into sharp focus.

IT'S ALL ABOUT THE REINFORCER

How, you may wonder, will teaching your child this time be different from before? First, we're going to approach skills as forms of behavior, and second, we are going to teach by reinforcing and shaping behavior. Most important, however, we are going to truly make your child's effort worth her while. We do this by reinforcing the behaviors we put together to make a skill.

What Is Behavior?

To many parents, professionals, and our culture at large, *behavior* has become a code word, a euphemism for someone doing something we really don't like. I suppose this is preferable to the old days when children were described as being "bad," "naughty," and "spoiled rotten." When teachers, parents, or Austin Powers warned us to "behave," they meant for us to stop doing something they didn't want us to do or to start doing something they did want us to do. As we all progressed to a more enlightened view of children and psychology, *behavior* became the new neutral, presumably nonjudgmental term that's been used so often it's become a mild pejorative in its own right. Now everyone, it seems, is trendily "behavioral": "Lucy has behaviors," "Jimmy had a behavioral episode," "Mark is very behavioral today." When I hear someone say that a child "has behaviors," my first impulse is to say, "Thank heavens"—because the only people who don't "have behaviors" are dead people.

We need to rescue *behavior* and restore it to its rightful place as a neutral, nonjudgmental description of an observable action. I remember feeling my back go up when teachers and others began talking to me about my son's "behaviors." And I have spent countless hours explaining to parents and others that "behavior" is not a bad thing. Really, all behavior is simply what we do that is perceptible to others (even if we are alone) or that makes a change, however slight, in the physical environment. (You might not see me breathe, but in breathing, I change the environment by moving air molecules.) It's that simple.

If you were with me in my home office right now, you would see that I am engaged in dozens of behaviors: I'm breathing, sitting in a chair, typing, reading a computer screen, applying lip gloss, turning some pages, sighing, sipping iced tea, cracking my knuckles, twisting my rings, asking my husband to turn off his Cheap Trick CD, and staring off into space while I'm clicking a pink highlighter. These are all behaviors anyone can observe, count, and describe in one or several ways. If you asked me later what I was doing at 1:25 p.m. on May 21, 2010, I would say only, "Writing my book."

I am doing some other things as well: thinking, feeling thirsty, hearing music, daydreaming. But you cannot see me doing those things. You cannot count or measure my daydreaming, though you could count and measure the behaviors that might be related: me closing my eyes or staring at something in the room not related to the task at hand. Generally, though, while you can perhaps make some good guesses about whatever's going on that you can't see, you can never really know. You have no way of knowing that I'm thirsty until I engage in some behavior that you can see—saying "I'm thirsty," taking a sip of tea, or staring longingly at your glass of tea. Am I twisting my rings because I'm daydreaming or because there's a mosquito bite on my finger?

A key strength of teaching approaches based on ABA is that, like *Dragnet*'s Sergeant Joe Friday, behavior analysts stick to just the facts, ma'am. Behavior is what people do that we can observe—period. Skills are behaviors that have a clear purpose. Teaching is a behavior, and so is learning. Remember: we are not concerned with "good" behavior or "bad" behavior, only with behavior we would like to see more of and behavior we would like to see less of. If your child has a tantrum, utters a naughty word, slams the door, mouths off, or kicks the ottoman, please say that he is having a tantrum, saying a naughty word, slamming the door, mouthing off, or kicking the ottoman—*not* he is "having behaviors" or "being behavioral." And when others discuss your child's behaviors in less than precise terms, request clarification and specifics.

SKILLS ARE REALLY JUST BEHAVIORS

Most of the teaching strategies that follow evolved from a scientific understanding of and decades of research on how living things learn.*
Yes, I said "living things," and, yes, that does include pigeons, mice,

---

*The only exception is Social Stories, which, because they are highly individualized and did not grow out of behaviorism, have not yet lent themselves to the kind of study that the other strategies listed have received.

monkeys, horses, dolphins, dogs, and people—all people, by the way, not just those with learning and developmental disabilities. You might be surprised to know that with the exception of Social Stories, each of these techniques is considered part of applied behavior analysis.

Although we will be using a select handful of other, non-ABA strategies throughout, ABA is undeniably the foundation for teaching

The Asperger "Exception"

You may have heard that "ABA is not for kids with AS" or "Kids with AS are too smart for ABA." That's simply not true. In fact, the principles that ABA applies to teaching are at work in your everyday life. Successful behavior-changing programs—from Weight Watchers to smoking cessation plans—run on the principles of behavior first identified by psychologist B. F. Skinner, as do the most effective approaches to training in any field where performance counts: from the military and professional sports to business and space flight. Just as ABA can explain why you work for a paycheck or continue to play a slot machine that's never paid off for you, it can also identify the reinforcement contingencies—the consequences of our behavior that prompt us to do something—that keep individuals with ASDs such as Asperger syndrome going.

ABA offers a wealth of strategies and techniques that work well for teaching a skill to anyone. But we also know that they seem especially well suited to the learning deficits and differences we encounter along the autism spectrum. As you will see, several of these teaching techniques seem almost custom-made to address the kinds of specific deficits we see in AS. Ironically, while ABA was finding greater acceptance among other communities in other fields (professional sports training, business and human resources, medicine), it was losing ground in education to decidedly unscientific approaches—particularly in regard to teaching "more able" youngsters. Meanwhile, young adults with AS emerged from years of such questionable interventions with alarmingly weak skills for independence.

these skills, just as its basic principles of reinforcement and teaching are widely reflected throughout our everyday lives. People who criticize ABA as being "unnatural" miss the point. It's important to keep in mind that ABA did not invent a new way to teach new skills or change behaviors; it simply provided a scientific understanding of the principles of learning as they apply to all people, and harnessed them into a consistent, research-based repertoire of teaching strategies that utilize our natural inclination to repeat behaviors that bring consequences we do like and to reduce or eliminate behaviors that result in consequences that we don't like. Then our behaviorist friends did what most proponents in education and psychology too often don't do: they conducted research, published that research, and made their oldest, most respected peer-reviewed journals, the *Journal of Applied Behavior Analysis*, available to everyone, online, for free.

One result of more than forty years' research is that ABA gives us a way to recognize and identify a highly consistent pattern that explains why we do the things we do. We can then use that information to create environments and change teacher behavior (what you say, do, how you prompt, and so on) in ways that set up a learner to learn. So rather than being some exotic, eggheaded approach to learning, the principles behind ABA are actually at work throughout our daily lives. Do any of the following scenarios apply to your life?

- You or someone else charts and applauds your weekly weight loss.
- You place a quarter in the "swear jar" for every bad word.
- You give your daughter $1 for every A on her report card, but only 50¢ for each B.
- You watch *Supernanny* and can accurately predict what Jo Frost will tell the parents within five minutes of watching the kids spray-paint the dog and squish Play-Doh into the carpet with their feet.
- You do volunteer work and feel good about it.
- You go to Vegas or another gambling town, or you play the lottery.

- You have harbored mean thoughts about or snarled mean words to a malfunctioning inanimate object, such as a soda machine.
- You have received or given someone an allowance for doing chores.

If you answered yes to even one of these, then you are well aware of the power of consequences to teach and shape behavior. While in all the instances cited, contingencies of reinforcement or punishment are influencing behavior, in none of these examples can we say that true applied behavior analysis is being practiced. More on that to come.

WHAT IS REINFORCEMENT?

At a recent seminar I gave, a woman asked me, "I know I'm supposed to reward our son when he is learning new things, but my husband"—and here she gestured to the man sitting beside her, his arms crossed over his chest—"doesn't believe in that. He's old-fashioned." Here the man gave me a strong, firm nod. "He thinks our son should just do things because he *should*. What can you say to change my husband's mind?"

The man seemed to be a good sport, so I said lightly, "And so when are you going to start going to work without getting a paycheck?" Everyone, including the gentleman, laughed, but I think they got the point. Giving something to someone in return for something he or she does is not bribery. If we do something, we do it for a reason; and usually that reason is because it leads to something that we want or because it helps us avoid or delay something we do not want. Sometimes it's a little of both. I go to Starbucks because I really like their oatmeal cookie; I do not get on the scale two days later because I do not want to face the consequence of eating that oatmeal cookie. (Three hundred and seventy calories? How is that possible? It looks so healthy!) I go for, toward, and after what I want; I avoid, move away from, and escape from what I do not. Any behavior that meets with reinforcement is more likely to be repeated as well as strengthened over time. Conversely, behavior that does not meet with reinforcement is less likely to be repeated and will weaken over time.

Reinforcers are highly individual; what works for one person will not necessarily work for another. And even the reinforcer of choice today may not have any appeal tomorrow. So we define a reinforcer not by what it is—a video game, a toy, a chocolate, a hug—but by how well it does what we want it to do: increase the likelihood that the behavior that occurred immediately before its presentation will occur again. A car that does not run is still a car, and a wedding dress is still a wedding dress even if it's never worn to a wedding. But reinforcers are different. A candy bar will still be a candy bar, and it may still be something Julie loves to eat, but it is not a reinforcer if access to it following a behavior does not increase that behavior.

When we systematically analyze situations and use that information to make changes in how we interact with someone to teach or improve a skill or reduce or eliminate an interfering behavior, we call it a behavior plan. Like so much in the world of education, the term *behavior plan* has taken on an ominous aura, because it tends to be invoked when there is a problem behavior. But as a matter of fact, a plan you might write to teach your son to keep in touch with friends on Facebook more regularly or show your daughter how to make pancakes is also a behavior plan. I prefer thinking of these as teaching plans for everyone involved, because in order for them to work, all of us must change something about what we do. For instance, as a teaching parent, you may be changing your voice tone, simplifying your language (yes, even if your child's verbal IQ is 130), and using more physical prompts than you ever have before. When we develop a behavior plan intentionally, we clearly see what works and what doesn't.

For a moment, though, let's turn our attention to the countless "behavior plans" that nobody seems to have consciously, deliberately written but which are running—and working to deliver reinforcement and sometimes less pleasant consequences—throughout our days. Nobody writes the plan for the dad who gives his screaming two-year-old candy while waiting in the supermarket checkout line, but it "works" in getting each of them what they want in the moment (candy for the kid, quiet for the dad). Nobody writes the plan for the woman in the parents' association who never complains (and gets all the work dumped on her) or for the one who always complains (and so is rarely asked to help out). But this plan "works" very effectively on the people who assign the work, since they naturally more often ask the person who seems happy to do it all (or is at least quiet about it) and less often ask the person whose complaints they would rather avoid.

There are two kinds of reinforcers: positive and negative. Both terms are often misused, so let's clarify. When we say *positive*, all we mean is that something is added or given. All *negative* means is that something is removed or taken away. Basically, a reinforcer is something that happens after a behavior that increases the likelihood that you will use that behavior again. Of course, we all tend toward the positive, but don't discount negative reinforcement. In some situations, removing an unpleasant condition can be as reinforcing and as powerful a teacher as a positive reinforcer such as praise or access to the Wii. Putting out the smelly garbage, opening an umbrella in the rain, or removing a whistling teakettle from the burner are all examples of negative reinforcement, because they remove something unpleasant from the environment (a bad smell, exposure to rain, and an irritating sound). For some kids, removing Mom from their getting-dressed routine in the morning is an example of negative reinforcement (because when Mom leaves the room, so does the sound of her voice). Again, we all believe we do these things—taking out the garbage, opening the umbrella, or picking up the teakettle—as a matter of course, but a lot of what we do is determined or influenced by the reinforcement produced. We do things that result in things coming into our experience or being removed from it because they're worth it to us in terms of consequences we seek or consequences we avoid.

WHAT KINDS OF REINFORCERS ARE WORKING NOW?

Even though we're talking about a wide array of skills, there are some general things we know about acquiring these types of skills and the behavioral reasons for some of the difficulties we encounter. We've already explored what may be going on in terms of learning and some of the neurological factors possibly at work. Now let's focus on what happens with your child and his environment—and that includes other people.

The Skill Is Just "Too Hard"

Yes, many independence skills are difficult for children to learn, but often that is because they either have not been taught systematically or they have a history of doing things in a way that is unnecessarily complicated and inefficient, physically or mentally. Praise for trying and giving it your best is not very fulfilling (reinforcing) if you walk away feeling frustrated and inept, and if that's the unpleasant consequence your child experiences for investing a great deal of effort, he's going to seek an alternative reinforcer: namely, avoid the task and/or engage in behaviors that reduce the likelihood he'll be asked to do it again.

It's Just Easier for Parents, Teachers, and Others to Do It Themselves

We're all busy, we all have deadlines, we all have just so many hours in the day to get things done. Kids' lives run on schedules, and most of our daily routines have time restrictions. Yes, your daughter could spend an hour getting dressed for school, but then she'd miss the bus, you'd have to drive her to school, and you would be late for work. When youngsters cannot manage their daily responsibilities in a timely way, their problem becomes our problem, and many parents' immediate reaction is to simply "fix it"—which usually means doing whatever they can to keep the child's problem from morphing into their problem. No doubt about it: this is an effective damage-containment strategy. That's how we end up micromanaging routine activities that kids should be doing for themselves. Why? Because we get something good (everyone out of the house on time) and avoid something bad (everyone late for the day). What we need to focus on are the secondary consequences, unintended but equally strong: limiting your child's learning and practice of these essential skills.

One way to address this is to teach routines that have time constraints during a more forgiving time. For example, your child can practice dressing for school or repacking the backpack after homework during a free half hour on the weekend. You'll want to stick to the same real-life time constraints (for example, if five minutes is how long the backpack routine should take each morning, the time it takes in practice should be less than five minutes), but at least this removes pressure from the equation.

"I Don't Want To! I Don't Have To! You Can't Make Me!"

There's no minimum age requirement for putting up the "I don't want to" kind of argument, but the chances of your hearing it increase with your child's age. As Dr. Tony Attwood observes of teens: "Parents have reached their use-by date." Again, it is never too late to start teaching people the skills they need. That said, let's be honest: younger children can sometimes be easier to persuade. Dr. Gerhardt suggests using behavioral contracting—essentially making a simple written agreement between you and your child that outlines clearly who will do what: "I tie it into what *their* goals are, but it truly has to be from *their* point of view. What is it worth to them?" Once again, the answer is reinforcement.

The Skill, the Supplies, the Purpose:
They're Just Not on Your Child's Radar

The pull of attention toward irrelevant stimuli results in children who are surprisingly unaware of basic activities that occur around them every day. The natural curiosity that typical children exhibit is virtually unlimited compared to the often highly restricted interests and curiosity typical of many with ASDs. Once you start working on household tasks, you may be surprised to find that your child never really noticed things such as when the garbage gets taken out, how you "burp" the lids of plastic containers, or where you keep cleaning supplies.

Applied Behavior Analysis Is Everywhere, Just Disguised

Our current education lexicon overflows with buzzwords such as "positive behavior support," "individualized teaching," "reinforcement schedules," "fluency training," "natural consequences," "time out," "token systems," "response cost," "Grandma's law," "direct teaching." The latest version of the Individuals with Disabilities Education Act (IDEA)—the federal law that mandates special education and related services—requires functional behavior assessments and behavior intervention plans in certain situations. All these have their origins in the science and practice of applied behavior analysis. Why? Because federal education and disability law requires that interventions be evidence-based. Currently, among all interventions and therapies for autism spectrum disorders, applied behavior analysis has met the criteria of being a scientific, evidence-based treatment with the longest history and largest body of supporting research of all competing treatments.

LOOKING AT BEHAVIOR BEHAVIORALLY IS NONJUDGMENTAL

Another positive aspect of approaching skill building behaviorally is that it offers a fresh, decidedly nonjudgmental way to look at why someone does or does not do something. Sure, Jimmy might not make his bed every morning because he is "lazy." But instead of jumping to conclusions, look at this behavior through your behavioral goggles. I can assure you that you will approach it quite differently, even if—especially if—you've dealt with it a dozen times before. This is difficult for professionals sometimes, and it is even harder for parents. After all, you probably share a history of tackling this problem with your child, and past attempts may have been unsuccessful or worse. In behavior-speak, we would say that your learning history has not been reinforcing. It is perfectly understandable, then, why it may be hard to gear up and give it another try—not only for you but for your child. Try to move past that. Don't blame yourself, your child, or the fact that he has an ASD. Your child can learn and will learn, and you can teach her. But she will most likely learn if you use an approach different from the one you tried before.

LOOKING AT BEHAVIOR BEHAVIORALLY IS REALLY SEEING

As Yogi Berra famously said, "You can observe a lot just by watching." When we look at problems behaviorally, we aren't looking solely at behavior. (See the sidebar on page 125.) What we are looking at, really, is what we can observe, which sounds ridiculously obvious until you realize how often we develop solutions for problems that we define, characterize, describe, and draw conclusions about based on things that we do not or cannot see: "attitudes," "deficits," "disorders," "abnormalities," "delays," "sensory issues," and so on. Though those factors certainly exist, remind yourself to look beyond or around them. They might provide important information to consider, but they aren't that helpful when it comes to solving a learning problem. Focus instead on what is happening that you can see, count, evaluate, and describe in a way so that someone else would know exactly what you are talking about. Make it concrete, make it visual, make it simple and to the point.

Even though we might both be describing the same situation—say, Ziggy making his bed—I trust that you will appreciate the difference between someone describing it as "I don't know what he did, but it's a mess!" or "He just can't get himself organized" or "What do you expect? He doesn't know where his body is in space" or "It figures. He has Asperger's" and someone else describing it like this: "Even though the bottom sheet and the top sheet were in place, the comforter was askew, and the pillows were lying on the floor."

Reading the first description, you might well ask, "Where do I start?" Good question! I'd have no idea. But the second description gives you a place to begin. Some even better questions would be:

What did Ziggy do well?

What did he do not so well?

What do we know about the skills Ziggy has from the parts he
   got right?

What do we know about the skills Ziggy has not mastered
   from the parts he executed poorly?

Those are the questions that someone observing the situation
from a behavioral perspective would ask. They're specific, concrete,
and based on what we see, not what we think Ziggy might be thinking
or a condition he might have. Suddenly, it all seems much clearer. The
problem is broken down and described in a way that is useful, because
it can point us in the direction of a solution. And the sooner we can
begin trying solutions, the sooner we find the right one. Expect a little
trial and error: this isn't a cake mix.

When we look at a problem like Ziggy making his bed or Aidan getting ready for school or Angela getting ready to go outside in the rain,
we are looking at three things:

1. A series, or chain, of individual behaviors
2. The behaviors we would like to see more of (or increase),
   like Ziggy getting the sheets back on the bed properly
3. Those behaviors we wish to see less of (or decrease), such
   as leaving items that belong on the bed lying on the floor

THERE'S GOOD PRACTICE AND THERE'S BAD PRACTICE

When we break down behavior behaviorally, we take a panoramic view.
We also think in terms of the skills a child has today forming a foundation for skills that will develop later. Some kids do not develop the best
early skills. For others who attempt new tasks, it is easier for Mom and
Dad to accept a not-so-careful job than to try to improve it.

Let's say that we want to improve Angela's feeding the puppies
and filling their water bowl. The seven-year-old loves her new pets and
enjoys the praise she receives for this daily chore. But after she's done,

you spot puppy food sprinkled across the countertop and a trail of water splashes across the floor. You were hoping she would get better as she went along, but she's been doing this now for a few weeks, and you wonder if you will spoil her pleasure in it if you insist that she carry out the task more neatly.

We all know the expression "Practice makes perfect," and it is true, but only when the practice is correct and accurate. Remember that the internal monitoring system and innate tendency to self-correct found in the typical child may not be as strong in some of our kids. What happens to many kids with learning problems is that they repeat a skill or a behavior the wrong way, and so we get a "perfected" version of that imperfect behavior or a skill—one that's not executed well enough to be effective or produce the desired result. Behaviorally, we describe this type of situation with the new saw "Practice makes permanent." In other words, just as perfect practice makes perfect execution so fluent and effortless that we seem to be doing it automatically, imperfect practice results in fluently imperfect execution. The difference is that when perfect practice of imperfect or substandard skills leads to a fluency and effortlessness in doing it wrong, it can be difficult for a child to unlearn the substandard skills and relearn the skills the right way.

Letting Angela keep on practicing a chore filled with errors does two things: First, it reduces her opportunities to experience doing it right. Second, it sets into place the habit of doing it wrong, with the associated motor memory and behavior chains. Angela will be using these skills or similar skills to do other things such as refill an ice cube tray, carry dishes of food from the kitchen to the table, and so on. If she is learning to carry plastic doggie bowls improperly, and spilling food on the floor, it may be difficult for her to relearn to do it correctly when it's time to carry a bowl of hot soup. When you consider how many things our children must learn and the effort they put forth to do so, it sure seems unfair to waste their time learning anything they may have to unlearn later on.

From beginning to end, what is happening? What does the task look like? What does Angela actually do—and not do? Later we will get into the exact steps for correcting incorrect behavior chains. For now,

though, start getting into the mind-set that a chore such as feeding
the puppies is made up of many other small component behaviors. In
Angela's case, she always fills both the food bowl and the water bowl
all the way up to the brim. She has not learned to determine by sight
or by weight when the bowl is full enough as opposed to totally full.
You might provide a photograph of the bowl filled correctly or make
a permanent ink mark inside the bowl at the correct level. It is also
likely that this inability to gauge the concept of "enough" may crop up
throughout the day: the toothbrush winds up smothered in toothpaste
and the juice glass is filled to overflowing. Ideally, teaching Angela to
determine independently the right amount of food and water will carry
over to these other tasks.

The ability to learn something under one set of circumstances and
then actively apply that knowledge to other situations is called *generalization*. Teaching Angela the rote steps of feeding the pups is great, but
by paying attention to and providing lots of errorless practice of each
step *and* encouraging her to make decisions about how high to fill the
bowls offers her a wider range of skill. Ideally, this will also produce
more independence and self-confidence.

In chapter 10, we'll delve into the nitty-gritty of your teaching plan.
For now, let's look at some of the most commonly used teaching strategies for independence skills.

Chapter 8

THE TOOLS FOR TEACHING

There are several behaviorally based teaching techniques that lend themselves beautifully to teaching independence skills:

Prompting that precedes the action
- Verbal instructions
- Modeling
- Physical guidance

Prompting that happens during the action
- Graduated guidance
- Least-to-most prompts
- Time delay

Changing the teaching sequence
- Behavior chains
- Forward chaining
- Backward chaining

Shaping

Visual supports
- Video modeling

ALL ABOUT PROMPTS

Prompts are truly wonderful when they are used effectively. It's easy to think of using prompts as helping your child, but, in fact, your goal in using prompts is to accomplish the following:

- Use the minimum level of prompts needed to support learning.
- Use the minimum level of prompting to prevent or immediately correct errors.
- Fade the prompt as quickly as possible without any loss of learning or performance.

Different Kinds of Prompts

Prompts are usually ordered in a hierarchy from "most" to "least." At the "most" end of the scale, prompts are more intrusive and restrictive; at the "least" end, less so. Try teaching a skill using the least intrusive prompt you can. Then, once your child demonstrates the ability to perform that step or skill, fade back to the next-least prompt.

Not all prompts are created equal; there are different levels of prompting, and some forms are easier to fade than others. Fading prompts is as important as the learning that the prompt supported, because independence will not be achieved so long as another person is still managing the prompts. (Kids using other methods to prompt themselves is a different matter entirely, which we'll examine on page 154.)

When people first encounter a prompt hierarchy list, they are surprised to find that spoken verbal prompts are considered a "last resort" strategy—and one that we try to avoid while teaching independence skills. After all, prompting through speaking is all around us; it's what everybody else seems to do. However, verbal prompts are uniquely susceptible to becoming embedded in a behavior, with the result being a child who will literally stand and wait to hear a verbal prompt before moving on to the next step of a skill. If you find your own child seemingly frozen or totally distracted in the middle of a familiar task, he may be waiting for that verbal prompt he's used to hearing when you or someone else notices he is off task.

	INDEPENDENCE/NO PROMPTS	
Least ↑	Visual or verbal-visual prompts; pictures or brief written instructions or reminders	
	Brief spoken verbal prompts: one- or two-word instructions, reminders, cues	
	Gestural prompts: pointing at, nodding toward, deliberately gazing at relevant object	
	Shadowing prompts: following from a distance without directly touching	Work toward fading your presence from the room
	Partial physical prompts: touch or light physical prompt at fingers, wrist, mid-forearm, elbow, mid-upper arm, shoulder	Use spatial fading (move your prompt the next step farther away from the last prompt)
Most ↓	Full physical prompts: Hand-over-hand	
	DEPENDENCE/FULLY PROMPTED	

TOO MUCH OF A (FORMERLY) GOOD THING: PROMPT DEPENDENCE

For kids who may receive special education and related services at school or other forms of extra help, prompting gets a bad name on account of another, albeit related development: prompt dependence (which some people call "learned helplessness"). I would estimate that the vast majority of parents reading this were advised against getting extra personal support for their child on the grounds that it could encourage prompt dependence. Often moms and dads are dubious about this concern, as I was when it was offered as a reason why my son should not have a one-on-one aide way back in kindergarten. What I heard then—and what many parents hear today—is a school district trying to avoid providing a very expensive service.

Well, my son got his aide; in fact, he had a number of wonderful people working with him for quite a few years, and I appreciate and thank them all. But thirteen years later, I can honestly say that prompt dependence is every bit the problem that some educators claim, and it is one enduring legacy of my son's school career that I'd have tried harder to avoid had I known then what I know now. (And, in some odd karmic boomerang, working to increase kids' independence claims a large percentage of my professional energy.)

Prompt dependence is one of the few things in behavioral terminology that actually is exactly what it sounds like. There are several causes, and they all seem to intertwine, so it's usually impossible to identify which is the chicken and which is the egg. If we look at the ASD learning style and view the back-and-forth between the person doing the prompting and the person being prompted as another environmental stimulus, it's easy to see how prompt dependence evolves. First, the highly socially reinforcing interaction that often accompanies prompts (after all, typically a kind person is helping you; what's wrong with that?) sometimes steals the spotlight of the child's attention. You think that by patiently explaining every step of using the blow dryer, you are helping. In fact, we know that people with ASDs often have difficulty with input overload. What your child should be focused on is his how hair looks, whether it feels wet or dry, where the air from the dryer is going, what he's doing with the brush in his other hand, and so on. Also keep in mind that helping—no matter how well intended and necessary—sends kids the message "I'm here because you can't do it." Of course, none of us think that, and none of us would ever do anything intentionally to give that impression. Yet for many kids, that is the take-home message.

Prompt dependence also has social and emotional ramifications. It undermines a child's sense of independence, interferes with his peers accepting him, and creates a false impression that the youngster is less capable than he truly is. Needless to say, none of this builds either self-esteem or social success.

There are several ways to avoid prompt dependence without reducing the support and help your child may need today. The first, and probably the most important, is to understand that prompt dependence is an unintended side effect of intervention and to plan for it. Make reducing and fading prompts as important as using them.

Every type of prompt has its advantages and disadvantages. Spoken verbal prompts are the easiest to use, the hardest to fade, and the type most associated with prompt dependence. Two words: zip it. As a general rule, independence skills should be taught using *no spoken verbal prompts*. None, nada, zero.

You want to teach the skill wherever it takes place in daily life. We call this the natural environment. When it comes to most independence skills—especially those involving personal care, hygiene, dressing, and so on—the natural environment is private and includes no one else but you and your child. Further, the cue for moving to the next step or activity already exists somewhere in the environment, for the goal of prompting is to help a child learn to seek out and attend to those naturalistic cues. Here's an example: approaching the door as you leave the bathroom is the cue for turning off the light, not someone saying, "Turn off the light." And certainly not someone saying "Turn off the light" ten minutes after you left the room and your parent just noticed the light still on. Talking can draw attention from and eclipse the natural environmental cues your child should be focused on. Again, remember how difficult it is for some people with ASDs to process information coming in on two channels. Turn off the volume as much as you can.

The presence of another person talking a child through the task is unnatural and in some instances inappropriate, especially with regard to personal skills. While you might not see a problem with talking it through at home, what about outside the home? Do you really want your child to require the presence of an adult for dressing and using the restroom at school, camp, a friend's home?

Prompts usually come with a big dollop of friendly adult attention in the form of social reinforcement (praise, hugs, smiles, and so on). We all like people to be nice to us; we all appreciate a little help now and then. The problem is that sometimes this social interaction becomes the point and the purpose of the prompting, and everyone loses sight of the skill we want the child to acquire. Some children learn quickly that staying dependent ensures continued adult attention. Again, this is not "manipulative" or "bratty" behavior. This is something the child discovered accidentally; it's another example of an unwritten, unintentional, yet highly effective behavior plan.

Quick Tip: Check Out Rethink Autism's Video Library of Behavioral Teaching Tools and Tips

---

Launched in 2009, Rethink Autism (www.rethinkautism.com) is an innovative web-based provider of ABA programming that includes evaluation, curriculum, program design, data management, and parent and therapist training. For a monthly fee, Rethink Autism makes it possible for parents, schools, and school districts that might not have access to trained ABA professionals to learn to run their own programs. You do not have to sign on for a full program to benefit from all the website has to offer, though. Rethink Autism offers a free email newsletter full of timely tips and links to demonstration videos that show exactly how to teach a skill, along with free, informative webinars with experts and limited access to a video library of programs. You can get a free month's membership to sample the more than one thousand video lessons and tips (all accompanied by written lesson plans) demonstrated by skilled

ABA teachers. The Rethink Autism curriculum offers programs in all domains, including self-help and socialization, for learners across the spectrum, including those with AS and HFA. I recommend you watch several of their demo videos just to see effective prompting, fading, shadowing, et cetera, in action.

Remember that we all have social appetites for interaction, support, and caring from others. Typical children satisfy much of this appetite by interacting with other children. But peers are rarely a sufficient source of social sustenance for kids with AS and other disabilities that profoundly affect social development. These children spend a much larger percentage of their social time with adults compared to what they spend with other children. Adults understand them, make accommodations, and appreciate qualities that maybe their peers either don't see or don't get yet. Not that there's anything wrong with this. However, one way to reduce the risk of prompt dependence is to save the good social stuff for other times. It's not being rude or mean to matter-of-factly stick to business when teaching and prompting. There's enough time for smiles, laughs, high fives, and talking when the task is completed and you can use social reinforcement for a better purpose: to really reinforce a skill, as opposed to creating a distraction and reinforcing dependence.

TEACHING BY SPOKEN VERBAL INSTRUCTIONS, DEMONSTRATION, MODELING

"Just watch me," "Don't forget to . . . ," and "See how I did that?" constitute just about all the teaching that most typical kids need in order to pick up most daily living skills. When you realize that the seemingly simple act of observing and then imitating someone else requires attention, executive function, working memory, mirror neurons, theory of mind, sound motor skills, and good receptive language abilities, it becomes a lot clearer why this does not work as well for all of our kids.

Do not be misled by the general idea that everyone with AS (or even ASDs generally) is a visual learner who "thinks in pictures." No doubt some are. However, a person can be highly adept at visualizing, say, the construction of a new kind of hybrid car engine and yet be unable to imitate the physical actions of another person. Yes, both situations are highly visual, but the ability to use visual images as a language (as Temple Grandin seems to do) does not depend on the same neurological processes that motor imitation does. Here again, we see the spectrumwide weakness in attending to and imitating the actions of other people, no matter how well your child learns visually or how bright she may be in other areas.

SPOKEN VERBAL INSTRUCTIONS, DEMONSTRATION, MODELING	
Advantages	**Disadvantages**
Quick, simple; no need for extra paraphernalia or materials	Not appropriate for all skills; may be weak or missing component skills
Can model the precise target behavior	Not all individuals with ASDs are visual learners; mirror neuron deficits can impede their ability to imitate, especially face-to-face; words or pictures may not convey the information well
"Just talking it through" sounds easy; doesn't take a lot of preparation; highly portable	Spoken verbal prompts are easily embedded into routines but foster prompt dependence; can be the hardest types of prompts to fade; undermine true independence

Does that mean you should never try to demonstrate or model a skill? Absolutely not! In fact, for kids who are not natural observers of others, using modeling in a highly reinforcing situation could conceivably support the separate, and crucial, skill of attending to others.

Then there is the simple fact that some skills can be taught *only* by observation and imitation. Of course, you will use this in addition to different combinations of prompts, but most independence-skills teaching includes modeling.

Before you get started, be sure that you have done the following:

- Conducted a task analysis, a detailed step-by-step inventory of each separate action. See task analysis on pages 159, 160, 206, and throughout the book.
- Gathered any necessary materials at hand (and that both your materials and your child's are the same in important dimensions of size, weight, and so on).
- Practiced your "choreography"—your plan to model the skill from beginning to end, then immediately repeat it with whatever prompts and other strategies you will be using. Even if the skill is to be broken down into small units or taught using backward chaining, it's important to demonstrate the whole skill, from beginning to end, so that your child begins to form a mental picture of the complete process.

Go slowly. There's no rush. Fluency comes later. And watch out for the "Houdini steps" (see box).

Houdini Steps

When you begin breaking down and analyzing a skill, be on the lookout for what I call the "Houdini steps." These are movements in the task chain that your child may have difficulty seeing accurately and imitating. When demonstrated by someone who performs the task fluently, these movements can seem incomprehensible—almost magical—to someone with poor mirror neuron activity, poor imitation skills, or poor motor planning and coordination. (See chapter 5 for more details on these.) For someone with AS, simply seeing these steps demonstrated does not provide all the information he may need in order to imitate them. A pizza man tossing and shaping a pizza crust, a hairstylist creating an elaborate hairdo, and a boy riding a bicycle are all examples of behavior chains that might appear to happen in part by sleight of hand, because the processes that make them work either are invisible (like the sense of balance, in the case of riding a bike) or can be seen but go by way too quickly (the hand motions that shape a crust in between tosses).

Try this: fold a towel or sheet the way most of us do—while holding it in front of us, without laying it out on a flat surface—and notice how many times you ever so subtly toss and catch the material, then make folds in midair. Now ask yourself, "How would I demonstrate this elaborate ballet of eye-hand coordination and motor planning so that someone else could learn it?" Chances are it would be difficult, not to mention extremely frustrating for your learner. This is one reason why it's essential to conduct your own task analysis, where you perform the behavior.

There are probably many Houdini moments in some of the skills you'd like to teach. (There are a good number in shoe tying, for sure.) Your child will learn more easily if you can pinpoint these and teach using steps that are slower, more visually relevant, and more noticeable, and if you make use of environmental supports, such as folding items on a flat surface.

Minimize talking during the task. You don't need to narrate what you're doing, but a few handy word cues that your child can integrate into his own internal checklist for the skill cannot hurt. Let's say you're teaching your son how to crack an egg. Instead of saying, "Okay, first you take your egg, and you hold it like this, from each end. Then you line up the bowl, and you hit the egg sharply against the edge of the bowl while you hold on to and separate the two ends," say: "Fingers. Crack. Separate" to narrate the particular step in the chain. Remember that kids with AS are attracted to language; when words start flowing in, their attention to most other stimuli goes out the window. Clear away the verbal clutter and use minimal language to help refocus your

First, a Word About Words

Educators, parents, and other experts have correctly identified the verbal channel as a strength in kids with AS. They have words, they use them, and they understand them to varying degrees. However, we have missed the target if we assume that simply because someone is good with using words, he or she will learn everything best by hearing or reading words. In fact, for many of the skills this book addresses, actual physical practice may be the key. For others, practice in noticing details and making judgments is the answer.

youngster's attention on what you are doing and on the natural environmental cues.

In one study, researchers helped a highly prompt-dependent nineteen-year-old man with Asperger syndrome improve the percentage of ten-second intervals during which he was on task simply by giving directions that included information about the expected outcome. For example, in sessions where he was told, "Here are some shapes; cut out as many as you can," he cut an average of 4.5 shapes. However, when told, "Here are some shapes; try to cut out at least five shapes in the next fifteen minutes," he cut an average of 15—more than three times as many. More specific directions stating the outcome expectations produced similar improvements in typing (from an average of 13.9 lines typed to 24) and reading (from an average of 1.5 questions answered about a short passage to 12 questions answered).

However, use antecedent (before the activity) verbal prompts judiciously: "Remember to wash your hands right after you crack the eggs," "For this we're using the microwave, not the stove," and so on. This may reduce the amount of talking you have to do later on. And keeping information like this in the forefront of your child's memory is an element of executive function it can't hurt to prompt.

Be aware that asking your child to "follow along"—to watch and then imitate you performing a step—requires her to do two (or maybe three or four) things at once, which can be very challenging for some.

Unless you know otherwise, assume that your child may be finding it difficult to maintain her focus on the relevant details of what you are demonstrating. You want her to pay attention to how to fold the napkin to fit into the napkin ring—not to the color of the napkin, the texture of the ring, or the Band-Aid on your hand. And, it should go without saying, you also don't want your child listening to her iPod or glancing at whatever's on TV. There are two schools of thought on this. One says to clear the field, or remove as many distractions as you can. But the other maintains that the world is full of distractions, so learning to attend to the relevant cues and disregard irrelevant ones is an essential skill that should be practiced and reinforced as often as possible. If attention is a particular problem for your youngster, try a sensible compromise: minimize distractions when you start the teaching exercise, but allow them to creep back up to natural levels as time goes on and the skill improves.

Plan the environment to work around mirror neuron and imitation deficits. Set up the demonstration so that your child sees the action from your perspective—working at your side, not face-to-face. (Also see "Graduated Guidance" below, and consider working from behind whenever possible.) Research has found that some people with ASDs have difficulty imitating someone facing them. That may be because in addition to doing the work of observing and imitating, the learner also has to mentally switch left to right and vice versa.

PHYSICAL AND GESTURAL PROMPTS

Hand-over-hand prompting is exactly what it sounds like: while standing behind or to the side of your child, you literally move his hands through the motions of an action. Guiding him on how to pull up his pants or wash his hands is usually pretty easy, but when a task involves fine-motor skills, it can take some patience and ingenuity. At first, you may find physical prompting a little awkward, and there's no question that it's easier to use with smaller kids than with bigger ones. Since, ideally, you will be standing or sitting behind or beside your youngster, you need to be able to do so comfortably. However you do it, position yourself so that you can prompt and correct as needed without being the focus of your child's attention. Part of absorbing these independence skills is learning to attend to the relevant cues, not to another person pointing out the relevant cues. That's why you want to keep yourself, literally, in the background.

PHYSICAL AND GESTURAL PROMPTS	
Advantages	**Disadvantages**
Reduce errors, provide immediate feedback	Learner may attend more to the prompt than to other, more naturalistic cues
Don't forget verbal antecedent prompts; naturalistic; "learning to remember" is another important skill for daily living	May inadvertently foster prompt dependence
Hand-over-hand prompting teaches child what the correct action looks and feels like; repeated physical prompting helps to build memory of the physical steps involved	Learner may have sensory sensitivites or aversion to some or all forms of touch
	A learner with a history of prompt dependence may need specific training to not wait for the prompt

Quick Tip: Righties and Lefties

If your child does not use the same dominant hand that you do, you may have a bit of extra work. Remember that we are trying to teach not only the physical motions of a skill but also fluency, which requires some level of grace. Since your child may imitate your actions, you want to be sure that you are modeling the right ones for his hand preference, not yours. Here are some tips:

- If possible, contact an occupational therapist who works with your child or find someone in your community who can help. OTs have great tips on righties teaching lefties and vice versa.
- If you know someone who shares your child's hand preference, ask her to show you how she does things, such as positioning paper for handwriting, using scissors, buttoning shirts, tying shoes, and so on. Be sure you have mastered these skills yourself using your child's preferred hand before trying to teach him.
- If your child is left-handed, be sure that you have scissors and other implements that are designed for southpaws. Not only are they more comfortable, they are also safer to use.
- Search online for specialty occupational therapy websites and equipment providers.

Once your child shows signs of being able to perform a step on her own, start fading the level by moving to a less intrusive prompt. However, do this systematically, so that you are still present to either offer some form of prompting or shadow your child to catch errors before they become embedded in the behavior.

Gestural prompts (pointing, waving, nodding in the direction of the next environmental cue) offered without words are less intrusive than verbal prompts. Kids with AS who are not strong readers of facial expressions, body language, and other nonverbal communication may not pick up on subtler gestural prompts, however, such as your gazing intently at the next item he should pick up, or your miming stirring when he seems stuck at this crucial stage of pancake making. If your child has trouble following basic, unambiguous gestures such as pointing, work on that separately. A surprisingly high percentage of our communication is carried out nonverbally, and being able to interpret nonverbal cues is important in all areas.

Having said that, gestural prompts can be very effective for three reasons:

1. They focus your child's attention on a relevant cue in the environment, which is what he must follow to be independent.
2. They do not use spoken words, so they're not as distracting.
3. They can be so fleeting as to go unnoticed by others around you.

This last point is especially important if your child is easily embarrassed by being corrected in front of others. For example, when Justin was first mastering improved table manners, he had a tendency to revert to holding his spoon or fork in his fist whenever he got tired. If I just held my own up for a second or lightly touched his wrist, he immediately changed his grasp. This nonverbal signal between us came in handy when we were out with friends and family, because no one else noticed it.

As you work with your child, you will no doubt learn where the "soft spots" are in a given skill or behavior chain. For instance, your child may have no problem putting away all the flatware in its molded plastic tray, but she gets stuck when confronted with the ginormous spatula that goes back on the gas grill outside or some esoteric piece of gadgetry such as an avocado knife or nutmeg grater. Hover in the vicinity and give a quick point before your child even has a chance to ask or get flustered. Save your words to praise the great job she's doing.

Quick Tip: Ready for a Lighter Prompt? Try a Time Delay

When is your child ready to graduate to a less intrusive prompt? One reliable test is to disrupt the usual timing and delay giving the prompt for about three seconds. If your child makes no move to proceed, then prompt as usual. However, if she begins without the prompt, it's time to start fading. Stay close enough to catch and correct any errors that might occur on that step or on others.

Quick Tip: Self-Prompting: Timers, PDAs, Smart Phones

Transferring prompts, reminders, Social Stories, and even video clips demonstrating skills to smart phones, notebook computers, PDAs, and other devices has never been easier. Discreet vibrating alarms on cell phones, timers (like my favorite, the MotivAider), and watches can replace a teacher's oral verbal prompts. One advantage these devices have over most other forms of visual or auditory prompts is that using them carries no stigma, since everyone is doing it.

A seventeen-year-old young man with Asperger syndrome struggled with managing his homework. Despite his above-average intelligence, he was inconsistent in writing down his homework and including crucial information such as deadlines, which worksheets went with which classes, and what materials he would need. Using a personal digital assistant (PDA), he was able to improve his accuracy in recording assignments by 29 percentage points. Dr. Brenda Smith Myles and colleagues suggest that using the PDA was effective because it reduced handwriting demands, was easier to use than the paper planner, and was highly motivating.

Dr. Peter Gerhardt and his team have used MP4 players and iPods to provide auditory and visual cues for participants who were working out at a fitness center. For another young man, they used Bluetooth technology so that no one around him noticed that he was receiving oral verbal prompts from a teacher standing some distance away.

Common devices can also be used to camouflage otherwise

attention-drawing behaviors. For example, engaging in self-talk looks quite natural if you're also wearing an earpiece; likewise, singing in public loses its stigma if it looks like you're singing along to your iPod or talking on your cell phone.

Carrying a cell phone and knowing how to use it are essential for safety. Be sure that your child has a cell phone and knows how to use it—and that he remembers to turn it on!

GRADUATED GUIDANCE

Graduated guidance refers to a systematic use and fading of prompts specifically to teach independence skills. Typically, graduated guidance is introduced as soon as the child demonstrates the ability to initiate an action or a step on his own. If you are using hand-over-hand prompting successfully, you will be able to feel when your child is ready to perform the action on his own. An excellent resource is the second edition of *Activity Schedules for Children with Autism*, by Lynn E. McClannahan and Patricia J. Krantz (Woodbine House, 2010). Although many of the examples concern children with limited verbal skills, the techniques and strategies are applicable to any learner.

Graduated guidance moves systematically through increasingly lighter prompts, from spatial fading to shadowing to decreasing physical proximity. The key word here is *systematically*. You move to a lighter prompt when the child is ready—not before, but not too long after, either. Another benefit of graduated guidance is that you should be positioned so that you can anticipate and increase a prompt to prevent an error, or spot an error in progress and provide corrective feedback immediately.

GRADUATED GUIDANCE	
Advantages	**Disadvantages**
Systematic approach to prompts ensures that learner doesn't get stuck on the prompt level for too long	Learner may have difficulty with prompts that involve touching due to sensory issues or feelings about someone invading his personal space; may be difficult to physically prompt learners who are larger, older, or in settings where touching learners is discouraged
Usually taught without speaking; reduces the chances of fostering dependence on verbal prompts	Being taught by a teacher who is not speaking may be a new experience for the learner

BEHAVIOR CHAINS

Most independence skills are not discrete, stand-alone behaviors such as closing a door or pushing a single button to turn on a video game. Rather, they are chains of such single behaviors that are joined together in a particular sequence to accomplish a specific goal. Behavior chains are a good example of the whole being greater than the sum of its parts. I could spend ten minutes demonstrating the many steps involved in making a bed, but if I don't do them in a specific order and within a time frame that is generally regarded as appropriate, I am not really making a bed.

As mentioned before, our daily activities are dominated by a series of behavior chains so familiar to us that we give them little, if any, thought. We think it's just common sense that we put on the bottom bedsheet first, then the top sheet, and then the comforter. But the reason we make a bed this way is that—as in all behavior chains—completing one step functions as a cue for the next step. In other words, the bare mattress cues "bottom sheet," the bottom sheet in place cues "top sheet," the top sheet in place cues "comforter," and so on. Nevertheless, even those of us who are attuned to environmental cues do not respond exactly the same. For some, a single dish in the sink is a cue to wash it; for others, there must be at least five plates stacked up to make it worth their while; for yet others, only a shelf empty of clean glasses or the imminent arrival of in-laws does the trick.

Something about ASDs makes it difficult for kids to register these cues and respond to them in ways conducive to developing a strong repertoire of independence skills. Always keep in mind that a hallmark of any autism spectrum disorder is the indiscriminate attention paid to elements in the environment that have little or no relevance to the task or situation at hand. You often hear people complain that our kids are "not paying attention," when in fact the opposite is probably true: they are paying a lot of attention but to the "wrong" things. One great reason to teach behavior chains (as opposed to discrete small-skill units) is that we naturally perform these behaviors in chains. Teaching a full chain allows your child to experience the complete skill from beginning to end and then to start building both mental and physical memories of what comes before and after each step.

There are two ways to teach a chain: forward chaining and backward chaining. Neither is considered superior to the other, although there are certain skills that it would be highly impractical, time-consuming, and maybe even a bit confusing to teach in a backward chain.

Forward Chaining

Forward chaining simply means teaching a behavior chain from start to finish in exactly the order in which the steps would occur naturally. After you have conducted your task analysis and listed the steps, you work on each step until your child has mastered it before you introduce the next step. The teaching sequence might look something like what you see in the box on page 159.

When you teach a forward chain, you may use different prompt levels at each stage. For instance, in the shoe-tying forward chain on page 159, Sally may be independent on the first three steps but require other prompts for the remaining steps (e.g., hand-over-hand for step 4, gestural for step 5). While you focus on an independent, correct response at each step during each trial, you prompt the rest of the steps to the end, using whatever level of prompting is needed. Ideally, you will be using only the degree of prompting needed for each step. Any behavior chain can be taught forward.

FORWARD CHAINING	
Advantages	**Disadvantages**
Any behavior can be taught	
Breaks down behavior chain into smaller, discrete steps	
Proceeds in a natural sequence from beginning to end	Places reinforcement at the end—the last step—of the chain; reinforcement may not be frequent enough for effective learning

Tying Shoes Using Forward and Backward Chaining

Which order of teaching is right for your child will depend first on the skill you want to teach—is it something you can teach backward? Next you would consider your child's current level of performance. There is no hard-and-fast rule about this. Have your child demonstrate the skill without prompting to the best of his ability and see where he needs the most help. If the beginning of the chain looks pretty good, move forward normally. If the end of the chain holds the most problematic steps, then maybe work backward.

The tables on pages 159–60 show two basic approaches to teaching Sally to tie her shoes.

Forward Chain

Goal	Task Components	Task Analysis
Sally will tie her shoes whenever necessary, independently.	1. Put on shoes.	1. Put each shoe on the appropriate foot.
	2. Tighten laces.	2. Grasp the right lace in the right hand, the left lace in the left.
		3. Pull each lace toward you to tighten.
	3. Make a knot.	4. Pull left lace across tongue, to the right.
		5. Cross right lace over left lace to form an X.
		6. Holding left lace with right hand, use left fingers to flip the right lace under the left lace and over it.
		7. Pull both laces tight to form the first knot.
	4. Make a loop.	8. Place your right pointer finger on the knot.
		9. With your left hand, fold the left lace to double it and make a loop.
		10. While pinching the loop on top of the knot, wrap the right lace around the loop.
	5. Make a second loop.	11. At the bottom of the new loop, push the right lace through.
	6. Tighten the knot.	12. Pull both loops outward in opposite directions to tighten.

Backward Chain (Start with shoes on.)

Goal	Task Components	Task Analysis
Sally will tie her shoes whenever necessary, independently.	1. Tighten the knot.	1. Pull both loops outward in opposite directions to tighten.
	2. Make a second loop.	2. At the bottom of the new loop, push the right lace through.
	3. Make a loop.	3. Place your right pointer finger on the knot.
		4. With your left hand, fold the left lace to double it and make a loop.
		5. While pinching the loop on top of the knot, wrap the right lace around the loop.
		6. Pull each lace toward you to tighten.
	4. Make a knot.	7. Pull left lace across tongue, to the right.
		8. Cross right lace over left lace to form an X.
		9. Holding left lace with right hand, use left fingers to flip the right lace under the left lace and over it.
		10. Pull both laces tight to form the first knot.
	5. Tighten laces.	11. Grasp the right lace in the right hand, the left lace in the left.

Backward Chaining

Backward chaining turns your task analysis upside down, so to speak, because it focuses on your child mastering the last step in the chain first, then working backward: next to last, second to last, third to last, and so on. This seems counterintuitive, but it actually makes a lot of sense when you consider that the natural reinforcement point for most behavior chains occurs upon completion. Backward chaining is a good choice when the skill has a behavior chain of many steps that your child may find especially challenging, The classic example of this is tying shoelaces.

With backward chaining, you would prompt every step until the very last—"Pull each loop away from the shoe to tighten"—which, conveniently, is also probably the easiest step, even for the most fine-motor-skills-challenged. Reinforce lavishly, and you're good to go for a few more trials. Once your child executes the last step independently, begin to fade your prompts on the next-to-last step, and so on.

BACKWARD CHAINING	
Advantages	**Disadvantages**
Breaks down behavior chain into smaller, discrete steps	Not every behavior can be taught
Places reinforcement at the end of the chain but the beginning of the trial	Proceeds in an unnatural sequence, from end to beginning; may be difficult for others teaching your child to follow up without training
	If the chain is unusually long or difficult, consider reinforcing throughout the chain; may impede fluency

SHAPING

Shaping is not a prompt level but a method of using reinforcement to increase the frequency and improve the quality of behaviors we wish to see more of, as well as to decrease undesirable behaviors. When we learn something for the first time, our performance is never as good as it will become with practice. So how do we learn to improve? What enables us to move beyond making beginner-level mistakes? For one thing, good practice usually helps to improve performance. Shaping works by providing reinforcement for the best approximations of what the final behavior should look like. In other words, just going through the motions at the same level as you did last time does not get reinforced. Doing it a little bit better than you did it the last time, however, does. At the same time, we also tend to provide less reinforcement for behavior that has already been mastered, comes easily, or is not the best that the child can do.

Shaping happens everywhere in the natural world. A classic example of shaping is a baby saying his first words. Parents provide a lot of reinforcement in the form of smiles, hugs, eye contact, and talking for baby's first *m* sound. It's such a hit; why doesn't he just stop there? Some would say that we human beings come hardwired for using language. Behaviorists, however, see it differently (and, by the way, use these principles to teach children with severe language problems to speak). What happens is that soon making the *m* becomes old hat not only for baby but for his adoring audience, too, which means less excitement and thus weaker reinforcement. But the day baby stumbles upon saying *ma* instead, the fireworks start all over again and continue until *that* becomes routine. And so it goes until he finally says "Mama." Of course everyone is thrilled, but over time, Mom and Dad will stop going bananas every time he blurts out "Mama," too. Is baby consciously thinking, *Hmm, now how can I top that?* No. But since vocalizing behaviors have been so highly reinforced—particularly new vocalizations—baby will engage in more vocalizing behaviors and take his chances producing a wider variety of sounds until he magically hits upon another winner: how about the *d* sound, *da*, or "Dada"? When it comes to talking, the people in the baby's surrounding environment "select"—in other words, reinforce—the sounds that are familiar to them as parts of words. Throughout the day, baby makes all kinds of sounds, and somewhere in there are surely bits and pieces that could be part of Chinese or Spanish or Russian, but we do not reinforce every single sound with social attention. We respond to those sounds that resemble approximations of the words we expect baby to use.

SHAPING	
Advantages	**Disadvantages**
By reinforcing closer approximations of the final behavior, the learner's effort is reinforced	Can be time-consuming; requires close attention of teacher
A positive approach	Progress can be bumpy; learner may respond emotionally when the same level of performance is not reinforced as intensely as before
Easily combined with other procedures such as forward and backward chaining, live or video modeling	

Using the shaping technique to teach skills similarly entails selecting behavior that will support the skill and raise the bar, so that the best attempt—the one closest to what the final behavior should look like—receives our reinforcement. The first, most obvious benefit is that we reinforce progress, not just the final product. In other words, you don't have to get it perfect right out of the gate to be reinforced. But at the same time, we are not reinforcing effort alone; there has to be a standard of performance, and that would generally be as good as the previous attempt, or preferably a shade better. Once you see the improved performance, turn off reinforcement for the lesser approximations—

that is, for performance that is a step backward in terms of what you know from experience the person is capable of doing. (There's a term for that, too: *extinction of reinforcement*. As a result, the lesser approximations are less likely to recur.) For example, if you are trying to teach someone to scrub the kitchen sink, and yesterday she did it completely (scrubbed and rinsed all the surfaces, emptied the crumbs out of the little basket in the drain, wiped down the faucet and the handles), you would not reinforce the skill today if she left carrot peelings in the drain; you would also not let it pass without being corrected.

Let's say that eleven-year-old Sam is learning to set the dinner table. He has all the component skills; he knows where things are and what goes where. The problem is that it takes him forever to complete the task. However, Sam gets the same level of praise and a sticker on his refrigerator token chart buying him an hour on the internet regardless of whether it takes him ten minutes or twenty-five minutes. His parents like to be positive and are just happy that Sam does the job, no matter how long it takes. But what is Sam missing? First, in the real world, most tasks are expected to be completed within a certain time. We do not give much thought to the role of fluency (the quality of a behavior that is accurate, fluid, and appropriately quick) until we're stranded in line behind someone who struggles for three minutes to pick out the correct change. To cite an extreme example: sure, you can pedal your bicycle *very* slowly, but gravity tends to enforce its own performance standards, because if you go too slowly, you'll fall over. Read too slowly, and you lose comprehension. Work too slowly, and you fall behind in school and your friends won't wait for you to come out to play.

There are mini-deadlines throughout Sam's day, and it is in his interest to learn to self-monitor and manage his time. Today it may be acceptable for Sam to set the table in a leisurely manner, but, life being what it is, someday it won't be okay. There may be a change in family plans; Sam or his parents might have other things for him to do. Keep in mind also that the work habits you want to establish in your child should be of a type and quality that can be generalized and will enhance her performance wherever they are applied. There is clearly a good argument against rewarding Sam for unnecessarily slow work.

Finally, when too much time elapses between start and finish, attention tends to stray, the power of the last step to cue the next step weakens, and those irrelevant stimuli come creeping back into view. Keeping a realistic time limit on tasks helps many kids sustain their focus.

To guide Sam toward a shorter, more useful table-setting time, his parents should set an optimal time—let's say twelve minutes, based on his previous performance or someone conducting a task analysis walk-through and timing it. Keep in mind that we are not aiming for the fastest time; for some kids, maybe it's not even the same time we would expect of another child the same age. We are looking at the time frame in which the skill can be applied completely without periods of being off-task.

His parents could sample Sam's usual times over a few days. If his times over five days were 14 minutes, 24 minutes, 15 minutes, 18 minutes, and 24 minutes, they would pick a time somewhere between his longest times and the target time. Our target here is 12 minutes, so halfway between 12 (target) and his longest time (24) is 18. Sam's parents would explain to him that while they're always happy that he sets the table, it needs to go more quickly. They should also let Sam know what's in it for him: more time on the computer. Once he has met his target time of 12 minutes or less for one week, he will earn a special reinforcer. In the meantime, however, tokens for internet access can be earned only by completing the task in under 18 minutes. Once Sam does that for three days in a row, move the targets downward: 17 minutes, 16 minutes, and so on until Sam reaches the target.

What happens on the days that Sam does not finish within his time limit? Simple: he does not receive the token for internet access. Contrary to what some people think, this is *not* a punishment. It's simply a failure to earn reinforcement, and so there is no reward for taking too long to set the table. Sam may be unhappy at first, but the chances are good that, going forward, he will meet his targets more often. There's nothing in it for him to do otherwise, whereas before, his parents had actually set up a situation in which there was no incentive for Sam to set the table more quickly, because he was still being rewarded regardless of his speed.

In Sam's case, we shaped his behavior to occur within specific parameters of time, but you can also shape for accuracy, fluency, neatness, initiation, appropriate stopping, and countless other aspects of behavior.

VISUAL SUPPORTS

Visual supports come in all shapes, sizes, and forms. Indeed, we all use visual supports every day: lists, calendars, schedules, menus, notes to ourselves and others. In particular, visual supports can be very useful in teaching children across the spectrum. Again, however, there is no one-size-fits-all method for teaching any particular skill, and what works for one child might not work for another.

That said, there are a number of commercially available products that can reduce some of your prep time. You can also make them yourself, which has the advantage of allowing them to be uniquely individualized—as complex or as simple, as large or as small as you wish. Ideally, though, for kids with AS, it is probably more helpful to see highly specialized, task-specific visual supports as a stepping-stone in learning rather than a permanent addition to daily life. At some point you will want to transfer the support function, if it's still needed, to a form that everyone else uses, such as reminders on a computer, smart phone, or PDA, or visual and/or verbal lists shrunk down to business-card size or smaller. And there's nothing wrong with using something as old school as a small pocket calendar.

VISUAL SUPPORTS	
Advantages	**Disadvantages**
Visual supports are commonly used in everyday life; can be discreet and not draw attention	Not every learner with ASD is a visual learner; always try to teach using verbal input alone first
Visual supports are commonly used in educational settings	Sometimes are overused; may foster prompt dependence; often, fading visual supports isn't addressed in behavior plans; failure of a behavior plan or teaching strategy may lead to the questionable conclusion that visual supports don't work
Research says we all learn best when verbal and visual information are presented together	Learners with ASD and other issues (ADHD, dyslexia) may find visual supports in their work area distracting, especially if they are made too interesting

Although visual supports can be incredibly helpful, you have to also consider their potential downside before you rush out and spend the weekly food budget on Velcro, a laminator, an expensive picture icon computer program, and a rainbow of Sharpie markers. Visual supports are very popular with schools and in home services, and I've seen toileting schedules, to-do lists, and visual recipes that were works of art. They were absolutely lovely, but they were also very time-consuming and expensive in the sense that they often addressed only one skill or situation. Once the child solved the problem addressed by the oh-so-cool laminated, illustrated, perforated morning schedule, there was little chance of recycling the materials for the next goal.

Sometimes people will try to discard a visual support or abandon the whole idea because of one that "doesn't work." As I assume you have gleaned by now, the process of teaching skills and changing behavior can be surprisingly complex. When we identify a behavior that we wish to address or a skill we would like to teach, there are many, many factors at work. What people usually mean when they say that visual schedules don't work is that a behavior they sought to address or improve using them didn't get magically fixed. I'm still surprised at the number of parents and teachers who think that just placing an agenda in a kid's backpack or a timer on the desk will change behavior or teach a skill. That's like assuming that you will engage in all the behaviors you need to lose weight just because you have a scale in the bathroom.

Visual strategies can be a crucial part of a behavior learning plan, but they are only a part. There can be dozens of reasons why the visual support wasn't helpful: it targeted the wrong skill, the teaching that went along with it was ineffective, the reinforcement was weak or nonexistent, and so on. Generally, one of the most common reasons a visual support system fails is that no one teaches the child how to use it or why he is using it. The art to using visual supports is not unlike the art of prompting: a visual support should be designed to fit both the task and the student, and it should be faded as much and as soon as is reasonably possible.

Over the past fifteen years, Linda Hodgdon, a speech pathologist, has become the guru of visual strategies. She has published a series of excellent books—the classic being *Visual Strategies for Improving Communication: Practical Supports for School and Home*—and also has a website rich with resources, including webinars, for more tips. As she points out, visual supports can be especially helpful for students who teachers and others assume are too smart, too poorly behaved, too attention-seeking, or too unmotivated to use them. If you or your child's teachers have rejected visual strategies or you have never used them before at home, please reconsider. Visual strategies have a lot to offer, and they have the added advantage of being a prompting method that does not require the presence of another person—a key step toward true independence.

Visual supports can do many things, but in the realm of independence skills, we're most interested in using them for these purposes:

- To give information: calendars, schedules
- To give or support directions: reminder lists, checklists, task organizers
- To guide or support organization: labeling, maps

WORDS OR PICTURES?

Most kids with AS do read, and for many, written words may be more age-appropriate than verbal prompts. That said, look at all the images, symbols, icons, and other pictorial prompts that surround us. (And by "pictures," we do not mean photographs, though they have their place, as we will see.) If your goal is to reduce the use of words in any form, we all know what pictures are worth. For example, if twelve-year-old Joey is carrying a business-card-sized prompt in his pocket to remind him of three steps for greeting friends at the school dance, you could have:

> 1. Approach a friend and smile.
> 2. Say hello. Stop. Wait for an answer.
> 3. Ask, "How are you doing?"

Or you could have something that looks like this:

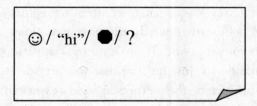

Again, the ultimate goal for teaching many of these skills is full independence. For learners with AS or an AS-type learning profile, stringing together several separate tasks into a behavior chain is more difficult than performing the tasks individually. These children might do best to learn the individual task components, then have a written or picture support to remind them of the order of steps for the complete chain. Kids elsewhere on the spectrum would benefit from having every step of, say, folding a towel or using a coffeemaker illustrated with a picture. However, some boys and girls with Asperger syndrome might do better with no visual reminders at all but rather your guidance and prompts as they perform the task, so that they learn and acquire the motor memory.

Some kids find visual supports distracting, especially for short tasks with few steps; furthermore, the constant stopping to refer back to the support can hinder their developing fluency. Some visual supports are so colorful and fun to look at that they are too distracting! Also, remember that visual supports, if not faded appropriately, can bring about their own form of prompt dependence. But, as always, every child is different.

Generally, visual supports work extremely well as scaffolding for executive function. This is true for all of us. Visual supports that target executive function are also more naturalistic; they are everywhere already. Such supports tend to take the form of lists that use words, words in combination with pictures, or pictures alone. Try to use the least restrictive, most naturalistic level of prompting you can. For example, if the task is gathering materials and packing up at the end of the school day, consider where your child will be using it. If she is in a regular elementary classroom or a special education classroom, pictures are probably okay and will blend in with the many other similarly designed supports in the room. If, however, your daughter attends a regular middle, junior high, or high school setting, words are most appropriate. Bottom line: use what works for your child. If you have to start with pictures for an older child, then do so. Just be sure that you provide words with the pictures and work to fade the pictures as soon as you can.

People with ASDs tend to be experiential learners—they learn and retain best by doing. (Just like everyone else, when you think about it.) Although you could construct a lovely series of photographs that illustrate each step in the process of folding a bath towel, there's a lot more to this task than merely positioning a rectangle of terry cloth and manipulating it in different directions. How do you decide where to make the first fold? How close do the edges need to be? Generally, any small hands-on task that requires ongoing evaluation of what's "just right"—buttoning, starting a zipper, rinsing shampoo completely—should be taught first without visual supports. You can always incorporate prompts that target the weak links later, if needed.

Photographs can be helpful, but they can also be confusing. There is an art to taking photographs that clearly convey the relevant information and nothing else. One common mistake is to create a photo visual support that looks like a storyboard or outtakes from a movie about the learner's day. Long shots with a lot of background and visual clutter are rarely effective at helping our kids selectively weed out the irrelevant cues and focus on the ones that matter. Think about it: as your child puts away his folded laundry, his visual perspective of the task is not that of a movie director or an audience watching him. His visual focus should be on the clothing and where it goes. If anything, with a wide-view photo we have added another bit of clutter. Instead the photograph should depict exactly what the learner should be looking at, from the angle he would see it, if he were working the task. Let's say you're assembling photographs to depict proper tooth brushing. First photograph: a toothbrush held in the right hand (for a right-handed kid). Second photograph: the left hand squeezing toothpaste onto the bristles, seen from the same angle as what your child sees when he's brushing his teeth.

Visual supports can be combined. For instance, you could write a list of the steps needed to use the washing machine, but it might be more useful to include a close-up photo of the exact placement of the dials for water temperature and cycle. Again, your purpose is to highlight the most relevant data from the environment, not to reproduce the entire environment as a documentary.

Visual supports that teach and visual supports that remind serve two different functions. Say that we have two children, Abe and Zoe, learning to water the houseplants each morning. Abe's main problem is executive function; he simply has not had enough experience performing the task correctly to have established a memory he can reference when doing the chore. After a couple of weeks of highly reinforced practice, with someone using nonverbal prompts and a little manual guidance, it becomes routine for Abe, and he can do it independently. Zoe, while she has the exact same learning profile as Abe and is taught using exactly the same strategies, has attention issues that still get in the way. She will need to use the visual schedule to prompt her attention to the task, even though we know that she knows how to do it. Visual supports that are used to help focus and sustain attention may need to be more detailed and may not be faded as quickly (if ever).

Using visual support is a skill like any other: it must be taught. In many cases where parents and teachers say that a visual support "just didn't work," a little investigation reveals that no one taught the child how to use it. While our world is full of directions and signs and other kinds of visual supports, the difference between kids with ASDs and most of the rest of the world is that typical people are hardwired to be attracted to these environmental cues: we almost can't help attending to them. Not so for many of our kids. Even though we see the visual support as something helpful, to many learners on the spectrum it's just another detail in the environment that may or may not scan as relevant. Merely telling your child what to do won't work, either. You need to guide her through using the visual support until she has really mastered it. Then you tackle the skill.

Ask your child what she thinks would help. You might be surprised to find that your color-coding system is too confusing, or all those little photos of Tony Hawk you glued onto your son's morning routine reminder card make him think about skateboarding (or playing a video game of skateboarding) instead of brushing his teeth. Before you create any visual support, talk to your child and find out what might help. Remember that a visual support will not get used if your child does not want to use it.

Generally speaking, when it comes to effective prompting systems, the simpler the better. Fewer prompts used also means there will be fewer you'll have to fade in the future.

At this moment, someone is reading this and thinking, "But what about his special interest? Can I use that?" Great question. Why *not* turn a special interest to our advantage? On one hand, it makes a lot of sense. And many experts seem to believe that if you can't beat 'em, join 'em. Often this is based on the idea that these children find it too difficult to learn to attend to anything else. Reinforcers, stickers, visual supports, and materials related to the special interest can be motivating and make learning or doing a task more fun. On the other hand, they can also prove irresistibly distracting. If you are working with a routine schedule using trains and your child starts enlightening you as to the differences in wheel configuration between a Super Chief and a Big Boy when the task at hand is matching socks, dash back to the drawing board. Remember that for independence to emerge, kids need to learn to attend to the relevant, task-related cues in the environment. Also, think forward: once the special interest digression starts, what will you probably do? Start talking, I'd guess. And that's exactly what we should not do. Think instead of using the special interest strictly as a reinforcer, available only once the task is completed in a satisfactory way. This way you get the motivational benefits with less risk of distraction. It should also be noted that special-interest-related supports may pose a particular problem for kids with attention issues.

Quick Tip: Reinforcement Helps Build Memory

Do not be surprised to find that your child can easily remember to pack everything he needs to play a video game at a friend's house but still has to be reminded which drawer is for socks. After all, he receives a lot of reinforcement for getting all his video game stuff to his friend's house (and reinforcement that is highly meaningful and valuable to him), but for putting away his socks? Not so much. So rig things your way. Try offering vastly richer forms of reinforcement for a task and see how it goes before putting into place an elaborate picture or labeling system, especially for a task that should be easily incorporated into the day's activities.

VIDEO MODELING

Video modeling—presenting a model of the skill or behavior in a video—has several advantages over static visual presentations and live modeling with a real person. First, it makes use of the fact that many of our kids are attracted to anything on a screen. Many of them have already gotten into the habit of rewatching videos or segments of videos repeatedly. A video model may feel more familiar and be more readily accepted than another type of visual support. Second, with a video model, the person doing the teaching and your child don't even have to be in the same room. Third, video modeling is consistent in a way that even the most conscientious of us probably cannot be. However I model hanging up a jacket on the video will be precisely the same every time the video is played. I don't have to worry about missing a step or getting a little sloppy here or there every time. Fourth, your child can watch the video anytime, not only when he's working on the task. He can also access the model when you or someone else who might teach him is not available. Super-portable screening devices can be used quietly and discreetly.

Technology has made shooting, editing, storing, and playing videos easier than ever. That said, it is still a somewhat unnatural type of prompt, and, again, you will want to consider whether watching a video while performing the task is a help or a hindrance (or even a safety risk). If your child can learn what to do by watching the video once or several times immediately before attempting the task, you would get the benefits of modeling without the intrusion of a live model or screen playing during the task. If your child cannot do that, consider other, real-time cues.

Think through the production of the video model before you start. You don't want the final video model to include a lot of stops, starts, or actions and words that are not essential parts of the prompt model.

Try to shoot the video from the perspective of the child performing the task. Remember: the goal of visual strategies is to teach kids to tune in to natural environmental cues. A video of Louisa brushing her teeth shot documentary-style (from a wide angle that takes in the whole room from a distance) conveys no information on the relevant cues. A video in which the camera focuses on the relevant natural cues and the discrete actions involved should help Louisa learn not only what to do but also where to look during the task.

VIDEO MODELING	
Advantages	**Disadvantags**
Can eliminate verbal prompts, direct physical prompting	May not address difficulties in motor clumsiness or poor motor imitation; learner may imitate movement inaccurately
Learner does not need the teacher present to learn	Concern about the amount of time individuals with ASDs spend not interacting with others and instead using screens: video games, computers, internet, iPhones
Has been demonstrated to be effective for teaching social skills	Not always very portable or discreet

SOMETHING DIFFERENT: SOCIAL STORIES BY CAROL GRAY

It's been more than ten years since I first heard Social Stories creator Carol Gray use the phrase "Abandon all assumptions." At the time, she was teaching a seminar on how to write Social Stories, but that sentence remains a mantra I have returned to daily as both a mom and a teacher. The idea that we cannot presume to know what a kid does not understand about the hidden social expectations and demands of life without investigating—and, ideally, asking him—is revolutionary. Social Stories is not a behaviorally based intervention like the others we'll review here, but the idea of "what we think we know" taking a backseat to open, objective investigation dovetails nicely.

In fact, one of the most important facts about Social Stories is that they are *not* designed to change someone's behavior. Rather, in Gray's words, the goal is to "share accurate information meaningfully and safely." Social Stories are also *not* about telling the child what to do. Instead, they explain the world situation by situation on the premise that just as a child's misunderstanding the world can result in behaviors that are inappropriate or not helpful to him, understanding it supports behaviors that are more appropriate and helpful. For kids on the spectrum with strong cognitive and language abilities and/or kids who are approaching or in adolescence, Social Stories also provide what Gray calls the "news": the who, what, when, where, how, and why about people and situations. Learners like these have a drive to understand not just what to do but also why they should do it; this understanding can be a very powerful motivator. In particular, kids with AS may be prone to not do something because it doesn't make sense to them. Once they have a fuller understanding of the hidden curriculum, they sometimes change their minds.

If your child has any interventions at all, you have probably heard teachers and therapists refer to "social stories," and they or you may have tried writing one. When I write about this kind of "social story," I'm not using capital letters (Carol Gray's Social Stories are a registered trademark) because these are usually quite different from what Gray intended. These other "social stories" may be based on fill-in-the-blank forms, or on templates downloaded off the internet or copied from books; they may read like to-do lists or itemized rules for class, the bus, the playground, and so on. They may be elaborate, detailed, even illustrated. But they are not Social Stories.

Fortunately, Gray just issued her latest version of the Social Stories "10.1 guidelines," which describe the ten criteria a "social story" must meet to become a Social Story. This brief review is selective and incomplete; upon reading it, you will not have all you need to write a real Social Story. However, I hope that this introduction to some of the key concepts will encourage you to consider learning more and incorporating them where appropriate, as well as give you some general criteria by which to judge Social Story–type written verbal prompts that may not conform to these standards.

Social Stories seek to convey information to a learner in a clear, carefully structured, accurate, respectful, and what Gray calls "unassuming" way. In other words, a Social Story about going to a carnival would never include the sentence "Everyone loves the carnival, and you will, too." Social Stories are written in the first person ("I am learning to clean my room") or the third person ("It is a good idea for kids to learn to clean their rooms"), but *never* in the second person ("You are learning to clean your room," "You must always clean your room," "You will be proud of yourself if you learn to clean your room"). A Social Story also reflects a concern about the child's sense of self, so statements such as "When I get angry, I hit people" are never used. (Instead: "Sometimes when people get angry, they may hit other people.") As Gray perceptively points out, "A person with an autism spectrum disorder is more likely to be challenged, corrected, and redirected far more frequently than his or her peers." The purpose of a Social Story is to teach alternative responses, not to scold, humiliate, point the finger at, or try to prompt a change in behavior in someone by making him feel bad about himself.

Social Stories also take into account—and help to prevent—the types of misinterpretations of language kids with ASDs are predisposed to make. For instance, an inept "social story" might say, "I ride my bike to school every day." Whoever writes that should not be surprised when Jasmine gets upset on a snowy Saturday morning and insists on riding her bike to school. By contrast, a real Social Story recognizes that, first, "every day" is not literally true (children don't usually go to school on weekends, on holidays, and during the summers) and, second, that someone with an ASD would benefit from having some of the "obvious" (to most of us) real-life exceptions to that statement explained: "I can ride my bike to school on days when Mom or Dad says it is okay. There will be days when Mom or Dad will say I have to take the bus. That could happen for many different reasons. For example, if the weather is bad or if I have to carry a lot of things to school."

In my decade or so of using Social Stories, I've also tried to carry over the Social Story formula to any kind of teaching. That formula sets a *minimum* ratio of two or more sentences that describe, provide perspective, or affirm for every sentence that coaches or gently guides the preferred behavior ("I will try to remember to raise my hand," *not* "I will always raise my hand"). If you believe that a Social Story would be a helpful addition to your teaching plan, I encourage you to read Carol Gray's beautifully written and illustrated tenth-anniversary edition, *The New Social Story Book*, which also comes with a free CD of real Social Stories templates that you can edit and personalize, then print. You can also find more information online from the Gray Center for Social Learning and Understanding at www.thegraycenter.org.

START BUILDING EXECUTIVE FUNCTION:
INVITE YOUR CHILD TO HELP

For many learners with more severely impacting ASDs who require high levels of intensive instruction or depend on visual and other support systems, parents and teachers determine the types of supports, how they are designed, and how they are used. One reason that kids with AS and similar learning profiles need these supports is that they lack the executive function, attention, or other cognitive skills to generate their own internal how-to manuals and real-time monitoring systems for the everyday jobs of life. But just because your child needs a visual strategy support does not mean that she cannot help design it. If anything, involving your child in conducting the task analysis, creating written verbal and picture schedules and reminders, and test-driving the plan will:

- Create a sense of ownership in the plan that likely will encourage more enthusiastic participation.
- Let her experience analyzing a problem and deciding on a possible solution. Due to theory of mind deficits, people with ASDs do not always realize that the rest of us do not "just know" things but rather reach decisions through thought processes that are largely private and invisible to others. Try to make your process visible by narrating what you are thinking, describing the choices you have, explain-

ing how you made your decision, and talking about a mistake you made and how you fixed it.

- Begin to problem-solve on her own. As you walk through a task analysis or test-drive a plan, stop and see what happens. Ask, "Next?" or simply make eye contact and shrug. Even though you are right there, poised to swoop in with a prompt or correction, try giving your child a few seconds (no more than three to five; practice this with a timer, because you'll be surprised how short it is) to do it herself.

Chapter 9

WHO ELSE CAN HELP? THE ROLE OF SCHOOL

Most parents of children with special needs have some dealings with special education and related services at different points. The severity of your child's challenges and how effectively they're being met by your school and school district can vary widely. When it comes to teaching many of the skills discussed in this book, parents often wonder what the school's role is. Here we will explore what special education and related services are designed to do and where independence skills fit in.

SPECIAL EDUCATION AND RELATED SERVICES

Many students with AS qualify for and receive through their local school districts special education and/or related services, such as speech and language therapy, occupational therapy, or physical therapy; the services of a consultant, counselor, or psychologist; and assistive technology, to name a few. The scope and purpose of those services depend on your child's age, your child's degree of disability in different areas, and how your school district decides how those services are delivered. In speaking to a number of experts with extensive experience in the field, I found that one theme always came up: the increasing school focus on academics, particularly the demands of mandated assessments. Not surprisingly, time during the school day that ten years ago might have been devoted to more practical daily living skills for some kids has been claimed by teaching to help children meet academic demands.

Early Intervention and Preschool Special Education Services Basics

Many readers' children will be past kindergarten age, too old to qualify for either early intervention (EI) programs (for learners from birth to approximately three years) or preschool special education services (approximately three years to kindergarten). If, however, your child is four or younger and there are ASD-related issues, contact your school district's special education administration as soon as possible and get the process started. Parents who are new to the diagnosis often have reservations about applying for intervention services; they sometimes worry that their child's future school placement will be negatively influenced by his having had these services. The other big concern is that their child will be "labeled."

First, research has shown conclusively that earlier intervention is a major factor in improving youngsters' abilities and skills, reducing problem behavior, developing social skills, and ultimately enhancing social abilities and preparation for school. As you will read, early intervention and preschool teachers and therapists teach skills—to both kids and parents—in the natural environment: the home. Further, these programs are designed to address the needs of both the child and the family.

Second, these services are there to help. It is your child's legal right to be evaluated for services at any age, at no cost to you, and to be provided services for which he is eligible. In preschool and elementary school, these services are provided to your child free of charge through your school district.* Some parents prefer that the district not know their child has

---

*However, each state sets its own policies for early intervention, so rules regarding the cost of services, if any, are set by states. Under IDEA, certain early intervention services are always free: evaluations, assessments, development of an Individualized Family Service Plan, service coordination. Your school district should be able to tell you everything you need to know about the cost of services. In most places where there is a fee, it is minimal, determined on a sliding scale, or can be waived under certain circumstances.

a problem, and so they seek out services on their own. Since most insurance plans either do not cover or place severe restrictions on the type and amount of these services, many parents are forced to pay out of pocket, and that's only if they can find professionals locally—many areas of the country suffer from a shortage of qualified practitioners willing to work privately with individual families. Often the most experienced qualified professionals work for school districts and for state-authorized agencies that coordinate and staff home programs.

In addition to accessibility, there is also the matter of cost. This highly specialized intervention is expensive. For certified teachers and duly licensed and certified therapists, fees can range up to or exceed $100 an hour. Six to ten or more hours of services per week is about average for a child with a mild autism spectrum disorder. Children whose behaviors or learning problems are more involved may receive up to thirty to forty hours a week. Many children fall somewhere in between. Financially and practically speaking, there is every reason to obtain these services through your local early intervention program and, later, through your school district.

As for keeping your child "out of the system" in the hopes of him not being labeled or categorized later on: it's usually not a good idea. For one thing, your child is your child. If she has issues today that are not being addressed or that are being tended to inadequately, she will enter school with those same issues. ASD-related symptoms and behaviors do not improve on their own; kids, unfortunately, don't "grow out of" them. Obtaining services as soon as your child qualifies is a good way not only to get her the help she needs but also for you both to benefit from the professional guidance of the therapists and teachers she will meet. By the time your child does enter kindergarten, everyone will have a clearer idea of her skills and deficits and how best to address them.

SPECIAL EDUCATION SERVICES BEFORE KINDERGARTEN: WHAT MANY KIDS WITH AS MISS

Early intervention services are those that children with disabilities receive from birth to approximately age three; the cutoff for transition to preschool services depends on a youngster's birth date and local regulations. When a child receives services for a suspected or diagnosed developmental disability, providers focus on all domains of normal child development: cognition, language, gross-motor skills, fine-motor skills, and self-help skills. Typically, a child with an ASD diagnosis who is receiving early intervention would be learning age-appropriate skills in eating (using a spoon, drinking from a regular open cup), dressing (taking off shoes and socks, "assisting" parent with dressing), and self-care and hygiene (wiping his face with a napkin, "helping" with brushing teeth) as part of the standard curriculum.

Early intervention usually takes place in the home, so parents—usually mothers—see what teachers and therapists are doing and learn hands-on techniques for helping their child. Depending on the diagnosis, the number of different services and the number of hours or sessions of each can vary from a few sessions per week to a few per day. For many children diagnosed with or suspected of having an ASD, applied behavior analysis (ABA) is often provided, with speech, occupational therapy, physical therapy, and parent training also usually included. The last of these is important, since it helps parents learn to integrate aspects of intervention into their daily routines and their parenting repertoire.

Sometime around age three, children with disabilities who are evaluated and found to still qualify for special education and related services transition to preschool services, which cover them until they enter kindergarten. At this point, service provision begins to move out of the home, and while some children continue to receive services at home, the importance of access to typical peers and experience in a school-type environment results in many attending either a special education preschool or a regular preschool, perhaps with a specially trained "shadow" or aide who can implement special strategies or provide behavioral support. With the move from early intervention to preschool services, parents usually have fewer opportunities to see firsthand what teachers and therapists are doing, and communication with professionals is usually less frequent and detailed than what they received at home. In addition, the preschool setting brings a new focus: social skills, such as turn taking, sharing, greetings, play, and so on, along with early academic skills, including using scissors, drawing, coloring, painting, and recognizing colors, shapes, letters, and numbers. Because teachers and therapists are not in the home so often, if at all, responsibility for the child's continued acquisition of age-appropriate daily living skills falls on Mom and Dad. While teachers and other professionals are happy to help and offer suggestions, that is sometimes simply not enough for children with ASDs—especially when you consider the schedule on which children are expected to acquire the skills listed on page 62. Also, teaching daily living skills sometimes takes a backseat if parents and professionals see skill acquisition in other areas or addressing problem behaviors as more pressing.

In many areas, there is a tendency for committees on preschool special education (CPSEs) to reduce special education and related services as a child gets older. This is partially because the objective of EI and preschool services is to bring a child's skills within a specific range of what is considered developmentally age-appropriate and is often outlined in local early intervention and special education regulations. Contrary to popular misconception, the purpose of these services is not to have every kindergartener functioning at a "normal" level or arrive at the schoolhouse doorstep indistinguishable from typical peers.

There is also the question of how best to spend a teacher's valuable time, and some in the field would say that while only a specialist can address a persistent articulation problem or help develop a functional pencil grasp, anyone can teach tooth brushing or shoe tying. "Anyone" would be—you guessed it—Mom and Dad. If the speech teacher has identified following oral two-step directions in the classroom as a goal on the child's individualized education program (IEP), for example, everyone should understand that what's being focused on is not just a problem in the classroom but a sample of a problem that is *pervasive*, that occurs throughout the day, in *every* setting, under *every* condition that the child encounters. Some experts believe that this division between "school skills" and "home skills," particularly for students with ASDs, is not helpful and may be at least partially responsible for the disappointing outcome statistics for young adults.

Children with Asperger syndrome often do not receive services prior to kindergarten because, in the absence of speech delay, they do not qualify (except if they have other problems that do qualify them). Even with the increased awareness of autism spectrum disorders, the majority of AS children are not identified as having a definable problem until they encounter situations that involve intense social contact with typical peers; for many, that would be nursery school or preschool. By then, they are usually too old for early intervention, though they may qualify for preschool services, with speech, occupational therapy, and special education being the most likely.

This may partly explain why a child with another type of ASD often has stronger independence skills than a child with AS, HFA, or PDD-NOS. I'm referring to kids whose verbal and other skills may not seem as developed as those of a child with AS from about ages two to five. What made the difference for those children? Three things:

1. Teaching began at or around the time the skill was expected to emerge naturally.
2. The teaching was specific to autism, recognizing and effectively addressing ASD learning styles.
3. Maybe the most important factor: Mom and Dad learned how to do it, too, so there was carryover and consistency.

In addition to receiving services, youngsters with other types of ASDs were probably also learning—and mastering—a specific repertoire of seemingly basic skills that we now know are essential to acquiring many independence skills. Not surprisingly, deficits in these areas often undermine kids with AS:

- Imitation
- Learning by observing the actions of others
- Age-appropriate fine-motor skills
- Age-appropriate gross-motor skills
- Following directions

It is not a coincidence that quality ABA programs of the type designed for learners with other forms of ASDs focus on these and learners are given countless structured, consistent, heavily reinforced opportunities to practice and learn. If you think that typical children acquire these same skills without intensive repeated practice, think again. They "practice" for thousands of hours through typical social development and play. Interestingly, play of the type typically engaged in by developing youngsters is usually not in our kids' repertoires, either.

Your Child "Does Not Qualify": A Green Light or a Caution Sign?

In most places, children with Asperger syndrome who present with age-appropriate or strongly emerging language skills and are found upon evaluation to fall within the normal range of IQ scores may not qualify for services in the EI years, but they may at the preschool stage. I doubt that you could find parents who wouldn't be thrilled to learn that their child does not qualify for services. But not qualifying for services isn't always a green light. Especially with AS, children can present with behaviors or learning differences that, while a little bit "off," are not deemed serious enough to qualify for services. Or, in a classic example of our being blinded by their strengths, a way-above-average vocabulary, an ability to demonstrate attention in the special interest for unusually long periods, and cognitive ability that falls into the fairly wide range of what is considered normal will probably result in nonqualification.

Does this mean that everything really is okay? Not necessarily. If family or friends, teachers, or doctors either suggested that you seek an evaluation or supported your inclination to do so, there's a good chance that something is up. Now, what's "up" may not involve the same issues exhibited by other children who qualify for these services at these early ages, and—this is classic AS—some of your child's deficits may test out as strengths. Another important factor is the doggedly prevailing assumption on the part of too many professionals (who by now should know better) that a high IQ or strong expressive language skills guarantee that a child "will just pick the rest up as he goes along." Outcome studies demonstrate that this faith is misplaced, to say the least.

KINDERGARTEN AND BEYOND

The first day of school! Most children will not remember it, but most mothers and fathers will never forget it. For parents of children with AS, it may signal some changes beyond those that usually come to mind. For one thing, if your child has received services prior to this, those services may or may not continue in school; if they do, they will probably be further reduced. In many areas, whatever home services may have been provided before will be at least severely cut back and most likely discontinued. The reasoning on the school's side is simple: the child is now in school, and that's where special education and related services will be provided. Further, the law requires that in the interests of promoting and supporting a more inclusive school, community, and world, these services be provided in the least restrictive setting. For many children with AS, the least restrictive setting is the regular classroom, although it may be an inclusion or co-teaching model. (Also keep in mind that "special education" is not a place. Good special education programs offer a range of placements, services, and supports.) Philosophically, most parents have no problem with this; in fact, many of them see the need for fewer services and a regular classroom full of typical peers as a good fit for Mikey and something to celebrate. Mikey might receive a few pull-outs or push-ins for speech or occupational therapy and perhaps a small group counseling session with the school psychologist or social worker each week. While special education and related services (or related services alone) do continue, the focus in school shifts more to addressing problems that have a direct impact on functioning in school, particularly academically. Surely exceptions abound, but generally speaking, parents should not be surprised to learn that for a child attending a regular public school—even if she is receiving services under an IEP or 504 plan—many independence skills, especially those considered personal (dressing, hygiene, toileting, et cetera), will not be addressed. Again, remember that, according to some educators, the purpose of special education and related services is to help the student meet the goals of their education plan, not necessarily to reach an age-appropriate or developmentally appropriate level in all domains. Dr. Ami Klin, however, is among those who see a larger role for schools. "The bulk of the work that needs to happen with our children should happen at school," he says. "It's the law; it's mandated that way. Sometimes people will have a rather narrow view of what education is, and they may consider that children go to school to learn to read, to write, and to do math. But I think that few people would disagree with the notion that kids go to school to learn skills that will make it possible for them to live successful lives."

IEPs and 504 Plans: What's the Difference?

The Individuals with Disabilities Education Act and the Rehabilitation Act are two federal statutes that work in different ways to ensure that disabled students have access to public education. IDEA is concerned specifically with the provision of special education and related services to students with disabilities between birth and age twenty-one. The Rehabilitation Act (which includes Section 504) is concerned primarily with access to education, or, in the words of special education attorney S. James Rosenfeld, "leveling the playing field." The two statutes are complementary and seem to overlap somewhat; for instance, all students who qualify under IDEA are also covered by Section 504, though not all students who receive services under Section 504 qualify under IDEA. The goal of Section 504 is to eliminate barriers to access to regular education. In other words, if a student in a wheelchair whose disability does not impact her ability to learn is provided with a ramp and any other help required for her to access the regular curriculum in her school, Section 504 is satisfied. IDEA, however, has much more stringent requirements. Under IDEA, a student with a disability is entitled to an individualized education that meets her specific needs and that she benefits from. The two also differ in terms of the types of disabilities covered. For example, Section 504 covers anyone who currently has and has a record of a physical or mental impairment that "substantially limits at least one major life activity." It can also include a student who has a temporary disability, a chronic health problem, or a communicable disease. To be eligible for special education and related services under IDEA, a student would have to qualify based on the findings of a multidisciplinary evaluation; fit under one of the IDEA categories (autism, deaf-blindness, deafness, developmental delay, emotional disturbance, hearing impairment, mental retardation, orthopedic disability, specific learning disability, multiple disabilities, speech or language impairment, traumatic brain injury, or visual impairment including blindness); and be demonstrably unable to benefit from a regular education. There is far more to it than this, however. For further information, visit the best special education website in the world: Wrightslaw, at www.wrightslaw.com.

Since our focus here is independence, parents should understand that the protections and services provided under IDEA last only as long as your child is enrolled in a school district. Usually, once a student earns a high school diploma and graduates, IDEA no longer applies. (There are exceptions: students whose disabilities prevent them from obtaining a high school diploma can continue to receive services through their school district to age twenty-one.)

THE FACT: SOME INDEPENDENCE SKILLS CANNOT—AND SHOULD NOT—BE TAUGHT AT SCHOOL

Another issue related to school-provided services for teaching independence skills is that most schools are not designed, in terms of either staffing or physical facilities, to teach some of the more personal skills. For example, it is not unusual for a specialized school for students with ASDs to turn a classroom into a mock furnished bedroom or bathroom, where they can teach related skills. Teachers have special training, and the schools follow special procedures to ensure that privacy is protected and the students are safe. Such facilities, personnel, and training generally do not exist in most public schools. Whereas in specialized schools, teachers and staff are expected to be involved in programs that teach self-help skills and toileting, in many parts of the country, public school teachers either are not required to do it or are allowed to decline to do it. So the highly complex teaching of such skills is usually left to an assistant, paraprofessional, or aide who probably has a heart of gold but might choose to follow her own program (often based on how she trained her own children or what worked with kids she babysat). It is right that school policies reflect a vigilant attitude toward keeping kids safe, and school staff tends to be acutely aware of any interaction with students that might be construed as inappropriate. However, this can present a problem for a third-grade boy whose female aide cannot accompany him into the boys' room to ensure that he zips his pants and tucks in his shirt before he steps back out into the hallway.

We are only beginning to recognize that even the brightest child with Asperger syndrome may need help in these areas. In an ideal AS program, at least one period per day would be devoted to social and independence skills in a class with a curriculum as clearly defined as that of algebra or American history, in every grade. To my knowledge, no such program exists. For now, though, most professionals with the necessary expertise either are school psychologists and counselors or are teachers working with students whose learning profiles require significantly less emphasis on academics and more on what are frequently termed life skills. It can be argued that these placements would fail to meet the mandated requirement for a student with AS to be educated in the least restrictive environment, even though, ironically, such a classroom is where you find the staff members experienced in teaching the practical skills of everyday living. Sometimes parents of students with AS who have significant learning disabilities are confronted with a choice between having their child pursue a typical academic curriculum and enrolling their child in a program that will address the learning disabilities and life skills concerns. As we are discovering, the ideal for many kids with AS is some individually tailored mix of the two.

DON'T LOSE SIGHT OF THE BIGGER GOAL

I'm not suggesting that these skills have no place being taught in school. As a matter of fact, they should be included as goals on your child's IEP and/or discussed with the appropriate service provider. And you may find the guidance from a specialist such as an occupational therapist invaluable. That said, do not adopt the attitude that since the school district should provide the services, only the school district can provide them. Yes, we should all be advocating for our children, and, yes, every child with a disability should receive all the mandated services for which she qualifies. That said, it's no secret that special education is not perfect anywhere. And in this time of rampant budget cuts and mandated changes in what schools do and how they do it (think of No Child Left Behind), gaps do form between the ideal as spelled out in the IEP or 504 plan and the real-life outcome.

Try not to let yourself—and your child—get caught up in waiting too long for "what should be" to materialize. If you believe, as many experts do, that teaching self-help skills to children with Asperger syndrome and similar ASDs falls under the requirements of special education law, certainly advocate for it. However, if your district or state education department chooses to interpret the law differently, lacks the resources to provide the services, or has a history of not viewing self-help skills as part of its job, do not wait. That your child learns the skill is more important than who teaches it. Don't let her fall behind or be in a position to miss out on important, life-enhancing experiences because you are waiting for a change in attitude or availability of services that may never come.

And even if you are in the incredibly fortunate minority and have a school district willing to take on the teaching of these skills, don't skip practicing at home. Remember, home is the natural environment and the place where most of the skills are put into practice. If you can work at home to help your child reach these goals that much quicker, that's even better. In short, wherever your school district falls on the helpfulness scale in this area, you should be teaching and practicing skills at home anyway.

Now, I know there are some who would argue that schools that admit students with disabilities are responsible for addressing all of their needs, whether the skills would be needed for school or not. Certainly that is the view of such renowned experts in the field as Dr. Ami Klin. However, having worked in schools, I think it's also fair to ask, just how much can a school do? If, for instance, we would like the occupational therapist to help Sally learn to button her shirt or tie her shoes, and everyone agrees to make this a goal, wonderful. Sally, who has between five and ten other occupational therapy goals for the school year, will be practicing using buttons or tying laces for a few minutes once, maybe twice a week. A fine-motor skill such as buttoning or shoe tying is mastered only through lots of practice. The amount of practice that Sally will get performing these skills in the OT alone is simply not sufficient for mastery.

Another thing to consider when we think about these skills is, where and when is this skill practiced the most naturally? In this case, the answer is at home, and this is true for most independence skills. As we know, the key to developing mastery and fluency is intensive, structured practice, and the more trials of practice we fit into a given period of time (say, a week), the more quickly we reach success. The rate at which our kids acquire these skills should be another important consideration. Given the fact that learning these skills may feel like a challenge to your child, who may find the process frustrating or uncomfortable, naturally it makes sense to do whatever you can to plot the shortest route from start to mastery.

Let's say that Sally's OT can devote five minutes, or about three trials—meaning three attempts to complete the task from start to finish—to shoe tying in each of her two weekly sessions. That's six trials a week. At home, however, you can easily set aside ten minutes a day, or maybe two separate sessions of five minutes per day, seven days a week, during which you can provide six practice opportunities per day instead of three. Over the course of a week, home teaching provides forty-two opportunities for practice compared to just six for school. In other words, Sally would have to attend both sessions of OT (and let's not forget schedule changes, holidays, and other events that routinely interfere) for seven weeks to receive the same number of practice opportunities that she would get in a single week at home.

Clearly, while parents have the primary responsibility for teaching essential life skills, there are ways to work with your school district to ensure that any educational program meets the full range of your child's special needs.

Chapter 10

CARING PARENTS MAKE EFFECTIVE
TEACHERS—ONCE THEY KNOW HOW

Parents of children with special needs wear many hats—advocate, protector, interpreter, coach, chauffeur, tutor, playmate, social guide—and they often wear at least some of them for years, even decades, longer than parents of typical kids. When we learn that our child has an ASD diagnosis, most of us bolt out of the gate, determined to win this race, no matter what the emotional, financial, or social cost. We will, as we tell anyone within earshot, "do anything" that might help. By late elementary school to middle school, most of us are still in the race, but the pace has slowed as we take in the weary realization that even the best efforts sometimes come up short.

As a teacher-consultant, I give a lot of advice to parents and other professionals. I'm full of suggestions, tips, and strategies for things that parents can do to help their kids, and I admit that I sometimes have a hard time understanding parents who freely admit that they try but do not always follow through on everything that professionals like me have to offer. Of course, as a parent, I know firsthand how hard it is to always follow through on each and every recommendation your child's teacher, behavioral therapist, or other professional suggests; it can be easy for professionals to lose sight of how much parents are juggling. If you could assemble all the wonderful teachers, behaviorists, occupational therapists, speech teachers, coaches, trainers, socialization therapists, audiologists, psychologists, psychiatrists, neurologists, special education attorneys, and other wise people who have helped my son, Justin, it would make the Verizon network look like a coffee klatch.

It would be wonderful to follow through with everything that I know might possibly help. That said, some suggestions are more likely to be followed than others: namely, those that work. The recommended strategy probably won't be easy or quick, but whatever effort you and your child put into it will be worth it. It's clear that parents recognize the value of these skills, and they are willing to do the work. But, like everyone, we too need some reinforcement to keep going.

What are some of the things that moms and dads find most helpful when trying to teach these skills? At the end of one of the surveys, I asked parents to respond to this open-ended question: "Please describe what you believe you need to help your child acquire or improve these skills." Because this was an anonymous survey, some parents apparently felt it was safe to be honest. One joked, "A loudspeaker with the tasks repeated over and over, so I don't have to say it anymore." Other replies included winning the lottery, hiring a full household staff, and having a "magic pill."

On a serious note, however, answers overwhelmingly highlighted the need for patience, time, repetition, and consistency. Even if their child was not in a school or program with a heavily behavioral orientation, most who responded recognized the value of that approach. They just weren't sure how to go about it. Some also mentioned that either they had no access to professionals with behavioral expertise or they simply could not afford the service.

Parents are different from teachers (and here I include any therapist or other professional whose intervention succeeds through teaching). Teachers are trained for this work; they know how to depersonalize a kid's anger, resistance, and whining; they have done this all before, so their faith in knowing it works goes far to carry them—and their students—through the rough patches. And they get paid and go home at some point. In contrast, parents do not come to this task as much as it falls upon them. Untrained, emotionally tethered to their child, unsure whether the work will be worth it, and "on duty" all the time, mothers and fathers start at a real disadvantage. That extra, emotional investment we bring to endeavors such as teaching our kids difficult skills can be both our noblest trait and our undoing.

For parents, some advantages of using behaviorally based strategies are the focus on objectivity, systematic teaching (that is, there is a reason behind everything you do), and consistency. Once I learned to use ABA strategies with my own son, I saw immediately how time-consuming and unproductive my earlier efforts had been. I'd been engaging in a lot of "mom talk," such as "I have shown you this a million times," "Isn't there something wrong with your socks?" "Don't forget to put the cap back on the toothpaste!" These nonteaching comments undermined teaching because they shifted his focus from learning the task to having a conversation with me. They also made learning less pleasant and less reinforcing than it needed to be for my son to succeed. For several years after receiving my son's diagnosis, I rejected structured teaching approaches like those based in ABA. I thought that caring, supporting, helping, doing for, and understanding would help him more. While those things are definitely essential to his well-being and to my sense of myself as a good parent, I missed a crucial reality: none of those things teach my son the skills he needs to no longer need me.

All that said, parents can be the *best* teachers for conveying these skills. Why? To begin with, you know your child better than anyone else does, and you already have a rapport with her. What's more, you don't have to work at establishing yourself as a reinforcing presence, and you control and inhabit the natural environment where most of these skills can be taught and practiced. Finally, no one in this world, no matter how dedicated and expert, cares more about your child than you do. This bears repeating. *No one* cares more about your child and her well-being than *you*.

When a child struggles to learn, and especially when it's for reasons that we do not expect or cannot fully grasp, the situation certainly can feel overwhelming. Often, though, our emotional response to our child's frustration and failure (and, I daresay, our own), is what complicates the picture. If you step back far enough to turn down the emotional static—yours and your child's—and focus solely on the task or skill and the behavior needed to complete or teach it, things will be much easier.

The idea of intensive practice being the key to mastery is hardly news to anyone. Who is going to the NBA, the player who shoots one free throw a day for thirty days or the player who shoots thirty free throws every day? Even if it feels artificial when applied to independence skills, we all know—almost instinctively—that a higher rate of practice (more opportunities over a shorter period of time) produces better learning. Another added bonus is that Sally masters and thus is done with learning shoe tying much sooner. Now, this may seem like a small thing until you consider how much time and energy our kids already devote to learning over the course of a typical day. Think of all the parent-child interaction—some of it fun, some of it not so much—around the issue of shoe tying. Don't you and your child have something better to do? I'm sure you'll agree that the quicker we can reach the magic "I can do it!" moment, the better for everyone. Again, it all goes back to reinforcement: the more you can get and the sooner you can get it, the better—and the sooner you can move on to tackling the next skill and guide your child one step closer to independence.

Other advantages to learning these skills at home include:

• **Home is the safe place.** Many youngsters with Asperger syndrome and other ASDs view home as a haven, a refuge, the safest place in the world. Generally speaking, home is the environment that they can predict most accurately and exert the most control over. Home is also where they are best understood by people who love them. It is the place where mistakes are forgiven and disappointments shared and understood.

• **Home has no deadline stress.** Sure, we all seem to live by the clock, but home presents a rare opportunity to take teaching and practicing these skills "out of time." As you will read later, the best time to learn and practice many skills is exactly when you do not have a deadline looming. At home, you set the stage. No one else will be lining up for recess while your child struggles with buttoning her jacket.

• **Home offers more opportunities for immediate correction and guided practice.** With general education classrooms averaging sometimes more than twenty students, it is unrealistic to expect a teacher to be standing by every time your child attempts a new skill. Yes, there are aides, paraprofessionals, and teacher assistants in many classrooms, but in some cases they lack the training to recognize when and how to intervene. And, if anything, they may actually increase your child's prompt dependence rather than help build his independence. In contrast, you can set aside the time to provide really good practice without interruptions and with just the right level of prompting.

• **Home offers unique opportunities for immediate and effective reinforcement.** Since the way you'll be teaching will rely on providing potent reinforcement, another consideration is what the school environment typically cannot provide in terms of type, frequency, and duration of reinforcement. For the majority of our kids who are learning in a regular school in a general education classroom, the facilities and equipment simply do not exist. Schedule-wise, it is often impossible to provide certain types of reinforcers without taking away from instruction time or time with peers (which you do not want to sacrifice, either); at home it is much easier to access the ten minutes of Wii or the favorite ice pop that makes the learning of truly hard skills worth the child's while. If we are concerned that a child with AS be viewed by his classmates as more like them than unlike them—and research shows that this is an important consideration in peer acceptance of kids with any form of disability—we should be honest in evaluating the social impact of a child being the only one in class to get a snack, special access to the computer, and so on.

• **Your home generally offers a much wider variety of reinforcers.** For some students, the most powerful reinforcer is available only at school: being chosen to run errands, take the classroom pet rabbit home on weekends, or erase the SMART

Board. But there is more diversity at home, not to mention many more opportunities to access and enjoy the type of reinforcers kids with AS tend to go for.

• **Home provides privacy and freedom from embarrassment.** Let's also keep in mind that while children with Asperger syndrome and other ASDs may be socially awkward at times, they are not completely socially unaware. Learning more personal self-care skills, such as how to use a zipper or how to brush one's hair, in the school setting may be uncomfortable or embarrassing. And, to reiterate, skills are best acquired in the natural environment where they will be used.

ACKNOWLEDGE AND EXPLOIT TO THE MAX YOUR UNIQUE ADVANTAGE

Does the compliment, high five, or big hug—served up with a smile—mean more coming from Mom, Dad, Grandma, or Aunt Danielle? As a mother, I'd love to believe that it's so, and in the absence of research finding otherwise, let's just say that it's true. There's something in it for you, too: the feeling of empowerment, knowing that, yeah, you really did teach that skill, not to mention the opportunity to share a happy moment with your kid. Again, let's consider how much of our communication with our child involves directing, correcting, and explaining. Don't we all wish we could do less of that? There's no research on this one, either, but if the number of times someone has remarked to us, "I don't know how you do it," "You must have the patience of a saint," or "I don't think I could handle this" can be considered a valid indicator, it's safe to say that the answer to "How much more valuable is reinforcement coming from parents or family?" is somewhere between "twice as much" and "a hundred times more."

CONSISTENCY IS EVERYTHING

Clearly, we all understand the importance of consistency for our kids. But while it's usually easy to recognize their need for consistency and predictability in terms of schedule, personal preferences, and other aspects of daily life, sometimes we fail to deliver consistency in teaching. Interestingly, consistency was among the most common qualities that respondents to the parents survey felt they needed to be effective. We all recognize the value of consistency, so what gets in the way? In the survey responses, time and patience were identified most frequently as prerequisites for effective teaching.

In practice, one thing we love about using behaviorally based teaching is that everything—and I do mean everything—is written down. Sure, you could concoct a plan of teaching in your head, give it a try, and see what happens, but you would miss capturing some essential information: namely, what parts of your plan work and what parts do not. Second, it is impossible to maintain consistency from one teaching trial to another if you do not have it written down, and it's even harder to recall what levels of prompting were used and any little adjustments and deviations that mysteriously slipped in. And, believe me, they will. Third, without a written plan, there is no way to track data—at least not accurate and truly informative data about your child's progress. If you recall that Kim did really well setting the table on Wednesday but not so well on Thursday, without data you might miss the fact that you were there prompting a lot on Wednesday but had to answer a brief phone call in the middle of things on Thursday. Or you might have offered Kim the same reinforcer for both days, or you might have overlooked the reinforcer both days, or you might have decided that Thursday's less optimal job was good enough and gave her the reinforcer anyway. What lesson did Kim learn? For one thing, that it doesn't really matter how well she does the job.

Again, we need to be crystal clear on this: I don't mean to say that Kim will become manipulative and start playing her parents to get away with it. That's what lots of typical kids learn to do by this type of parental response, and we should not be surprised. And when our kids are subjected to substandard teaching—poorly planned, undocumented, inconsistent—and consequently fail to learn, we parents too often hear that they're being manipulative or trying to get away with something. Sometimes we even think that ourselves.

The classic "Terrence did it yesterday, so I know he can do it today—he's just got an attitude problem" probably would look, to anyone focused on the data, a lot like this: Terrence had been assigned the job of reorganizing the class homework bins. Yesterday the teacher hovered about, offered a few prompts and corrections, and gave Terrence a chance to run an errand to the principal's office (one of his favorite reinforcers) if he did a good job. And he did—with lots of sound, appropriate prompting. Today, however, the teacher is distracted dealing with the SMART Board (everyone's finger writing is coming out in plaid), and Terrence is left on his own. Although he is aware that he's probably not doing as good a job as he did yesterday, he's not sure how to make it better. Put yourself in Terrence's place: it's frustrating, to say the least. Hello, bad attitude. The sadder truth of the matter is that while our kids may not always know what they're doing, the interpersonal exchanges that revolve around these so-called teaching methods deliver some totally unintended lessons that have far deeper implications.

First, remember that Kim and Terrence were tackling chores that were not easy for them to begin with. If you are inconsistent with directions, prompts, corrections, and reinforcers, it will be hard for them to get a firm idea of what constitutes setting the table or organizing the homework bins.

Second, if you do not offer consistent prompts and corrections, you may be inadvertently teaching Kim and Terrence to incorporate mistakes into how they learn the skill. Teaching a learner to make errors through our own inattention to these details is not as bad as deliberately setting out to teach someone to make mistakes, but the end result is precisely the same. To quote my friend and mentor Dr. Bobby Newman, "The universe does not care what you meant to do; it only cares what happens."

Third, just as our kids do not always know when they are doing what they should not, they do not always know when they are doing what they should. There's no hard science behind this statement, but I think we have all seen it often enough to know that it's so. We know that the ability to self-observe and self-monitor is generally weak in people across the autism spectrum. Having told your child that he did a good job yesterday probably will not carry over to today, because understanding that he is doing a good job today requires a certain level of self-awareness and the ability to judge his own performance with, if not a degree of objectivity, at least a very clear idea of what a good job entails. Terrence, for example, has an idea of what constitutes a good job reorganizing the class homework bins, but his brain and his body have not practiced this enough for the task's many facets to come to him easily. I know exactly what a job well done looks like when it comes to sewing a wedding dress or wowing the judges on *American Idol*. Can I do either of them? Nope.

Fourth, Kim received the same degree of reinforcement whether she did a good job or a not-so-good job. Terrence, on the other hand, received reinforcement for doing a good job with a lot of teacher support, but he received nothing (and, in fact, may have picked up on a bit of his teacher's attitude about his attitude) for trying his best to figure it all out without that support. It's ironic that as we focus on preparing our kids for greater independence in the real world—where reinforcement and consequences tend to be pretty consistent—at home and in the classroom we end up teaching exactly the opposite by offering supports and reinforcement inconsistently.

Fifth, in both Kim's and Terrence's cases, we have also sent out an engraved invitation to our old friend prompt dependence. With Kim, who received the same reinforcement no matter how well she did the job, chances are very good that the next time Mom or Dad takes time to notice what Kim is doing, they will be more demanding—or at least it will certainly look that way to Kim. You can easily see why the next time she's presented with that task, she is more likely to engage in behavior, such as going off task or complaining, that will keep someone around to help her do a good job. Terrence, on the other hand, probably won't forget the anxiety he experienced trying to do his best when he knew that he could not. Like Kim, he will associate an adult presence with success and—maybe even more significantly—less stress. Are these kids being manipulative? No. But one thing I would say is that they are much more astute observers of human behavior than anyone who is currently trying to teach them.

WHAT GOES INTO A TEACHING PLAN?

Writing up a teaching plan is the best way to think it through thoroughly and make sure that you've covered all the bases before you start.

The Goal

The goal is the big-picture, long-term skill or behavior that is independent and accurate. Goals should also include:

- Who will perform the task (your child)
- What task will be performed (be specific and describe in a way such that anyone reading it could recognize the correct behavior vs. an incorrect behavior)
- Where it will be performed (usually at home, but other places should be considered to promote generalization)
- When it will be performed, and how often (every day, once a week, several times a day, whenever needed). Here consider what type of "schedule" will make the skill truly independent. Yes, you do teach Mary to brush her hair when she gets dressed in the morning. But she also needs to learn to brush her hair when she recognizes that it's messy.
- How it will be performed (with prompts or independently)

Examples of goal ideas include:

- Sally will tie her shoes.
- Tommy will perform all the tasks needed to get ready in the morning and get ready for bed at night.
- Aidan will set the table.

Without further elaboration, though, you will be left to decide, from day to day and even from trial to trial, "What is this thing we call shoe tying [or getting ready in the morning, or setting the table]?" Without a more fully developed goal, it's hard to decide whether Sally will tie her shoes every time or only sometimes, if she will do it independently, or if Mom or Dad will always do that first loop; we never know precisely which tasks Tommy will be expected to do or what dishes Aidan should put on the table. If we don't know, they don't know, and that's the real problem.

- The goal idea: Sally will tie her shoes.
  The goal: Sally will tie her shoes independently each time it's
    necessary.

- The goal idea: Tommy will perform all the tasks needed to
    get ready in the morning and get ready for bed at night.
  The goal: Tommy will independently perform all the tasks
    needed to get ready in the morning (respond to alarm
    clock, place dirty clothing in hamper, shower, brush
    teeth, comb hair, dress) and get ready for bed at night
    (pick out clothes for tomorrow, place dirty clothing in
    hamper, shower, wash hair, brush teeth, dry hair, put on
    pajamas) every day using a checklist of tasks.

- The goal idea: Aidan will set the table.
  The goal: Aidan will set the table (wipe the table, arrange
    place mats, and put down plates, flatware, glassware,
    salt and pepper shakers, and serving flatware as needed)
    using a visual map and checklist of questions to ask
    about what the evening meal requires (condiments,
    trivets for hot dishes, extra napkins, and so forth) every
    other evening. (He alternates with his brother, Adam.)

Think of your goal as the ultimate destination, the end of the road, the point of arrival at which you will be able to say, "She knows how to do it!" Next we plot the route to success with objectives and other details.

Objectives: A Goal in Bite-Sized Pieces

Each of the goals above has numerous steps or tasks within the larger task that must be executed in order to achieve the bigger goal. Breaking down tasks and routines makes them manageable, in terms of both teaching and learning. It also helps those of us who have perfunctorily performed these tasks for decades without a moment's thought to really think about what goes into bringing each one all together.

The table on page 206 shows different levels of breakdowns, or task analyses, for Joey making oatmeal.

There are a couple of excellent books on teaching these skills that were designed for parents of more learning-disabled children. Even though these books are full of useful information, parents of kids with ASD profiles like Asperger's find them a poor fit because the directions and steps are so completely broken down. It's a good guess that your child will not need explicit teaching to know how to locate the middle of the placemat or how to discriminate between when her hands are wet or dry. That said, however, do not overlook steps in a task that your child may not know. Remember, it's not very likely that your son has ever consciously observed how you wipe down the dining room table (unless his special interests involve sponges or evaporation rates). To help your child achieve a level of performance that will produce a clean table, you may have to do a couple of test drives and see what he actually does. For some of our kids, it's the little things that adversely impact task performance. In this case, the little things include not rinsing the sponge, not squeezing it out, and not wiping the table thoroughly. How you wipe the table may appear to an observer to be haphazard, but you cover every inch. Our kids, however, may need to learn to work in some systematic fashion—up and down, left to right, from the center outward, whatever you prefer—to do a thorough job. They may need to be reminded to wring out the sponge. Or they may even need to be taught "right," "left," and "middle."

Goal Idea	Goal	Task Components	Task Analysis
		Joey will take oatmeal from cabinet.	
			1. Open oatmeal packet and pour into bowl.
		Joey will prepare oatmeal in bowl.	2. Read package directions.
			3. Measure 1/3 cup of water and pour into bowl.
			4. Stir.
			1. Read package directions.
		Joey will cook oatmeal in microwave.	2. Place bowl in microwave.
			3. Set microwave to 100% for 2 minutes.
		Joey will remove oatmeal from microwave.	1. When microwave beeps, open door and carefully remove bowl.
			2. Remember to use an oven mitt or pot holder.
Who will do what, when, where, and how. Example: Joey will prepare his own oatmeal in the microwave every school day morning when asked.	*What will the task look like as Joey is learning and practicing it today?* Joey will prepare his own oatmeal in the microwave every school day morning with supervision and needed nonverbal prompts. *Also note that Joey could use visual prompts or cues or a written list of instructions, or be learning it with graduated guidance.*		

What Behavior Will Be Reinforced and How

Each time we consider reinforcement, we have to ask the following question—and our child has to answer it: is it worth it? The more difficult the task or the more important the skill, the richer the reinforcement should be. It should be a fair deal for everyone. As a general rule, for early skills that feature more components and may take more effort, you should reinforce 1:1—one reinforcer for every correct action—through the learning (acquisition) phase. Once the skill is on board, fade your reinforcement to every other time, then every third time, every fourth time, and so on, provided that the skill is still demonstrated at the same high level.

Teaching often fails because the reinforcement isn't rich enough, consistent enough, or meaningful enough to work. It's important to understand that a reinforcer is not just something your child likes or thinks is cool. And it is usually not what you or anyone else (and that may include 99.99 percent of kids your child's age) likes or thinks is cool. A reinforcer is neither a reward nor a bribe, because neither is given with the idea that it will change future behavior. By definition, something added to or removed from the environment is a reinforcer only if it changes the likelihood that a behavior will or will not occur in the future.

Reinforcement is another part of a behavioral or teaching plan that people like to claim "doesn't work." The first problem there is that, by definition, a reinforcer that doesn't work is not a reinforcer. A thing that you give someone after she performs a task is merely a consequence. Many times people choose a particular reinforcer because they think it's something the child really likes. Maybe she does really like it. But even so, if we look at human nature, it's easy to see that while you can like or enjoy something immensely, there are usually limits to how much effort you would exert to obtain it. There is a limit to how much anyone will do for anything, and it may be easier to see that if you look at reinforcers in purely economic terms.

For instance, Sally likes her Dora the Explorer doll a lot; she plays with it throughout the day and sleeps with it at night. Sally is also learning to brush her own hair. Despite how much Sally loves Dora, brushing her hair might be just hard enough that even having extra access to Dora is not worth it for her. Remember that when it comes to working at something difficult, in the background often looms a very compelling competing reinforcer that's amazingly easy to access: it's called "I quit," or, more formally, "escape from task demands."

One of the biggest problems with this type of competing reinforcer—and make no mistake, quitting is a powerful one—is that you can do nothing to control it. Remember, the learner determines the value of the reinforcer. It then becomes your job to revalue the reinforcer "currency." In this case, you would have to find some way to make access to Dora more "valuable." Or you might have to find another reinforcer.

Aidan, on the other hand, loves his Wii and, according to his mother, uses it too much. She could make access to the Wii contingent upon Aidan successfully setting the table. That probably would be a potent reinforcer, boosting his motivation for setting the table. Also, since Aidan's setting the table every other day, that would mean he would only have the Wii every other day. If Aidan seeks more access to his Wii, his parents could suggest a second chore to learn, and he would probably go for it.

Using Food as a Reinforcer: It's Not a Bad Idea

Some years ago, I met with a teacher who was totally against using a favorite snack to reinforce the behavior of a student learning a very difficult task. Seated at a desk covered with files and test results that had to be inputted into the computer by that afternoon's deadline, she had a small package of dark chocolate M&M's and a venti Starbucks cappuccino with four pumps of dark mocha syrup and an extra espresso shot. Every few computer entries, she washed down a couple of M&M's with a sip of coffee.

"I just don't get it," she said between sips. "And I don't like it. I think food reinforcers look very babyish." She tossed a few more M&M's into her mouth. "What else can we do?"

Let's face it: we enjoy food. And we do use food to celebrate and reward ourselves and others. Food is the universal currency. It's quick, it's easy, it fits nicely into our evolutionary preferences. The lollipop at the doctor's, the thank-you basket of cookies for the teacher, the nice lunch your boss takes you to after the big project is all done: in our culture, food is a well-appreciated reward. So while it's true that food reinforcers may not be appropriate at school, they don't have to be entirely ruled out. For better or worse, most kids in the elementary grades have a midmorning snack, then lunch, and then a little something later on; students in middle school, junior high, and high school often have access to plenty of treats at the school store or in vending machines. Formally or informally, in structured behavior plans and on a teacher's whim, kids are often being rewarded with food. How this influences student nutrition and health is beyond our scope here. Let's just say that food exists throughout schools as something that is desirable and enjoyable. The circumstances under which they are allowed to access it (outside of scheduled times such as lunch) make up another unwritten "behavior plan" that keeps on running.

Food has come into the behavioral teaching repertoire as a common reinforcer, especially for younger students and those who are unable to enjoy other types of reinforcers, and this has happened for a good reason: it really, really works. Certainly we should all be moving toward using more naturalistic reinforcers such as social praise. That is why, when you do use food, it should always be delivered with intensive social reinforcement.

But you're teaching at home. Except for siblings, there are no other children's feelings to consider. Your child is probably eating some foods he enjoys a lot but which are not really necessary and maybe not even so healthy. I'm not here to judge. If your child has some favorite foods that you can make available as reinforcers, it's not the worst idea. Foods are handy because you can offer small portions, they disappear quickly, and you don't have to waste time transitioning from a midtask reinforcer back to work (as you might if the reinforcer were computer time or going outside to play a few minutes). Or you can offer the whole minibag of chips or the orange when the task is completed.* If overeating preferred foods is a problem in your home, you might be able to control some of that by making those foods available *only* as reinforcers, and then fading the reinforcement.

---

*Somewhere, surely, there are kids who do eat as healthfully as we wish.

LET'S GET STARTED

Whether you have a short list of a just a few skills you would like to work on or a veritable laundry list, your basic approach will be the same.

- List all the skills you believe your child either should have acquired by now or needs to acquire soon.
- Prioritize the skills based on the Wish List on page 73.
- Is there an immediate or serious safety issue?
- Is there a health issue?
- Is the skill necessary for the acquisition of another skill or the ability to complete a routine or a behavior chain?
- Does your child consider it a problem?
- Does the lack of this skill lead to social problems or limit access in other areas?
- Does the current state of this skill function as a starting point for interfering behaviors or problematic emotional responses?
- Is it age-appropriate for your child to have this skill?
- Are you ready to teach the skill?
- Whom else can you count on for support in teaching this skill?

• Is teaching this skill something you can think of the same way you think of a recipe?

• Create a time in your daily schedule for addressing the skill. Then pencil it in and stick to it.

• Do a task analysis. Rehearse the skill yourself and write down every single step and every item needed for teaching and practice.

• Ask your child to perform the task cold.. Do not provide any instructions or prompts or direction. See what happens. What does he do well? What does he do not so well? What skill components does he have? What skill components does he need? Ask your child what he is thinking and how he feels when asked to do the task. Listen carefully. Also ask him what he might need to help and support him.

• Write down the steps and begin thinking about what strategies might be useful. Remember, there will be some trial and error. A teaching program that doesn't work like magic the first time out is not a failure; it's a source of valuable clues as to what will work the next time.

• In addition to the items needed for the task, think about the tools of the trade you will be using: clipboard, data sheet, pencil or pen, timer, counter. If you will be using visual supports such as labels, lists, recipes, schedules, pictures, and so on, prepare them before you start, then incorporate them into your teaching plan.

• Write down what you will say and not say. One very good way to ensure that you trim the spoken words you use is to give yourself a script and follow it to the letter. Also incorporate in your list of steps the types of prompts you might be using. Keep track of what worked and what did not.

• Pick a reinforcer before you start and discuss it with your child. Remember that a potent reinforcer can override the influence of countless other factors. Why? Because the right reinforcer makes the hard work of learning worth it to your child.

THE TEACHING ZONE

Teaching one skill really involves teaching several skills. Let's go back to our recipe. When we teach a skill, here are all the bases we need to cover:

- Approximately how long it should take
- Equipment, ingredients, and techniques you will use
- What to do with each and in what order
- When to begin and when to end each step
- What to expect at each step
- What the final result will be

IS IT A SKILL?	
Is it a skill? If you can provide answers to all of these questions, you have a skill you can teach.	
1. The environmental conditions	
2. Approximately how long it should take to complete	
3. Equipment, ingredients, techniques you will use	
4. What to do with each piece of equipment, ingredient, and technique, and in what order	
5. When to begin and when to end each step	
6. What to expect at each step	
7. What the final result will be	

Is it a skill? If you can provide answers to all of these questions, you have a skill you can teach.

	Math homework	Fixing ramen noodles in the microwave	Taking a phone message
1. The environmental conditions	After school, at the desk in the den	Lunchtime, in the kitchen; you feel hungry	The phone rings and no one else is there to answer it; Mom or Dad has told you that it's okay to answer the phone
2. Approximately how long it should take to complete	Between 45 minutes and 1 hour	Between 5 and 10 minutes	Between 1 and 2 minutes
3. Equipment, ingredients, techniques you will use	Backpack: take out daily planner, math book, math notebook, math folder, ruler, pencils, eraser	Package of ramen noodles, bowl, spoon and/or fork, microwave, measuring cup, water	Phone, paper, pencil or pen, someplace to put the message after you write it down.
	Daily planner	Ramen noodles	Phone
	Math book	Bowl	Paper
	Math notebook	Spoon and/or fork	Pencil or pen
	Math folder	Microwave	Message
	Math worksheet	Measuring cup	
	Ruler	Water	
	Pencils	Napkin	
	Eraser	Oven mitts or pot holders	

Is it a skill? If you can provide answers to all of these questions, you have a skill you can teach.

	Math homework	Fixing ramen noodles in the microwave	Taking a phone message
4. What to do with each piece of equipment, ingredient, and technique, and in what order	Remove items from backpack.	Read instructions.	Answer the phone and say, "Hello, the Starbucks residence."
	Open planner to today's page.	Open package of ramen noodles.	Listen for the caller to answer.
	Read assignment.	Pour into microwave-safe bowl.	Say, "Can I take a message?"
	Open math book; turn to page.	Measure water in cup.	
	Open math notebook; date blank sheet.	Add water to noodles.	
	Do the first problem.	Place noodles in microwave. Set timer.	
		Wait in kitchen for microwave to stop.	
		Using oven mitts or pot holders, carefully remove bowl from microwave.	

5. When to begin and when to end each step	Copy problem from math book into notebook.	Read instructions until you know how much water to use, how long to cook the noodles, and at what microwave setting.	After the caller gives you the message, read it back to the caller.
	Look at the operation signs: add or subtract?	Fill the measuring cup with only as much water as the instructions say.	If the message is okay, say, "I will give him/her the message. Good-bye."
	Question? Ask!		If the message is not okay, make the corrections. Then read it back to the caller. When the message is okay, say, "I will give him/her the message. Good-bye."
	Write the problem in notebook.		
	Solve the problem.		
	Question? Ask!		

Is it a skill? If you can provide answers to all of these questions, you have a skill you can teach.

	Math homework	Fixing ramen noodles in the microwave	Taking a phone message
6. What to expect at each step	You may not know the answer right away. That's okay. The operation signs might change with every problem. That's okay. If you get stuck, someone can answer your question.	The noodles might start to smell different as they cook. The water in the bowl may boil over a little if it gets too hot. That's okay; you can wipe it up after it cools. The noodles might not be as soft as you like when you first take them out. You can put them back into the microwave to cook for another 30 seconds.	The caller may not want to leave a message. That's okay. The caller may talk quickly or not be clear. It is okay to say, "Excuse me. Could you please repeat that for me?"
7. What the final result will be	Every math problem will have an answer.	You have a bowl of hot ramen noodles, ready to eat.	Most times, there will be a message for someone.

Many times we get so focused on the final result that we do not pay as much attention to the necessary steps that have to take place for that result to come about. As a result, our kids never really learn those steps. Remember that within each phase or step are the kernels of other skills that can be applied to other problems and situations.

To detour around the familiar roadblocks and potholes, we want to follow a teaching routine for each instance (or teaching trial).

Teach Following the Three-Term Contingency: ABC (Easy as 1, 2, 3)

If your child has ever experienced behavior that you or someone else was asked to document, you may be familiar with an ABC chart. ABC stands for three steps in teaching:

A: antecedent, or whatever occurs that the behavior is a response to (in teaching, this is your direction and/or a prompt)

B: behavior, or what your child does in response to the antecedent

C: consequence of the behavior (for a correct response, the consequence is reinforcement; for an incorrect response, it's correction)

Effective teaching follows this pattern consistently, whether you're teaching just how to turn on the washing machine or the whole array of skills involved in washing, drying, and putting away a whole load of laundry. When you approach teaching from this ABC framework, it's much easier to see what fits and what doesn't.

For me, it helps to think of the brief period between the moment just before you give the direction and the moment you hand over the reinforcer or offer the correction as the "teaching zone," a special time where any comment or action that does not belong on the ABC itinerary simply does not occur. This takes some practice and maybe some self-discipline on your part, but when you see the results, you'll wonder why you ever did it any other way. Some people have problems with the clear, no-frills teaching behavior used in the teaching zone. They like to talk to children, point things out, and sprinkle in praise, commentaries, constructive criticism, and little reminders throughout the teaching period. They think this is nicer, or more supportive. You know what it really is, from the child's perspective? It's incredibly distracting, adding more irrelevant, competing stimuli to the mix, and hijacking his attention from what he should focus on. Don't do it.

That said, after your child has practiced the skill well, and before you give your direction, feel free to be as chatty, playful, affectionate, and charming as you want. For most basic skills, a teaching trial runs from a few seconds to a few minutes. It's not as if your child will be starved for attention in the meantime. Besides, when you are teaching, she should have your full attention, which means you must also make a time and a space that is as free of distraction as possible.

Again, we are reducing or eliminating the extraneous environmental cues and distractions in order to focus on the relevant cues for teaching and reinforcement. You're part of that environment, too. Unnecessary talking, overprompting, changing your mind about how a task should be performed, and so on undermine your teaching and your child.

Make a Special Time and Place

Create a calendar and write down when and where you and your child will be working on the skill. Make sure to post the calendar someplace conspicuous where the two of you can see it.

Daily practice is best, and daily practice with several trials, when feasible, is even better. Practice in the natural environment—the place where the skill will be applied in the real world—as often as possible. If the natural environment is too distracting, start someplace that's more conducive to learning, but always with the goal of getting back to the real-world setting.

Plan for—and Eliminate—Distractions

Remember that learning to attend only to the cues relevant to the task is crucial for independence. View this as a competition in which the irrelevant stimuli and vital cues are vying for your child's attention. If necessary, remove as many interfering distractions as you can. If your child keeps looking at himself in the mirror, cover the mirror. If your daughter is fascinated by her jewelry, put it away. If your son keeps glancing out the window because someone is riding a skateboard, close the curtains. Needless to say, TVs, radios, iPods, computers, and anything else—and that includes other people and pets—that can intrude auditorily or visually is either off or out of the room. Clear the field.

Have a Plan and Follow It

Write down your plan and follow what you have written. Have it in front of you; don't try to wing it. Remember that consistency is crucial.

Establish Your Reinforcer

Whether it's fifteen minutes on the backyard trampoline, a few chocolate chips, or a token toward a bigger reward, have your reinforcer in hand. If circumstances preclude using a regular reinforcer (perhaps it's raining outside, so no trampoline), be sure you discuss with your child what the substitute reinforcer will be. Before you start, remind your child what the reinforcer will be and give her a chance to make another choice, if that's possible. Better yet, give her a choice between two or three proven reinforcers. This keeps things more interesting and reduces the chances of your losing a reinforcer to overuse (also known in the trade as satiation).

A note on timing: Schools and parents are often fond of reinforcement schedules that promise a big something at the end of a long period—a day or a week, usually—of "good behavior" or demonstration of a skill. Of course, the reinforcement schedule depends on the task itself and on the skill level of your child. If Doug has been unloading the dishwasher proficiently and independently for several weeks, there is nothing wrong in offering a weekly big-deal reinforcer. (Though he should also be getting some nice social reinforcement every time he does the job; that's just being polite.) However, if your child has not yet mastered a skill, delaying reinforcement can be a mistake.

First, when you base one chance for reinforcement on several opportunities over a period of time, children learn quickly that after a certain number of failures, all is lost. This means that the opportunities that were successful do not get reinforced at all, and if the first opportunities fail, then why even bother with the rest? Talk about a buzz kill. It's not surprising that this can have exactly the opposite effect: decreasing—rather than increasing—the likelihood of seeing the skill demonstrated next time.

Second, it is a scientific fact that effective reinforcement is immediate. The longer the wait between good performance and access to the reinforcer, the less valuable and potent that reinforcer will be. Furthermore, the more likely that performance will "fall off."

Correct Errors Without Criticism

For many of our kids, the hazard area is not the teaching itself but the moment when something goes wrong and we feel we must correct. Corrections are unavoidable, but remember that it doesn't matter what we intend to convey with our words—what's important is what our kids hear. Youngsters with Asperger syndrome are notorious for a tendency to catastrophize mistakes and overreact. Offering corrections in the teaching zone—no matter how well intended and neutral in tone—should be done thoughtfully and with care. Remember that the point of correcting is not to criticize or to talk about what went wrong but to teach, and we teach nothing by referring to what someone did that only demonstrates what we still have to teach them. Corrections that do not show or tell what to do are not teaching.

Get in the right frame of mind: be calm, positive, and relaxed. If you feel yourself anticipating mistakes or problems, make a conscious effort to ignore those thoughts. Instead of looking for the mistakes, try looking even harder for whatever you can praise in terms of your child's attitude, willingness, cooperation, effort, and execution.

Live in the now. Remind yourself to respond to just what's happening now, in this moment. Yesterday? Last week? Next year? Two minutes ago? They don't exist. Forget 'em. Further, alluding to your child's poor past performance and what that may bode for his future is never a good idea. He can't change what happened in the past (no one can), and conveying the idea that the future is somehow predetermined and beyond his control plays into a common perspective among kids with AS that what they do really does not matter. The fact is, responsibility for whatever happens today that will shape the future tomorrow lies in *your* hands, not his.

Wherever possible and effective, correct without words: gesture, silently refer to a visual support, physically prompt. If your child makes a mistake at some point in a chain—say, he squeezes out too much shampoo into his hand—anticipate the error and try to catch and correct it nonverbally before it happens.

Make use of an exception to the no-talking rule: oral verbal antecedent prompts. In the shampoo example, you might say, "Remember, put only one squirt of shampoo in your hand," or ask, "How much shampoo should you put in your hand?"

If an oral verbal error correction is in order, follow these guidelines:

- Explain what to do, not what not to do.
- Avoid "you" comments, as in "You need to look at your chart," "You forgot to add detergent to the wash," and so on. Instead say, "Next time, looking at your chart might help," or "Remember the detergent next time."
- Avoid using your child's name. I admit this sounds a bit unusual, but hear me out. In teaching, I have found that so many people, in so many settings, precede questions, task demands, and criticisms with the child's name, as in "Jeremy, get to work" or "Lisa, stop doing that!" Parents get a lot of behavior-control mileage out of pairing a child's name with an infinite variety of tones of voice. Simply by saying a child's name with the right tone of voice, they can convey everything from "Come here; I'm so proud of you" to "Go to your room and don't ever ask to use your cell phone again." Many kids on the spectrum are inconsistent in responding to their names, and no wonder. They—like their typical peers—may have learned that hearing

an adult say their name signals that something unpleasant is on the way. Or as they say on the bridge of the *Enterprise*: "Incoming!" Not surprisingly, they take evasive action: ignoring, moving away, shutting down, or blowing up. Not using your child's name with instructions and corrections takes a little discipline and forces you to think about what you are going to say.

DATA CAN BE YOUR FRIENDS (YES, IT'S PLURAL)

Reports, evaluations, report cards, grades on tests: these are all forms of reporting data on performance. Most parents have a big, fat folder filled with all kinds of data on their child. We tend to think of data as a measure of some aspect of an individual's performance, and some of us, almost instinctively, have a problem with that. Evaluative data should be objective, but it's still difficult as a parent to get past some uncomfortable feelings about our children being "judged" and "measured," deemed "below average" or worse.

Quick Tip: Data Help You Judge the Effectiveness of the Program—Not the Learner

Understandably, some parents react strongly to the word *data* or the idea of taking data. As one mother said to me, "It's so science-y. It doesn't sound like we're talking about my kid; it sounds like we're talking about a robot." Others have a hard time with the idea of measuring performance and "judging." One father complained, "It seems like it's all they do in school these days; now I have to do it here at home, too?"

I hear you.

First, behavior-based teaching relies on specifically defined terms that help us paint a complete, accurate picture of what's going on. This focus on consistency in terminology and methods helps ensure that everyone involved is speaking the same language and is being consistent in application.* Those are good things (and all too rare in other approaches).

Second, data measure programs, not people. And the most important question that a day's, a week's, or a month's collection of data answers is this: "Is the learning plan working? Is it effective? Is it making it possible for Wyatt to do better today than he did last week?" Notice that it's not about what Wyatt "scored." These are not grades. If anything, data are more a reflection on the performance of the teacher and the plan than on that of the child.

Third, there are kids across the spectrum who find looking at their charted data highly reinforcing. It's visual, it features numbers and dates—hey, what's not to love? Kids of a certain age can acquire some pretty solid math skills charting their own data, if that's something they are interested in doing. If you choose to share the collected data with your child, keep it a joint venture. When things are not going well, try saying, "Let's see how we did," or "What do you think of what we did today?" or "Let's see how this way of teaching is working for you." When your child is doing really well, though, don't hesitate to shower him with praise and give him all the credit.

Behaviorally based teaching runs on data to an extent rarely found in other teaching methods. That's because decisions about what's working and what is not working, what should stay the same and what must change, are made based on the data. When you do not use data, you're left with some pretty unreliable sources to evaluate how well

---

*If you find some of the behavioral intervention terminology baffling, you are not alone. Even experts in the field recognize the problem. If you wish to pursue more behaviorally based interventions for your child, or if your child is receiving such interventions and you've ever wished for a translator, please check out Dr. Bobby Newman's smart and fun *Behaviorspeak: A Glossary of Terms in Applied Behavior Analysis.*

things are going: someone's recollection of how Daryl did yesterday or last week, or a prediction of your child's probable course based on past experience with so many kids "just like her," or someone else's personal opinion of what's best based on anything from a seminar she attended last week to something she heard in teachers' college twenty years ago. Not only does your child deserve better, but none of the abovementioned practices comes within a country mile of meeting the legal requirement of evidence-based practice.

For kids with AS and similar ASDs, data can also work as a potent reinforcer. Many of our kids really like factual information and numbers. For some at this end of the spectrum, rising bars on a graph are a lot more compelling than a star chart. And for those who are computer savvy, charting it out in a spreadsheet program such as Excel and playing with the different graph formats can be a lot of fun. (I plead guilty!)

Working as a consultant, I often hear people say that although they really want to work a teaching program, they find dealing with data too time-consuming. Perhaps you're thinking the same thing, so let me try to convince you why collecting data actually saves time and yields teaching programs that are more efficient and easier for both your child and you.

Time Waster #1: Seeking the Unknowable, Ignoring the Obvious

As well as we know our kids, their having an ASD accessorized with some co-occurring conditions and learning disabilities introduces an element of mystery. When they struggle to learn, we cannot always say with certainty where the problem lies. And even when we can pinpoint the problem, there is often little we can do to address it. This is all the more reason for the teaching to be systematic and documented, because when it is, there is one crucial element that you can see, evaluate, and change. Data are obvious only if they exist, and they exist only if you record them.

Time Waster #2: Hiding the Crucial Cause-and-Effect Tie Between Effort and Result

When your teaching plan is unsystematic and goes with the flow, the odds are that you are doing something a little (or a lot) different from teaching opportunity to teaching opportunity. For your child, the cause-and-effect relationship between performing action A and producing outcome B gets very blurry, if not entirely lost. Remember that consistent reinforcement is the real teacher here. Without it, you can ensure that whatever learning does occur will not happen as well or as quickly as it could.

Time Waster #3: Throwing Reinforcement Out the Window

Let's remember why we are taking on the job of teaching these skills: because our kids are struggling to learn, because there is a lot at stake for them, and because we care more than anyone else in the world. While you or I may have a very powerful motivation at our backs, no one will keep fighting the headwinds if they don't see some progress. No one exerts tremendous effort for a payoff that does not, in his or her view, make it worthwhile—not you, not your child. Reinforcement can be your child's best teacher and your strongest ally—don't throw it out the window.

Time Waster #4: Not Recognizing and Planning for the Competition

Think of reinforcement as a crucial component to learning for all of us. It is a tool with a special kind of power that can work either for you or against you. Always keep in mind that whatever reinforcer you have to offer, there's always a competitor out there vying for your child's attention. The reinforcer can be the escape of quitting the assignment or not cooperating, the social attention and understanding that might follow an emotional outburst, or avoidance of the task through distractions such as arguing or drawing you into a discussion of how doing laundry damages the environment or why personal hygiene is just a socially imposed value and not a real need.

And let's talk about reinforcement for you, too. It was sobering but not surprising that between 28 percent and 53 percent of those who responded to my survey stated that they had taught a skill ineffectively more than once. Despite the repeated failures, only a very few (from 1 percent to 8 percent, depending on the skill) had given up. Clearly, parents seem determined to keep at it, even when our efforts don't pay off. After all, we are parents. Still, think of how much easier it would be, how much more patience you might have, and how much more pleasant it would be if your teaching achieved your goals. Remember: a really reinforcing program works for everyone, even parents.

Time Waster #5: Flip-flopping and Going Eclectic

When teaching doesn't seem to work, it's easy to blame the ASD, the ADHD, or even what Caitlin had for breakfast. Worse, though, and what happens most often, is what I call the "flip-flop": whatever you tried didn't work, so you decide to try something that is, or least looks, a lot different. On the micro level, you decide that rather than repeatedly verbally prompting (also known in everyday parlance as nagging) Barry to brush his teeth, you'll wait until he comes down to breakfast, ask him if he did it, and if he says no, you'll send him back upstairs to the bathroom sink. Yes, it is a different approach, but notice that neither one is teaching Barry to brush his teeth and to evaluate his own performance. After plan B fails, what comes next?

On the macro level, we have a mishmash of strategies culled from a number of programs or philosophies.* The fancy word for it is *eclecticism*, which barely hints at the frequent end result: a mess. Some experts on education for students with ASDs advocate eclecticism, and there is an argument to be made for using a number of different approaches for teaching *different* skills. A behaviorally based approach can be the ticket for learning to ride the bus safely, while a cognitive

---

*Teachers and therapists sometimes proceed with interventions that are a little bit of this and a little bit of that. Interestingly, most of these programs' developers specifically state that their programs need to be implemented completely, using all the recommended components, to be successful.

behavioral therapy (talk therapy) approach or a good Social Story is the key to more positive social interaction while on the bus. No problem there. Where eclecticism causes trouble is when you apply two or more different approaches to teaching the same skill or types of skills. Again, it's difficult to know where you're going or to look back and evaluate what you have done if you never planned a route and never noted all your stops and turns.

HOW TO COLLECT AND USE DATA

Throughout the book and in part III, I provide a sample of data collection sheets that you should find useful. Taking data does not have to be a big production, but it does have to be productive. To do that, and to begin thinking in terms of what you'll be collecting and why, let's look at what good data do:

- Good data provide an accurate, objective way to measure and compare performance from one trial (or day, week, or month) to another.
- Good data can help identify which parts of your teaching plan are working and which are not. This lets you make time-saving, timely, helpful adjustments rather than time-consuming and wasteful flip-flop overhauls.
- Good data provide good feedback, because they capture subtle changes—both in the right direction and in the wrong direction—that you would miss if you tried to keep it all in your head. This can keep you from abandoning a good plan too early or sticking with an ineffective plan for too long.
- Good data make the teaching plan portable. If you write down what you do and how it works, it may be easier to convince others who work with your child, like other family members, to use the same approach.
- Good data give clear guidance in helping you decide when to fade prompts, lighten up on reinforcement, or add more steps or greater complexity to the task.

• Good data make your input about how your child learns and how your child can learn better more convincing to those you may be in a position to convince.

Tips on Collecting Data Painlessly

Be clear about what you will be taking data on. Taking data can be dauntingly complex, but we don't need to go there. What kind of data you take will be determined by what you are teaching and how you are going to teach it.

What Kind of Skill Are You Teaching?
• Basic, with one or a few steps: hang up jacket, turn off computer.
• Basic, with more than a few steps: dressing, setting the table.
• Complex chain made up of a series of basic skills, each with either a few or multiple steps: getting ready for school, doing homework.

Where Is the Child in Terms of Learning the Skill?
This could be quite complex, but for simplicity, we are going to focus on two general points in learning. In the first, your child has or is close to having attained the skill. In the second, your child is still learning the skill and needs some level of prompting. For each type of skill, assess whether:

• Skills are at about the same level (mastered or nearly mastered); there may be visual supports but there is no direct prompting from a person.
• Skills are uneven and require different levels of prompting.

What Will You Be Counting?
See the charts, sample data sheets, and graphs that follow.

What is the easiest way to count? Sometimes the type of data you're collecting more or less determines this, but there are some time-saving tricks. You may experiment to find what works best for you. Just be sure that recording the data does not distract you from teaching or cause you to miss opportunities for error correction or reinforcement. In addition to writing it down on a data sheet as you go along, you can also try these strategies:

- For counting the number of consecutive occurrences, use a counter. Click it each time the behavior occurs.
- For counting the number of occurrences that are correct, to derive a percentage, use two counters. Place or keep in a pocket on your dominant-hand side the counter for correct responses. (If you are right-handed, then correct answers are on the right side.) Place or keep in a pocket on your nondominant-hand side the counter for errors. When the two counts added together equal the total number of trials—for example, 7 on the right-hand (correct response) clicker, 3 on the left-hand (error) clicker, for a total of 10 trials—you're done. Divide the number correct by the total number of trials for the day's percentage correct: 7 of 10 = 70 percent.
- Where keeping a clipboard or notebook would get in the way, place a strip of first-aid adhesive tape on your inner forearm and write on that in ink. Those with less sensitive skin can use regular masking tape.
- If you are offering a token or food reinforcer for each correct response, count out the total number of trials. Move any unearned tokens or reinforcers to one side or pocket them. When all the tokens or reinforcers are gone, count your "leftovers" (errors). Deduct those from the total number of trials and divide the remainder (which will be the number of correct trials) by the total number of trials for the day's percentage. For instance, for 20 trials of putting one piece of flatware in the right spot, you end up with 4 leftovers from incorrect responses: 20 total trials − 4 errors = 16 correct. Divide 16 by 20 = .08, or 80 percent correct responses.
- To save time taking data on multistep skills, where all the steps are indicated on your sheet, fill in only the data for incorrect or prompted responses. You can fill in the correct responses (all the remaining blank boxes) later.

• If the skill you are teaching is very complex and you cannot imagine how you will be able to record data and keep your hands at the ready when physical guidance might be needed, consider having someone else record the data, or videotaping or audiotaping your session. Then review and fill out your data sheet later. Seeing the teaching session on videotape will also give you an opportunity to see how well *you* are doing in terms of being consistent with your teaching plan, error correction, and reinforcement.

BASIC ONE- OR FEW-STEP TASK

Hangs up jacket, turns off computer, puts used glass in the sink, puts away toothbrush, etc.

What is the question?	What are the possible answers?	How can you capture the answer?	What does that information tell you?
In each opportunity presented, was the task completed?	Yes/no	Frequency chart; calculate the percentage of opportunities during which the behavior occurred. Of the 7 opportunities per week to turn off the computer, Liam did it without prompts 5 times. Divide 5 by 7 = 71 percent.	How close your child is to acquiring the skill. In what percentage of opportunities the task is completed correctly without prompts.
In each opportunity presented, was the task completed with prompts?	Yes/no, plus what level of prompt was used	Frequency chart that includes what prompt level was used for every yes. See Liam's graph.	What level of prompting is required? Is it decreasing (good) or increasing (not so good)?

BASIC ONE STEP, OR A FEW STEPS

Task or Skill	*Liam turns off the computer*			
Day	**Date**	**Yes/No**	**Prompt**	**Notes**
Monday	2/14	Yes	None	
Tuesday	2/15	No		Bus late
Wednesday	2/16	Yes	None	
Thursday	2/17	Yes	None	
Friday	2/18	Yes	Verbal	
Saturday	2/19	No		
Sunday	2/20	Yes	None	
Percentage yes (divide yeses by total days)	$5/7 = 71\%$	5 yeses		
Percentage yes + independent (divide yeses that are independent by total days)	$4/7 = 57\%$		4 independent yeses	

BASIC ONE STEP, OR A FEW STEPS			
Task or Skill	*Liam turns off the computer*		
Weekly Summary	**Date**	**% Yes**	**% Independent**
	2/21	71	57
	2/28	42	35
	3/7	42	42
	3/14	57	57
	3/21	86	57
	3/28	86	71
	4/4	100	100
	4/11	100	100

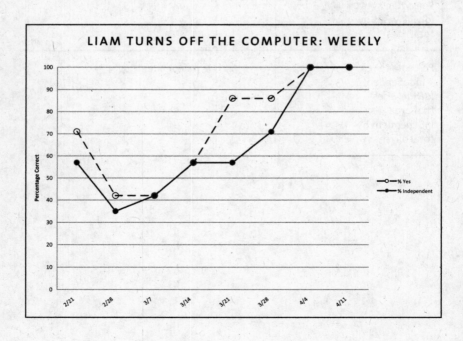

LIAM TURNS OFF THE COMPUTER: WEEKLY

BASIC TASK WITH MULTIPLE STEPS

Skills even through steps: dressing, setting the table, gathering materials for homework, feeding a pet, putting away groceries

What is the question?	What are the possible answers?	How can you capture the answer?	What does that information tell you?
In each opportunity presented, was the whole task completed?	Yes/no	Frequency chart; calculate the percentage of trials during which the behavior occurred. Of the 7 opportunities Kevin had to gather all materials for homework, he did so without prompts on one day, Sunday. Divide 1 by 7 = 14 percent.	How close your child is to acquiring the skill. In what percentage of opportunities the task is completed correctly without prompts.

BASIC TASK WITH MULTIPLE STEPS

Task or Skill	Kevin Gets Ready for Homework		
Day/Date	Yes/No	Prompt	Notes
Monday/Mar. 1			
1. Retrieves backpack.	Yes	Yes	Verbal
2. Consults homework agenda.	Yes	Yes	Verbal
3. Collects folders.	No	Yes	Verbal
4. Collects books.	Yes	No	
5. Collects notebooks.	Yes	No	
6. Collects worksheets.	Yes	Yes	Verbal
7. Collects supplies.	No	Yes	Verbal
8. Starts work.	No	Yes	Verbal
Percentage yes (divide yeses by total steps)	$5/8$ = 63% 5 yeses		
Percentage yes + independent (divide yeses that are independent by total steps)	$2/8$ = 25%	2 independent yeses	

BASIC TASK WITH MULTIPLE STEPS

Task or Skill	Kevin Gets Ready for Homework			Notes
Day/Date	**Yes/No**	**Prompt**		
Tuesday/Mar. 2				
1. Retrieves backpack.	Yes	Yes		Visual: Post-It on fridge
2. Consults homework agenda.	Yes	Yes		Visual: Post-It on fridge
3. Collects folders.	No	Yes		Visual: Post-It on fridge
4. Collects books.	Yes	No		
5. Collects notebooks.	Yes	No		
6. Collects worksheets.	Yes	Yes		Verbal
7. Collects supplies.	No	Yes		Verbal
8. Starts work.	No	Yes		Verbal
Percentage yes (divide yeses by total steps)	5/8 = 63% 5 yeses			
Percentage yes + independent (divide yeses that are independent by total steps)	2/8 = 25%	2 independent yeses		

BASIC TASK WITH MULTIPLE STEPS

Task or Skill	Kevin Gets Ready for Homework		
Day/Date	**Yes/No**	**Prompt**	**Notes**
Wednesday/Mar. 3			
1. Retrieves backpack.	Yes	No	
2. Consults homework agenda.	Yes	No	
3. Collects folders.	No	Yes	Visual, task list
4. Collects books.	Yes	No	
5. Collects notebooks.	Yes	No	
6. Collects worksheets.	Yes	Yes	Visual, task list
7. Collects supplies.	Yes	Yes	Visual, task list
8. Starts work.	No	Yes	Visual, task list
Percentage yes (divide yeses by total steps)	$6/8 = 75\%$ 6 yeses		
Percentage yes + independent (divide yeses that are independent by total steps)	$4/8 = 50\%$	4 independent yeses	

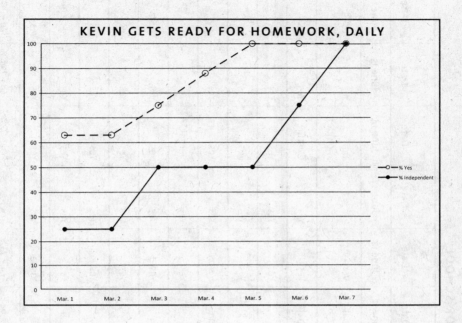

KEVIN GETS READY FOR HOMEWORK, DAILY

- —○— % Yes
- —●— % Independent

MARY GETS READY FOR SCHOOL

Task Components	Task Analysis	Date	Date	Date	Date	Date	Date	Date
	Independent (no prompts) Yes/No	June 10	June 11	June 12	June 13	June 14	June 15	June 16
Get out of bed.	1. Get out of bed at alarm.	Verbal	Verbal	Verbal	Yes	Tap shoulder	Yes	Yes
	2. Turn off alarm.	Verbal	Verbal	Yes	Yes	Gesture	Yes	Yes
	3. Make bed.	Verbal	Yes	Yes	Yes	Yes	Yes	Yes
Go to bathroom.	1. Take shower (wash hair, too).	Yes	Yes	Yes	Yes	Yes	Yes	Yes
	2. Brush teeth.	Yes	Verbal	Verbal	Yes	Yes	Yes	Yes
	3. Do skin care.	Yes	Yes	Yes	Yes	Verbal	Yes	Yes
	4. Dry hair.	Verbal	Yes	Yes	Yes	Yes	Yes	Yes
Get dressed.	1. Pick out clothing.	Yes	Yes	Yes	Yes	Yes	Yes	Yes
	2. Get dressed.	Yes	Yes	Yes	Yes	Yes	Yes	Yes
	3. Put on shoes and socks.	Yes	Visual	Yes	Yes	Yes	Yes	Yes
	4. Put on watch, jewelry, accessories.	Visual	Yes	Visual	Yes	Yes	Yes	Yes
	Percentage of steps independent (divide number of independent yeses by total)	$6/11 = 55\%$	$7/11 = 64\%$	$8/11 = 73\%$	$11/11 = 100\%$	$8/11 = 73\%$	$11/11 = 100\%$	$11/11 = 100\%$

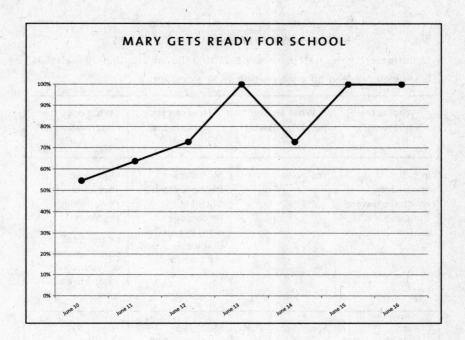

BASIC TASK WITH MULTIPLE STEPS

Skills uneven through steps: dressing, setting the table, gathering materials for homework, feeding a pet, putting away groceries

What is the question?	What are the possible answers?	How can you capture the answer?	What does that information tell you?
In each opportunity, which steps were completed?	Yes/no	Multistep frequency chart; calculate the percentage of steps in each trial that were carried out correctly.	How close your child is to performing all the steps. Of the total steps, how many did your child complete each day?
In each opportunity, which steps were completed with prompts?	Yes/no, plus what level of prompt was used at each step?	Multistep frequency chart that includes what prompt level was used for every step.	How close your child is to acquiring the skills and/or demonstrating the skills independently. What level of prompting is required? Is it decreasing (good) or increasing (not so good)?

COMPLEX CHAIN WITH A SERIES OF MULTISTEP TASKS

Use of skills even through steps: getting ready for school, getting ready for bed, doing homework, cleaning room, raking leaves

What is the question?	What are the possible answers?	How can you capture the answer?	What does that information tell you?
In each opportunity presented, was the full chain completed?	Yes/no	Frequency chart; calculate the percentage of opportunities during which the behavior occurred. Of the 7 opportunities per week to get ready for school, Mary did it without prompts 3 times. Divide 3 by 7 = 43 percent.	How close your child is to acquiring the skill. In what percentage of opportunities the task is completed correctly without prompts.
In each opportunity presented, was the full chain completed with prompts?	Yes/no, plus what level of prompt was used	Frequency chart that includes what prompt level was used for every yes	How close your child is to acquiring the skills and/or demonstrating the skills independently. What level of prompting is required? Is it decreasing (good) or increasing (not so good)? See Mary's graph.

PATIENCE

You have your teaching plan, your materials, your data collection systems, and everything else in place. You have read about and promise to follow the rules of the teaching zone and restrict your engagement to the ABC three-term contingency. You understand and accept the value of reinforcement and the use and misuse of prompts. What else could you possibly need (as if you haven't guessed already)? Patience.

Earlier we explored how professional teachers and therapists are different from parents. Sometimes mothers and fathers feel they are less capable of teaching their children than professionals because good pros have a way of making it look easy. True professionals do not personalize issues; they see things objectively; and, no matter what happened yesterday, they're back today, rarin' to go again. How do they do it?

Like all teachers, I've spent a lot of time reflecting on how my personal experience might influence my work. Having been the parent on the other side of the desk made me think about it even more. For example, I had always believed that everyone who worked with my son was born with endless patience. Over time, I've learned that professionals learn to be professional. In fact, if their own children have special needs, they don't always consider themselves their child's best teacher at home. Even parents who naturally have a patient disposition feel taxed by the intensive needs of their own child with ASDs.

I was not one of those.

I wouldn't call myself impatient, but I was always quick to spot mistakes and offer a "better" way of doing things under the guise of "only trying to help." (Both excellent skills for an editor and author, by the way.) If my son became upset, I became upset. While he was thinking only about why he didn't or couldn't do that thing in that moment, my mind took off on a tour of every possible negative future implication. Basically, my intentions were good and my motives were strong, but the results were neither. I had to change my act.

Think for a moment about your basic parenting style and how you approach correcting mistakes. Whether we can change our natural dispositions and become more patient, I don't know. What I offer below are what I think of as patience extenders: self-prompting tricks and strategies to help keep your teaching interactions positive, bright, and, yes, patient.

- **Take a step back, literally.** If your natural inclination is to help and do for your child, take a step back and put your hands behind your back or in your pockets.
- **Stop yourself from commenting.** If you tend to correct with comments, press your lips together or touch your fingertips to your lips for a second to remind yourself not to. By the way, saying "I'm only trying to help" doesn't fly because it has two problems: it's a comment, and it teaches nothing.
- **Show, not tell.** If there is a correction you can make by gesturing, silently referring to a visual support, or physically prompting, do so. Try not to speak.
- **"If you can't say something nice . . ."** Use your words only to comment on what your child is doing well. Forget the rest. Also, a change of setting does not change the rules. If it should not be said in the teaching zone, it should not be said out of it, either.
- **Check—and correct—your style of giving feedback.** Dr. Tony Attwood points out that many children with AS also have a parent who either has AS or has a number of related traits. Often that parent is the father, but sometimes moms have AS tendencies, too. Dr. Attwood notes that such parents "are often very good at criticism, not very good with compliments." He adds, though, that these parents do not intend to be mean; they simply believe that their child will learn better if his mistakes are pointed out. In fact, though, often it is better to correct errors without further comment than to talk about them.
- **Keep it in perspective.** Sure, there is a lot to do. Sure, these skills are important. Sure, they can be difficult to teach and to learn. But look on the bright side: you're doing it! Acknowledge every effort—your child's and your own.

- **Don't let perfection be the enemy of good.** Nobody's perfect—ASD or not. Sometimes, though, professional programs to teach these skills set a higher standard for acceptable performance than most of us aspire to ourselves—if you forget one item on your shopping list of ten, no one reprimands you and sends you back to the store to practice doing it correctly! Focus on completion, independence, and a consistently acceptable level of performance rather than perfection. (Keep in mind, though, for some skills, perfection or 100 percent accuracy may be necessary for reasons of safety or health.)

  People make mistakes. Discover what your child may need to learn to do or practice (or, perhaps, how you might teach, prompt, or reinforce more effectively), do it, then move on.

- **Be understanding of mistakes and forthcoming about your own.** Kids with AS sometimes have an inaccurate view of how the rest of us do the things we do. Think of Carol Gray's observation about how our kids have their mistakes pointed out to them far more often than most children—it's no wonder they often develop an overly negative opinion of their abilities and themselves. This sometimes takes the form of a negative view of those who teach and correct them, too. Everyone makes mistakes, and you will be doing your child a huge favor by narrating your own, how you feel when you make them, the steps you will take to avoid the mistake next time, and what you say to yourself—the actual words you tell yourself—to help you go on.

- **If your child makes a mistake, even if you know the reason why, stick to the script.** If your child drops some plates, say, "Uh-oh. Let's try using two hands to carry those plates next time," not "You made a mistake. You only used one hand to carry all those plates. No wonder you dropped them . . ." Blah, blah, blah.

- **Understand how powerful the motivation not to try is to your son or daughter.** Dr. Peter Gerhardt recalled asking a client why he kept refusing to do or learn new things: "He said, 'It's easier to succeed by not trying than to try and keep failing.' They have such a history of not being able to do things correctly, they just give up." Keep this in mind when someone questions your use of errorless teaching and supportive prompts.

• **Help your child expand his own perspective.** Kids with Asperger syndrome tend toward a glass-half-empty worldview. Dr. Tony Attwood views the tendency to overreact, to "catastrophize," as another expression of the weak central coherence problem. As a result, when things go awry, the child with an ASD may overfocus on select details as opposed to processing the whole. The classic example is the student who gets a 90 on a spelling quiz but agonizes over the one word she got wrong. Some children spot their own mistakes and overreact instantly, and sometimes it's you who realizes what's happened; in either case, try not to reinforce this with discussion. Model dropping the issue and moving ahead. It's okay to talk about it after the moment has passed and everyone is calm.

• **If at first you don't succeed, try again.** Demonstrating perseverance is almost always a good idea. But don't fall into a loop of demanding encores of performances that show minimal or no progress. If you see improvement, certainly try again. But also be aware that "try, try again" may not be the best course. Sometimes kids do not succeed because something that you control and they don't—the program, the materials, the teaching approach, the reinforcer—is not working. Don't let more than a few trials or days pass with no progress before you return to the drawing board.

• **If you and your child have one of *those* moments . . .** You know better than anyone when your child is on the verge of shutting down, melting down, or blowing up. Before you begin your teaching, review your child's day. Did he have a rough time at school? Is he tired? Maybe he's coming down with something? Has he just experienced a surprise or disappointment? While consistency truly is important, it is better not to start teaching than it is to find yourself having to stop for a "difficult moment." Doing that risks creating an association between acting out during learning and providing reinforcement for the behavior in the form of escape from task. Avoid this at all costs.

If the difficult moment occurs during teaching, quickly size up the situation. If it looks like an isolated incident— something he can move past after a period for calming down— by all means do your best to resume. If the incident is mild, you might consider reducing the number of trials or steps and/ or increasing the reinforcer. (Remember the reinforcing power of your competition: escape from task.) If recovery is highly unlikely or impossible, just stop. Don't get into a big discussion about why. Let it go. Yes, you risk your child repeating inappropriate behavior to get out of having to do the task in the future. But you have to balance that against the reality that under the circumstances, learning might be completely unproductive and may become aversive. This will only increase his motivation to avoid it in the future. If you do stop after you started, be clear with your child why and take responsibility: "I see you have had a rough day. This might not be the best time. We'll try again tomorrow."

TASK BREAKDOWNS

Goal Idea	Goal	Task Components	Task Analysis
Aidan will set the table.	Aidan will set the table (wipe the table, arrange place mats, dishes, flatware, glassware, salt and pepper shakers, serving flatware; ask about what else might be needed: butter, salad dressing, condiments) every other evening.	Wipe the table.	1. Rinse and squeeze sponge.
			2. Wipe table thoroughly.
			3. Using dish towel, lightly dry table.
		Arrange place mats.	1. Find out how many will be at dinner.
			2. Take out that number of place mats.
			3. Center each place mat on the table before a chair.
		Arrange dishes.	1. Get the number of plates and salad bowls needed.
			2. Place one plate in the middle of each place mat.
			3. Place one salad bowl to the upper left of each plate.

TASK BREAKDOWNS

Goal Idea	Goal	Task Components	Task Analysis
		Arrange napkins and flatware.	1. Place one napkin to the middle right of each plate.
			2. Place one fork and one spoon on each napkin.
			3. Place one knife to the left of each plate.
			4. Place serving flatware as needed.
		Arrange glassware.	1. Get the number of glasses needed.
			2. Place one glass to the upper right of each plate.
		Place salt and pepper shakers.	1. Place salt and pepper shakers, butter, and salad dressing in the middle of the table.
		Ask and retrieve anything else needed.	1. Ask whoever's making dinner what else you might need to put on the table.

PART II

The Skills

for Independence

Chapter 11

ALL ABOUT CLOTHES

Getting dressed seems to come to us so automatically. Most of us have been at it since before we can remember. In fact, one early developmental milestone marks when a toddler assists in his own dressing—for example, by raising his arms in anticipation of an adult putting a pullover shirt on him. Another milestone is a child's experimenting with dressing and undressing herself. Interestingly, a lack of initiative in this area is not unusual for very young children who are later diagnosed with an ASD. Problems with general coordination, fine- and gross-motor skills, and a sometimes inaccurate sense of where their different body parts are in space (problems with proprioception) can also complicate matters.

And let's not forget sensory sensitivities, some of which your child may have experienced long before he could express himself. Scratchy fabric, the annoying tag on the back of his shirt, other clothing-related sensitivities that may not be obvious to us but cause discomfort—any of these can undermine a youngster's learning to get dressed. Here I would urge you to think about the following potential sensory offenders: scents left behind by detergents, fabric softeners, or dryer sheets; the feel of certain fabrics or closures (such as buttons, zippers, and so on) against the skin. Some kids with ASDs have difficulty tolerating the feel of clothing on specific parts of their body, and so they may not like to wear long sleeves, hoods, or socks. Another possible problem area is sometimes the fit of clothing. While many kids on the spectrum seem to go for the looser, less restrictive feel of sweatpants and T-shirts, others can be comfortable only in more structured, even tight-fitting garments. One possible reason is that tighter clothing or items made from materials that tend to cling to the body (like spandex) provide a level of sensory input that is comforting. (This also explains some kids' preference for wearing hoods, long sleeves, gloves, and heavier fabric than the weather calls for.)

THE SURPRISING IMPLICATIONS OF DRESSING SKILLS

It seems obvious that learning to dress oneself is an important basic skill. But let's look a little more closely at the implications of not having these skills on board. First, when kids have trouble with an aspect of dressing—say, zipping up a pair of pants or tying shoelaces—it often eliminates all clothing items requiring that skill. On one hand, you could say, it doesn't really matter if Larry wants to wear only pants with elastic waistbands as opposed to a standard fly, or there will always be Velcro sneakers and slip-ons, so why bother?

Admittedly, at certain points in your child's life, there might have been more pressing concerns than learning how to dress. Fashion alert: once kids grow out of boys' and girls' sizes, the availability of elastic-waist anything depends on trends—unless they want to wear yoga pants everywhere or dress more like Nana and Grandpa in Florida. As for Velcro shoes, some years the choices are endless, other years nil, especially as your child moves into larger sizes. Certainly elastic-waist pants and shoes with Velcro closures have made many of our lives a lot easier. But is easy always the answer?

Maybe not. In many cases we decide to go with the accommodation rather than teach the skill when our kids are pretty young, and in the moment the decision probably makes a lot of sense. Unfortunately, before we know it, we've moved on to dealing with other pressing matters. Now it's five, ten, fifteen years later, and Larry still cannot zip a fly or tie his shoes. If Larry knows how to zip up a pair of pants and tie shoelaces yet still opts for elastic in the waist and Velcro at his feet, fine. More often than not, however, we find a temporary solution to a problem and leave it in place, sometimes long after it may be needed.

It is highly likely that one day Larry will need these skills for a formal event such as a high school prom or a job interview. Both occasions are anxiety-provoking enough for many of our kids without the added stress of feeling uncomfortable in a sports jacket, panty hose, or some other article of clothing that he or she has rarely worn before.

Nor should we assume that just because Larry once didn't like to wear the same kinds of clothes as his peers, that will always be the case. Often parents are forced to teach some of these dressing skills because their kids suddenly decide they want to dress differently. The Seattle grunge look of the 1990s—the loose pants and shirts, and casual (to put it mildly) grooming—made lots of young people with ASDs look very fashion-forward without any effort. But times change, and your child may just want to change her look. Whether it's to be like everyone else or to be totally different, your child should at least know how to wear anything she chooses. Ultimately, it's all about choice. And when we limit the skills needed to exercise choices, we limit choice.

Most important, I would argue, is that dressing is a private, personal activity that should not involve other people. Skill deficits in this area leave a child dependent on others—possibly, as he ventures out into the larger world, on people you may not know well. Independence in dressing, like independence in toileting, hygiene, and other personal areas, should also be viewed as a hedge against unwanted and potentially inappropriate contact.

LET'S GET STARTED

Finally, as you'll see below, these are not difficult skills to teach if you remember the following guidelines:

- Analyze and break down the steps; write them all down.
- Test-drive your task analysis; be on the lookout for movements or manipulations of the materials that might be difficult for your child.
- Ask your child to perform the task without advance notice or preparation, just to see what comes easily to him and what

does not. Note where it goes smoothly and where it breaks down. Write down on your list what type of prompt might be needed at each step. Don't forget to note where no prompt will be needed.

• Pay attention to where additional help is needed. Let's say that he's learning to button. On a full-length mirror in his bedroom, you might attach a photo that highlights a shirt buttoned evenly. You might also consider modifying a piece of clothing; for example, a zipper might be easier to work if it has a larger pull tab, and a bra that fastens in front might be easier than one that fastens in the back.

• Present the skill by modeling it for your child.

• Demonstrate for your child how to use any visual prompts or modified materials that you will be using.

• Ask your child to perform the task with you at his side or behind him, offering whatever prompts are necessary.

• Write down how it went: which steps were independent, which were prompted, what type of prompt was used.

• Praise your child's effort and offer whatever reinforcement you have determined beforehand. Emphasize what he did well and ignore what still needs practice. Remember, however, to watch for the rough spots in your next trial and try to prevent the same errors.

• Depending on the skill, repeat immediately. Many individual dressing skills take so little time to complete that five or ten teaching opportunities a day is not only feasible but recommended.

• Run the last trial of the day without any prompts to get an idea of where your child is at and how productive the prompting has been. Ideally, prompt-free execution at the end of the teaching session should be at least a bit better than the first trial.

• Look at your data: which direction are you headed? Even if your child is learning, the changes may be so incremental that you don't really notice them (which is why written data are so important). Don't throw in the towel if you do not see significant improvements right away, but if the data flatline or start to head south, reassess what you are doing.

THE BASIC BASICS

What's the problem? Usually a combination of deficient motor skills and proprioception, and not always having a good idea of what goes where when. Sometimes children have the ability to put on the shirt, but they fail to recognize the front from the back or inside out from right side out; maybe they don't have a clear idea about how to handle the clothing as they put it on. For instance, your son may try to pull on crew socks without bunching up the top portion of the socks before slipping them over his feet. Or your daughter may pull up her pants until they are on in front—which may be all she sees in the bedroom mirror—but sit far too low in back. Here are some tips for conveying basic skills that your child needs to deal with on any clothing issue. As you will see, it is often all about knowing which cues matter.

- **Discriminating inside out from right side out.** Granted, sometimes it's not so obvious with tops and pants that lack fasteners. There are a couple of clues that something is inside out:
    - Labels and tags are now on the outside.
    - The seams are visible. Some kids may not be able to see the difference, so ask them to run their fingers along a seam on both sides to feel the difference.
    - The fabric might appear smoother on the inside, or patterns are sharper than on the outside.
- **Knowing when clothing is on straight and properly.** Children with ASDs do not always have the degree of body awareness most of us rely on to signal us that our buttons are misaligned or our cuffs aren't where they should be. You might try:
    - Pointing out the physical landmarks of clothing that

has been put on properly. For instance, when you button a shirt or jacket, its hem should be even on both sides and there should be no empty buttonholes. When you wear a sweater or jacket over a shirt, you can pull down the shirtsleeve so it's not bunched up.

• Teaching your child to look—really look—in a full-length mirror. You might want to devise a quick list of things to check: buttons buttoned, hem of pullover shirt pulled down evenly all around, pants fastened and up where they belong, skirt down and even all around.

• **Noticing when clothing is too soiled, worn, or damaged to wear.** A light stain, a missing button, a small rip or tear—these are some of the finer details of dressing that our kids might miss. If your child seems oblivious to these things, take time to point out when something needs to be cleaned or repaired. And if this is a chronic problem, consider making a small checklist your child can refer to.

• Consider composing a Social Story that will help your child understand why wearing worn or unclean clothing may not be a great idea. But at the same time, also teach that there are times when this kind of clothing is okay, such as for play or for doing chores in which you get dirty.

• **Choosing appropriate clothing.** What your child wears should be appropriate for the season, the weather, and the day's activities.

• If your child is young, you might consider stocking his closet and drawers with only clothing that fits the season.

• Before your child gets dressed, mention the expected weather for the day, if that's a factor, and his schedule. Help your child use that information to decide what to wear; don't just decide for him every time.

• If your child makes a poor choice, patiently but briefly explain what would make a better a choice and why.

• **Helping your child make choices.** If your child takes a long time to decide what to wear, goes through a number of changes before finally settling on something, or makes poor choices:

- Consider planning tomorrow's outfit the night before. The more you involve your child in making decisions and exercising good judgment, the better.
- If you do plan the night before, however, be sure you are also teaching something about flexibility in case the weather or your child's schedule changes.
- Explore the possibility that she may have too many choices. It's wonderful to have choices, but for some kids with ASDs, having too many choices of anything can be overwhelming. You might want to streamline the process by designating separate drawers or separate parts of the closet for clothes for school, play, horseback riding, chores, et cetera. Mark or color-code the different groupings.

The Shirt/Hat/Socks/Skirt That Will Not Die

There are countless reasons why someone with an ASD might become attached to an item of clothing: familiarity, comfort, security, sensory issues, or simple habit. Most of us have a favorite item that we wear more often or have trouble parting with. Even if we know better than to wear that much-loved jacket with the space cadet shoulder pads or comfy jeans with the hole in the knee out to dinner or to work, we might still have a hard time letting go of it. For kids with ASDs, however, this preference for a piece of clothing or outfit sometimes becomes extreme.

Often these attachments begin when children are young, and they usually begin or at least look like a routine object attachment for security. One difference for kids on the spectrum, though, is that there may also be sensory sensitivities at work, so little Evan may not be wearing that blue-striped train engineer's hat all the time just because he likes the way it looks. Chances are he's wearing it partly because of some form of sensory hypersensitivity. He may like the gentle pressure of the hat around his head or the way the brim shields his eyes from the harsh (to him) overhead lights. Or maybe he wears it constantly for a little bit of both reasons.

When is attachment to an article of clothing a problem? Generally, when insistence on wearing the item or resistance to the possibility of not wearing the item interferes with whatever needs to happen at that moment. For example, if Evan loves wearing his hat, fine. But if he refuses to leave the house because he knows he'll have to remove it at the restaurant or during the school play, or if the idea that he won't be able to wear it provokes anxiety, you have a problem. You also know that things are out of hand when you find yourself buying two (or three or four) identical replacements or plan your laundry schedule around making sure the item is always clean and available, in order to avoid a meltdown.

There are several problems with just letting it go, even though that may seem to make a lot of sense. After all, what's the big deal? The first problem—one that we don't always think of until it's too late—is that clothing doesn't last forever. If your child doesn't outgrow it first, the well-worn item follows its natural course to decrepitude: the elastic inside the engineer's cap gives up the ghost, the shiny spots in the fave baggy cargo shorts give way to holes, zippers break irrevocably, cuffs fray to pieces. This doesn't even cover laundry accidents or (my personal nightmare) just plain losing it.

A secondary issue is how adults respond to these attachments. Of course, you want to be a good parent, and you want your child to be comfortable. But think carefully about the message you send when you go to extraordinary lengths to make sure the item is always available. Sometimes a child has long outgrown the initial reason he felt he needed, say, his black-and-white rugby shirt, but by then everyone around him has been treating the shirt as if it's as sacred as the Shroud of Turin; who can blame him, then, for feeling uncomfortable about giving it up?

Finally, situations will arise in which wearing that item is not only inappropriate but downright unsafe. The day I watched my son struggle to fit his bicycle helmet over the baseball cap we had allowed him to wear everywhere, with him trying to convince me this was okay, I realized how out of hand things had become. Wearing the hat underneath simply didn't work with the helmet. Fortunately, he loved riding his bike enough that we were able to reason with him: take off the hat or get off the bike. He reluctantly handed over the hat, but still, he was more upset about it than he should have been. And that was my fault.

What to Do?

If you can spot it, try not to let the habit start. If Evan likes his train hat, there's nothing wrong with that. But try to introduce—gradually—slightly different colors, textures, or styles, and insist that he change every day or so.

Out in the real world, we are all expected sometimes to wear things that may not be our first choice or that we would not wear any more than we had to, from a power suit to a garish uniform that clashes with our personal color palette. To whatever extent you can, try to subtly, gradually but consistently broaden your child's choices.

Out in the real world, there are also times when something we would like to wear is inappropriate or even unsafe (for example, flip-flops, backless Crocs-type shoes, and open-toed sandals when playing sports). Gradually place some limits on wearing the item. Think twice before you or others make exceptions. Use your common sense. There will come a day when your child's school will not allow him to wear his hat in class or the group of girls your daughter hangs out with will remark unfavorably on her wearing the same jeans every day.

Start small. Establish short time periods or short daily activities when the item is placed on hiatus. If you can, make these times ones that are enjoyable and/or unavoidable. If you would like your daughter to eventually stop wearing the same turtleneck sweater every day, you might insist that she wear something else while she's watching her favorite TV program. Then work your way back until the turtleneck is off-limits during mealtimes or between certain hours.

If there is a sensory issue, try introducing small items that usually go unnoticed if they're worn every day, like a wristwatch or bangle-type bracelets. Interestingly, these and other accessories (belt, fanny pack, backpack, shoulder bag, pocketbook with a strap that crosses the upper body diagonally, like a messenger bag) can provide comforting sensory input.

Another way to address the need for familiar, comfortable clothing is to consider undergarments. It's very easy and relatively inexpensive to find a dozen identical undershirts, camisoles, or pairs of underpants that may be especially comfy than it is to locate a dozen T-shirts or pairs of pants that look and feel exactly the same. And your child can wear what others don't see every day without anyone being the wiser.

If security is the issue, do what parents of young "blankie" aficionados do: gradually make it smaller or offer your child a piece of the garment to carry discreetly in a pocket or bag.

Don't shy away from making rules and sticking to them. Bunny slippers are for in the house *only*; ditto the aqua nylon mesh tutu and the sweatpants with the big chocolate stains. Kids with AS especially are what we call rule-governed: rules matter to them, and they generally tend to respect them. Don't be afraid to impose them.

FOR ANY TYPE OF CLOTHING

Sometimes kids know the motions to go through for putting something on, but they have not quite developed the repertoire of what I call "material management": picking up the garment and holding it in a way that makes it easier to put on, knowing when and how to adjust different parts, and recognizing when it fits just right (seams straight, buttons where they belong, collar out and lying flat). In addition, because of fine- and gross-motor problems and/or problems with motor planning, they may do things in a way that is inefficient and even tiring. The classic example is trying to put on shoes without opening the laces or the Velcro closures first or trying to get out of a jacket that is not fully unzipped.

Once you've seen your child perform the task and written up your task analysis, you will have a good idea of where and when to step in with your prompts. Remember to work from behind or beside your child whenever possible. Here are some ways to help your child learn how to handle garments for easier dressing:

- **Model side by side.** It's okay to talk a little bit here, but keep your words brief and limited to narrating the action.
- **Think about body position.** Many of us can put on our pants and socks while standing up, for example, but that may just make things more difficult for a child with coordination and motor problems. Some kids may also benefit from the sense of their bodies being grounded (literally) by sitting on the floor, the bed, or a chair when putting on pants, shoes and socks, leggings and tights, or dresses and skirts (especially if they are long).
- **Teach off the body.** If your child is learning a skill that requires him to manipulate material on his body (zipping, buttoning, and so on), you can teach it off his body as long as his hands and eyes are in the same relative position to the garment. For instance, if it would be easier for your child to see and practice how to start a zipper on a jacket he is not wearing, place it on, say, a chair (or a bed, or a table), so that the relative positioning remains the same. He stands behind the chair that is "wearing" the jacket, with the back of the garment closest to his body. Or if he works on tying a shoe he is not wearing, the toes should point away from him, just as they would if he were wearing them. If you teach the skill from a nonwearer's perspective—your child facing a jacket or shoe—you will have trained a series of movements that will be ineffective and "backward" when it's time to use them for real.
- **Consider a special vest.** You can purchase from an occu-

pational therapy supply company a vest that has buttons, zippers, buckles, snaps, and other fasteners your child can use to practice from the right perspective. Be aware, however, that the skills learned on the practice garment may not easily generalize to real clothing. Whenever possible, opt for the most naturalistic teaching materials.

• **Check for hand and finger placement and an effective, efficient grasp.** The most efficient way to pull on pants or a skirt, for example, is to place the thumbs inside the waistband and all four fingers outside the waistband, and then pull up firmly on both sides simultaneously, using the side seams as a guide. Again, kids with ASDs can usually put their hands and fingers where they need to be, but they may not apply the right amount of pressure or coordinate all the movements effectively. A child may simply not get a firm enough hold on the material to pull it up easily. Or she might curl her fingers but leave her thumb inside the waistband flat, and so the lack of a firm grips lets the material slip away. Be prepared to go hand-over-hand if necessary to give your child a clear idea of not only where to place fingers and hands but also how to position them and how much pressure to apply to work efficiently.

• **Make invisible steps visible.** For some kids, the invisible steps, as I call them, are just too elusive. They might have trouble getting a belt through the belt loops in back that they cannot see or fastening a bra that closes in back. You can teach your child to thread the belt through the loops before stepping into the pants or skirt. Bras can be fastened in front and then turned around and pulled up, or consider a front-closing bra or pull-on style.

• **Pay attention to the "helper hand."** When you teach a skill such as buttoning, pay close attention to what the "helper hand" is doing. Kids can sometimes pick up the motions of buttoning but find it frustratingly difficult because they don't pull the material with the button on it far enough over to provide the little bit of ease that allows the button to slip through the hole more easily. Or they may not automatically pull down on a zipper to ensure it's well aligned before they begin pulling up.

• **Use something to mark the spot.** For kids who have trouble with getting their hands on the sides of the garment, place a small tactile "marker": a small spot of textured fabric paint that puffs when it dries, a tiny iron-on fabric patch, or a couple of brightly colored stitches or spots of permanent marker. (Obviously, check the fabric in an inconspicuous spot first to be sure that you won't damage the garment. Remember that permanent ink markers, like Sharpies, saturate quickly and might bleed through.) If you do not wish to make your markers permanent, consider small nonpermanent label dots or mini Post-it notes that can be placed before dressing and then removed once the clothing is on.

• **Use a visual prompt.** Try a photo or a drawing with arrows, circles, or other indicators to map the terrain. There are drawbacks to this technique, however. It could become one more prompt to fade; what's more, referencing a two-dimensional image to learn to navigate a three-dimensional object may not be all that helpful. I recommend working with a real garment with built-in prompts (as described above) first before you go this route.

• **Try using old clothing.** Get an old piece of clothing, even a size larger than what your child usually wears, and mark it up to use in practice. You can reduce a lot of talking and modeling (in other words, another person's presence) by embedding the instructional cues into an actual garment. Fade the prompts by replacing the garment and using lighter and smaller markings until your child can perform the task on an unmarked garment. For example:

  • *T-shirts.* Number garment parts by the order in which they are put on. Opening the bottom would be 1; the right sleeve, 2; the neck, 3; the left sleeve, 4; and the front bottom hem, 5 (with arrows pointing downward to remind your child to pull it down).

• *Socks.* Place permanent marker dots indicating where to place the thumbs on the inside and index fingers on the outside, and label that 1. At the point in the foot of the sock where the top should be scrunched down to, make another dot, marked 2. Draw lines and arrows from dot 1 to dot 2 on each side. You can use this same method for leggings, tights, and panty hose, though you might also want to mark the heel as a reminder that it should be on the bottom and not creeping up the top of the foot.

• *Buttons.* Find a white or light-colored solid shirt. Make the buttons and the holes more noticeable by circling the outside edge of each button and each buttonhole with a permanent marker. To make sliding the button through the buttonhole easier to start, make a very small cut to widen the buttonhole—no more than $1/8$ inch. As your child becomes more adept at buttoning, tighten the hole with a couple of stitches or get another shirt and have your child practice with normal-sized buttonholes. If lining up the buttons with the proper holes is a problem, number the order of buttons and corresponding holes from top to bottom. You might also give the bottom button and its hole a different color to cue your child to check if all the buttons are correctly aligned once she's done.

• *Zippers.* Another common problem is learning to position the slider against the box—the end point on the slider side of the zipper—and then set the pin (the smooth metal piece at the bottom of the opposite side) inside the slider. You might line up the slider, box, and pin, and place small permanent marker dots to indicate the right position.

• **Modify a garment.** Of course, you are probably shopping for clothing with your child's skill level in mind. But if you find that the perfect jacket comes with a gnat-sized pull or the perfect pants have very stingy buttonholes, make some modifications. For instance, your son might be better able to manage button-up pants if the button and the hole are a bit larger. It helps to be handy with a needle, but if that's not your forte and you're up for a little adventure, the internet is full of information on how to do things like replace a zipper pull or modify a buttonhole. Or your dry cleaner or tailor can probably help.

Craft stores, jewelry and bead stores, and online sources make it easy to find parts and gadgets that can be used to make dressing easier. Velcro is excellent for this. As another example, many kids have trouble learning to zip because the pull tab—the little handle thingy that pulls the slider up and down—is simply too small for less agile fingers. If the pull tab has a hole in it, you can make it easier for your child to grasp by attaching a larger item, like a small key ring (split ring) or a small decorative item with a snap hook.

TYING SHOES

Tying shoes is perhaps the dressing skill that kids with ASDs are most likely to fall behind on, and if you were asked to verbally explain how to execute it, it would immediately become clear why. Shoe tying, a complex chain chock-full of Houdini moments, is not easy to teach! Search "shoe tying" on the internet, and you will be rewarded with dozens of tried-and-true approaches. Chances are, though, you will teach your child to do it the way you do, if only because it's just easier. Nothing wrong with that! So rather than my offering "the" way to tie shoes, here are some tips on teaching the skill however you choose:

- It is especially important to task-analyze this one and to then teach it consistently every time. Before you begin, streamline your verbal prompts or, preferably, figure out how to teach without using any at all.

• Decide whether you will use forward chaining or backward chaining. Some folks prefer backward chaining for shoe tying, but test-drive your teaching plan and see what happens. If your child is stronger on the last steps than on the first, forward chaining may make the most sense. You can prompt the earlier steps, and he may be close to independent toward the end. If the early steps are easy but the later steps are rough, try a backward chain, which will provide more guided practice on the later steps.

• Teach using the visual perspective and positioning of the wearer. If it's easier for your child to learn on a shoe she is not wearing, be sure it is placed with the heel closest and toe farthest from her and that she is working from behind the heel.

• Consider using different-colored laces and other visual cues. Some kids find these very helpful, while others find them utterly confusing. Depending on age and personal style, some kids love wearing them; others reject making this fashion statement. The cautions about generalization apply; your child may end up mastering tying with the color cues but may be unable to execute the task once those cues are removed. Check with your child before introducing a visual cue that may not be that helpful or that may take a long time to fade.

• If your child would benefit from visual reminders, embed them into the laces if you can. For example, at the point where the laces first form an X before the first pass under to start the first tie, you could place a dot of the same color where the two laces intersect and perhaps a small arrow on the lace that will be going underneath next. You could add matching dots for these steps, using a different color for each—for instance, the place where you pinch the first lace to form a loop.

• Although as a general rule oral verbal prompts should be avoided, there are countless helpful sing-along instructions and poems for shoe tying. Rhythm and rhyme do make learning easier and maybe even a bit more fun. Be on the lookout,

though, for signs in your child's performance that more auditory input is not helping.

WEARING NEW STYLES OR TEXTURES, DRESSING UP

Your sister wants your seven-year-old son to be ring bearer at her wedding. Your eleven-year-old daughter gets invited to a fancy birthday
party. Your college-bound son needs to wear a suit and tie for an interview. Don't panic. While these outfits may range well outside your
youngster's current comfort zone, there is a lot you can do to help make
him or her feel at ease in clothing for special occasions.

Of course, events that call for dressing up often have special social
demands attached as well. If you want your daughter to enjoy the party
or your son to focus on his interviewer and not the weirdness of wearing a necktie, do whatever you can to make the clothing familiar and
comfortable long before the big day arrives.

- Don't assume there is a problem. If your daughter fought
  her way out of a crinoline skirt at seven and you haven't dared
  try to introduce anything like it since, you don't really know
  how she will respond now. Remember that for certain social
  events that call for special clothing, your child's desire to be
  part of things can be motivating enough to override minor sensory issues or the need to learn how to use a button or put
  on stockings. Approach the situation optimistically until you
  know for sure you have a problem.
- Discuss with your child what she is being asked to wear and
  why. While your daughter might be able to choose an acceptable party dress from a wide array of styles and fabrics, choices
  for boys and men are often fairly limited. Have your child try
  on some clothing and find out what exactly it is about a garment that bothers him. Sometimes "I can't stand wearing this
  shirt!" really means nothing more than "The collar is a little
  too tight" or "The cuffs are too loose." Some kids want only

the soft feel of well-washed 100 percent cotton, while others prefer the slightly smoother feel of a cotton-polyester blend. Find out what kinds of adjustments can be made to improve comfort and wearability. Consult a tailor or seamstress if you're not handy with a needle yourself.

• Think undergarments. To many of our kids who spend most of their time in soft, stretchy, unstructured clothes, it just feels weird to wear clothes that are more structured, closely fitted, or made of less pliable fabrics. Sometimes having them wear a soft, well-laundered cotton undershirt or camisole under a new shirt or dress can make a difference.

• Conduct a full dress rehearsal. Ideally, do this every day leading up to the event. Often a child may just need time to get used to the new article of clothing in order to feel comfortable. Take a few minutes a day for your child to wear the clothing or part of it around the house and become accustomed to how it feels. Being in familiar surroundings and knowing that he'll get to take it off in ten or fifteen minutes can reduce sensory sensitivities.

CREATING HIS OR HER OWN STYLE

Though there are times we all have to conform to expectations, there is also room for personal style. For many people on the spectrum—and, let's face it, a lot of the rest of the world—everyday wear can become pretty close to uniform. We each like a couple of styles of pants or sweaters or shoes more than we like others. We prefer one fabric blend, type of shirt cuff, heel height, or cut of jacket to all the rest. Kids with ASDs may be equally committed to clothing they like; the difference is that their range of choices might be narrower, and so, in terms of style, season, and function, they may dress a bit unusually, if not inappropriately in some settings. Dr. Temple Grandin's trademark look—Western-style button shirt, bolo tie, and classic jeans—is a great example of someone on the spectrum who has created a unique style based on what makes her comfortable. Expanding your child's wardrobe repertoire should be done primarily to help him feel more at ease outside his current comfort zone. Sometimes people with ASDs are denied or decline a job or membership in a group, like a sports team, because they refuse to wear something required. It's easier to accept a lost opportunity if we know that the problem was addressed, discussed, and perhaps worked on before your child decided that the compromise in his clothing or other personal style was not acceptable. If, on the other hand, he refused because no one had ever taken time to figure out why the required clothing was hard for him to wear or how he might become less sensitive about wearing it, then his decision was not really a choice at all but a foregone conclusion determined by lack of a skill or experience.

Chapter 12

PERSONAL CARE

When it comes to basic personal care and hygiene, kids on the autism spectrum run the gamut from obsessively neat and clean to the opposite extreme. There are numerous possible explanations for why someone might seem to neglect to bathe or brush his teeth adequately: sensory aversion to some aspect of the task, simple forgetfulness, lacking awareness of social expectations and the responses of other people, or—perhaps the most egregious of all—never having been adequately taught how. With younger kids, it's easy enough to shepherd them through their self-care routines. But by the late elementary years, and certainly beyond, it's not only inappropriate but a serious intrusion into your child's personal space and a blatant vote of nonconfidence in your child's ability to handle these matters on his own.

Obviously, poor grooming can severely undermine social, educational, and employment opportunities. Throughout childhood and especially in adolescence, peer pressure and the prospect of rejection or disapproval are highly motivating forces. Most typical kids have strong theory of mind skills, so they almost cannot help stopping to wonder what others will think of them if their fingernails are dirty. But this is not how it is for many of our kids with ASDs. Their problems with theory of mind may render them oblivious to other people's reactions to their flaky scalp or bad breath; in fact, it might not even dawn on them that anyone might react negatively to someone else's lack of hygiene. Many times they do not notice these things about others. They might also have trouble recognizing aspects of grooming that require attention. So what can parents do? Instilling daily routines and sound self-care skills can eliminate the need for guesswork and put many of the tasks and skills on autopilot.

FIRST, TEACH THE SKILLS

Hand washing, bathing or showering, hair washing, hair care, tooth brushing, skin care, and toileting each involves a behavior chain of actions and constant self-monitoring to determine if the job has been done correctly and thoroughly. A kid who thinks that "Wash up for dinner!" means thrusting his hands under running water for all of two seconds isn't deliberately trying to put one over on Mom and Dad. Nor is the child who shampoos only the ends of her hair and somehow always manages to miss soaping her armpits. It's just that their concept of the steps needed to complete these chains may be a lot different from the actual steps necessary to do the task efficiently. One common example is the child who washes her hands while looking in the mirror and then exits the bathroom with dirty hands because she didn't notice that they weren't clean. Once again, an irrelevant (to the task) environmental cue draws the attention away from where it is needed.

Whatever the skill, run your task analysis as you would for any other teaching plan:

- Analyze and break down the steps; write them all down.
- Test-drive your task analysis; be on the lookout for movements or manipulations that might be difficult for your child, such as remembering to brush the teeth he can't see in the mirror or comb out tangles in the back.
- Ask your child to perform the task without any preparation or instruction. Note where it goes smoothly and where it breaks down. Write down what type of prompt might be needed at each step. Don't forget to note where no prompt will be required.
- Also pay attention to where a visual prompt or modification to the material might be helpful (e.g., liquid soap instead of bar).

- Present the skill by modeling it for your child.
- Demonstrate for your child how to use any visual prompts or modified materials you will be using.
- Ask your child to perform the task with you at his side or behind him, offering whatever prompts are necessary.
- Write down how it went: which steps were independent, which were prompted, what type of prompt was used.
- Praise your child's effort and offer whatever reinforcement you have determined beforehand. Emphasize what he did well and ignore what did not go so smoothly. Remember, however, to watch for the rough spots in your next trial and try to prevent the same errors.
- Depending on the skill, repeat it if you can. Repeating teaching trials is not always possible with many self-care skills. For that reason, you will want to strive for practice and prompting that is as close to perfect as you can get. If there are only three or four opportunities to practice tooth brushing, make each one count. Be there, watch what happens, and correct mistakes before your youngster settles into the routine.
- Every few days, run the last trial of the day without any prompts to get an idea of your child's progress and how productive the prompting has been.
- Look at your data: which direction are they going? Even if your child is learning, the changes may be so incremental that you don't really notice them (which is why written data are so important). Don't throw in the towel if you do not see significant improvements right away, but if the data flatline or start to head south, reassess what you are doing.

MORE THAN GOING THROUGH THE MOTIONS

A child can imitate the motions of many self-care skills and yet not really do the job. Once again, problems with proprioception, motor skills, and coordination come into play. She can apply deodorant too lightly to be effective or brush her hair so lightly that the tangles remain. For teaching some of these tasks, you may need to demonstrate hand-over-hand, just to show your child how hard to rub shampoo into his scalp or what it looks like and feels like to thoroughly soap up a washcloth.

At the other end are kids who tend to be heavy-handed about everything. They hate brushing their hair because they scrape their scalps with the brush bristles, or they scrub their hands until they become chapped. Again, hand-over-hand prompting can help if you are not sure that your child is feeling the appropriate amount of force or pressure to apply.

As with any other skill, be mindful of inefficient or awkward ways of doing things—for example, gripping a comb or hairbrush so tightly that muscle fatigue sets in before the job is done, or holding the toothbrush in one hand while trying to squeeze the toothpaste tube with the other (the preferable way is to set the toothbrush on the countertop and use two hands if necessary for applying the toothpaste). This may seem like a minor concern, except that when our kids start shaving, clipping their own nails, or doing anything that involves cutting, using the wrong touch or the wrong approach can be dangerous. Address it now.

One of the most important skills to teach in any self-care routine is how to tell when something is clean enough, dry enough, wet enough, soaped up enough, rinsed enough, brushed enough, and so on. If your child tends to rush and do things incompletely, consider getting her a timer, clock, or other device to track time. Then assign her a specific amount of time for the task: "Set your timer for two minutes, and don't stop brushing until it buzzes." Do not be arbitrary about this time. Set it by timing yourself, or, ideally, a sibling or peer about the same age. Then adjust the time up or down based on your child's current skill level, fine- and gross-motor and executive function issues, and so on.

You can help your child keep track of how much time he should spend on a hygiene task by matching it to one of his favorite songs, which can be played on his iPod, MP3, CD, or tape player. When the song-ending power chord or old-school sample fades out, he's done. Or sync up several songs to a whole morning or evening routine. By the end of track one, he should be in the shower, totally soaped up, and rinsing off. Track two is over? He should be rinsing out the last bit of conditioner and getting ready to step out. By the end of the third track, he should be dried off and have applied deodorant, brushed his teeth, and so on.

Consider providing visual written reminders of how to tell when the job is done. Use photos to show anything from what your child's hair looks like when it's really brushed to what the right amount of shampoo looks like in the hand. You might also draw on the shampoo or conditioner bottle in waterproof permanent ink a circle approximately the same size as the dispensed product.

For kids who forget to wash everyplace they should, get two laminated sheets of poster board (preferably about 11 by 14 inches). On one of them, draw a fairly large gingerbread figure with permanent, waterproof marker. Next, lay a sheet of thin white paper over the figure and trace it. Cut out the paper figure to form a pattern from which you can cut a second figure from the second sheet of laminated poster board. On the image on the large sheet, affix Velcro dots (the ones with the hard loops) to the figure's hair, face, neck, chest, arms, underarms, and so on. Take the second figure and cut into separate body parts. Affix the soft Velcro dots to these, then place a strip of hard loopy Velcro along the bottom of the big picture to hold the body parts. As your child washes, he can place each part on the body until it's complete, and he's done. You may want to make two sets: one for the front and one for the back.

SENSORY ISSUES IN SELF-CARE

Self-care involves using liquids, powders, gels, sprays, and, for girls, sanitary supplies that might be offensive to someone who is sensitive to a particular texture, feel, or scent. Sometimes responses to these products color the whole experience, so kids rush through the routine to escape the sensory assault, or they avoid the offending products altogether. When working with little children in early intervention, I learned that more kids disliked brushing because they hated the taste, smell, or texture of toothpaste than had sensory issues from the actual act of brushing. (Think about it: there is nothing on this earth that isn't poisonous that tastes anything like most toothpastes.) Most times, a change in toothpaste (or briefly eliminating it altogether, with a dentist's permission, of course) made it possible to teach tolerating the brush. Try unscented products or those formulated for sensitive skin; they may be a bit more expensive but just might do the trick. If your child can describe what it is that's bothering him about a product—for example, "The deodorant feels yucky!"—it's easy enough to switch from stick deodorant to spray or roll-on. While you're scoping out the bathroom for potential sensory offenders, don't forget about the scents and texture some laundry products can leave behind on towels, washcloths, and bathmats, or the overall sensory assault your child may experience from cleaning products or from potpourri, air freshener, or scented oils and candles.

On the other hand, your child might really like and be more inclined to use something with an appealing texture or scent. I've yet to meet a child on the spectrum who couldn't wait to wash her hands with foaming hand soap, for instance. Experiment until you find products that make self-care routines pleasant and fun.

START BY MAKING ROUTINES ROUTINE

Some daily routines can be skipped now and then, but self-care is not one of them. Set a routine and a schedule, then really stick to it. It might be helpful to post a daily schedule. Given the importance of self-care skills, you might want to up the ante in terms of reinforcement by making access to preferred activities contingent upon your child's having completed his personal hygiene tasks. This approach leads to less nagging—for both of you. This is not to say that your junior partner will be happy at first. That's okay.

Establish some basic, unbendable rules for routines that naturally precede or follow other predictable occurrences, such as:

- Brush your teeth after every meal and before you go to bed.
- Every time you use the toilet, wash your hands.

- Every night before bed, take a shower, wash your hair, and brush your teeth.

Convey to your child that while there may be nights he can skip feeding the gerbils or days when it's okay to stay inside reading *X-Men* when the family's out raking leaves, it is never going to be okay to skip a bath or shower, go to bed with unbrushed teeth, or leave the house with dirty hair. Period.

DEALING WITH PHILOSOPHICAL ISSUES

Sometimes kids are lax about self-care for reasons that might best be described as philosophical. They may have logical, reasoned thoughts on why it is okay not to shower every day or why it's silly for other people to care about how they look or smell. You might hear something along these lines: "But, Mom, we Americans are a lot more uptight about natural body odors than people in some other parts of the world!" (True to some extent, but . . .) Or this: "Showering every day wastes water!" Or this: "I don't care what other people think." Be prepared.

As for the argument that current prevailing social conventions about personal care are arbitrary and silly, get ready to present Reality 101. Be completely clear: the world is not going to change its ideas about this anytime soon. And people who choose not to get with this part of the program set themselves up to be judged not for who they are or what they can do—in other words, the wonderful things about them—but by how they look or smell. Classmates, friends, teachers, employers, and others you may wish to impress are turned off by people with poor personal hygiene. It is not a decision they make or an opinion they think through: it's a natural reaction that most people cannot control. If you want to get all science-y about it, you can talk about the health benefits and the evolutionary value of good hygiene. But ultimately, you have to come down to the practical: even the most brilliant video game designer will lose his job if his grooming offends others. Period.

Interestingly, because of hypersensitivity to smells, some people on the spectrum find lapses in the personal hygiene of others intolerable. If that is the case for your child, talk about it. Also, don't forget the side order of manners. We all chuckle when an expert recounts the "cute" story about the boy with AS who tells his teacher that her breath smells gross, but it's not funny when it happens in real life. What those stories often leave out is scene two, wherein the teacher (or a stranger or a friend or a crush) responds unhappily. These can be stressful, anxiety-filled moments for our kids.

There is a loving way to talk about these matters. I like to put it in terms of how uncombed hair and dirty fingernails "can keep someone from seeing you for the wonderful person you are." You can also frame it this way: does it make sense to let something that you can so easily fix stand in the way of things you may want, like making a friend (including of the boyfriend/girlfriend type), getting a job, or being admitted to a school? When my son was younger and he asked about things like this, I would start off with, "Well, people who don't have Asperger's think and do things that don't always make sense if you look at them logically." And that's true. But do not follow—or lead your child down—the primrose path by promising a more accepting world that will overlook greasy hair and whiffy clothing. That world does not exist, and especially not in many of the places our kids want—and deserve—to go. Bet on autism being accepted long before smelly armpits come into vogue.

GET A HEAD START

Shortly after Justin was diagnosed, I started attending parent support groups and hanging out on the OASIS message board, where parents' and teachers' concern about kids' hygiene was a popular topic. Parents whose kids were not handling their own grooming had a real problem. It's easy enough to put a five-year-old in the tub, brush his teeth, and monitor his toileting practices. After a certain age, however, parental options are limited, while at the same time, the social ramifications of poor personal care increase exponentially.

Given that most personal care is a habit, I decided to start some habits early, while Justin was young enough to feel that these made him more grown-up yet too young to have written a treatise on why BO is okay because it's "natural." At around eight, he was using a hypoallergenic, unscented stick deodorant, and a couple of years later, he was routinely swiping his face with a cotton ball and a mild astringent. (Many kids will have skin care problems that require some kind of daily care regimen.) We reminded him that the cool teenagers who were his camp counselors all did this, so it was the cool thing to do. A couple of years later, this could have been a much harder sell.

NEVER FORGET THAT WHAT COMES NATURALLY TO YOU MAY BE A STRUGGLE FOR YOUR CHILD

You might find that you will need to monitor these routines more closely over a longer time than you would for a typical child. Unlike doing homework or house chores, these tasks are not in the public arena, so there is more risk of your child lapsing back into poor habits. Be prepared to turn up the volume on the reinforcement for a while. When you praise your child, focus on what practicing good personal care will mean to him, not necessarily to others, unless he has indicated that he cares what they think. If your child wants to make a good impression on others, certainly use that: "Wow, your breath smells great! So minty!" If their opinions don't matter to him, use a different tack: namely, what's in it for him? "College recruiters get distracted when they see dirty fingernails. I'm glad you're not going to let that get in your way." One of the most effective caveats around our house after my son entered his teens and started expressing an interest in girls was a simple "Girls don't like that."

PERSONAL PERSONAL CARE

Parents whose kids have more *personal* personal care issues often don't know where to turn. Pediatricians and other professionals may know a lot about toileting or dealing with menstruation for typical kids, but they may not be as helpful when it comes to the unique issues ASDs bring to the mix.

Problems with toileting are surprisingly common among children with ASDs and run the gamut from simple inefficient wiping to health-threatening patterns of holding urine or feces. If your child is having a serious problem that goes beyond the realm of hygiene, consult your doctor and ask for a referral to a specialist such as a pediatric gastro-enterologist. Before embarking on a major behavioral intervention, you should have medical clearance from a physician who has ruled out any physical cause for these problems. Note that no ethical behavior analyst will treat a toileting problem without that clearance, and do not work with any therapist from any discipline who does not insist on a medical clearance first. Sudden changes in toileting patterns and related hygiene may have other causes: stress, anxiety, a sudden fear of using the bathroom at school or elsewhere. You will also want to explore these possibilities before you proceed. Here we are addressing the simple hygiene-related aspects of toileting. This section presumes that your child is toilet-trained, uses the toilet independently, and does not have accidents. If those are problems for your child, see Maria Wheeler's *Toilet Training for Children with Autism and Other Developmental Disorders*, second edition. Another good resource is "Teaching Toileting Skills," in Stephen Anderson, Amy Jablonski, Marcus Thomeer, and Vicki Madaus Knapp's *Self-Help Skills for People with Autism*. Though both use illustrative case histories of children who probably would not have an Asperger's or HFA-type profile, the principles and strategies can be applied to any learner. If you cannot resolve the issue quickly on your own, consider working with a Board Certified Behavior Analyst with experience in this area (see page 110).

Hygiene-related concerns include problems with getting to the bathroom on time, wiping, keeping hands clean in the process, washing and drying hands afterward, and recognizing when underwear needs a change.

Getting to the Bathroom on Time

I doubt anyone has studied this formally, but it is not uncommon for kids with ASDs to seem to wait until the last minute. We know that people on the spectrum can be hypo- or hypersensitive to physical sensation, and that includes internal sensations, too, such as pain, hunger, and other internal biological cues. So it also seems to be the case with "Gotta go!" signals for some of our kids. While this can result in accidents, more often there is a slight soiling that may not seem sufficient to warrant a change of clothes but still poses a problem. Sometimes, for a whole host of reasons, kids feel uncomfortable using the restroom at school, at a neighbor's or family member's house, or anyplace but home, so they end up waiting too long.

If your child's early internal signals are not making a timely impression, build visiting the bathroom into the daily routine. Whether he thinks he has to go or not, he is to stand at or sit on the toilet at designated times—for example, upon waking up, before he leaves for school, after lunch, before he gets on the bus to come home, after a snack, before bed, and so on. It's important that he focus on completing the task. Make his access to fun activities and playthings contingent upon his using the bathroom regularly.

If your child seems to never have to go, she may not be drinking enough water and other liquids.

Teach your child that any degree of soiling calls for a change in underwear. No exceptions. Explain that even a small spot can cause a bad smell.

If your child is holding urine or bowel movements because he doesn't like using the bathroom anywhere but at home, provide lavish reinforcement for using, say, the bathroom at school and one or two other places where he spends a lot of his time. The insistence on going only at home may be simply a problem with generalization: the ability to practice a skill in an environment different than the one in which it was originally taught. Provide opportunities for practice at friends' and relatives' homes, a place of worship, a favorite family restaurant, day camp, and so on.

Don't Forget the Charmin

When you break down the task of wiping one's bottom, it's easy to see why doing a thorough job can be a challenge for our kids. First, you cannot see what you are doing while you are doing it. Second, handling toilet tissue in such a way that it covers the hand yet does its job requires a surprising degree of fine-motor skill. Third, what feels like a complete job may not really be so thorough. This is the classic example of a problem too easily solved by adult intervention that may continue way past its appropriate expiration date.

While it is easier to help your child, remember again: who will help your child when you are not there? This is not something that any youngster should need help with past the age of five or six.

In a nontoileting moment, teach your child how to handle toilet paper. There are a few approaches to this, but whichever you use, make sure that there is enough toilet paper, that it covers the fingers and hand, and that it is positioned to stay in place as it moves from being visible to being out of sight.

Be specific about how much toilet paper to use, how to fold it or wrap it around the hand, and so on. You might have your child count how many squares to use, or measure a length that covers the distance from the roll to your child's outstretched hand or some other marker.

Teach your child how to discriminate when she is done. Some children cannot do this by sensation, but they can be taught to look at toilet paper before it gets dropped into the bowl and continue wiping with fresh paper until the sheet comes away clean.

Consider using flushable wet wipes (not baby wipes, which usually are not flushable). The same guidelines for determining when he's done apply, but your child will probably get through the job more quickly.

Teach girls the correct way to wipe: front to back, to prevent introducing bacteria from the anal area to the urethra and vagina.

While, yes, independence is important, be in the vicinity to teach and monitor progress until important hygiene skills like this are completely mastered. Left on his own, your child probably will not improve, and you may find yourself back at square one, though now perhaps with a host of interfering behavior and ingrained, poor practice to deal with.

Hand Washing and Drying

Hand washing is an easily taught chain that every child should have mastered by age three. The degree of prompting your youngster needs may vary, of course. The important thing is that he learns it as a chain, from start to finish, so that it goes on autopilot. If your child is going to the bathroom on his own but still requires some level of monitoring to ensure that his hands are washed, he's not really independent.

Hand washing provides health benefits that Purell and other waterless hand cleansers simply cannot match, despite their promises of killing a lot of germs. The physical act of rubbing the hands together and contact with soap and water destroy many pathogens on contact. Further, products such as Purell are made up mostly of alcohol, which dries the skin, and also contain antibacterial agents that can be rough on sensitive skin or that you may not wish to expose your child to several times a day. Further, a good scrub with soap and water is as effective in removing most bacteria and viruses as special chemicals.

Teach your child to scrub long enough (singing "Happy Birthday" through twice is good, or "Yankee Doodle") and to look at his hands when he's done, especially under his nails. And when he dries his hands, they should be thoroughly dry.

Hand Washing Behavior Chain

Obviously, this is a chain best taught forward. Before you begin, be sure that all necessary supplies are at hand. How much detail you need to provide really depends on your child. Safety tip: Children should always be taught to turn the cold water on first and off last to reduce the risk of burns from hot water. The numbered steps are the actual steps in the chain. The subsections are tips and comments.

1. Turn on cold water first.
2. Turn on hot water last.

When I teach turning water on and off, I say this aloud because turning faucets on and off in the correct order is a serious safety issue. Be sure to include the words first *and* last *in your instructions and stress the words* on *and* off *and* first *and* last. *You could further shorten it to "Cold on first, hot on last" and "Hot off first, cold off last."*

3. Wet hands.
4. Apply soap.

For some kids, you may need to be very specific; for example, "one pump of liquid soap" or "rub the soap bar between your hands for a count of five." Sometimes soaps and other products that are more "fun" are actually more distracting. There may be a fine line between your child being more willing to wash his hands with the blue gel stuff that turns magically to a foam and it being such a distraction that the actual hand-washing task falls apart.

5. Rub hands until they are completely covered by soap.

To ensure that your child learns this, you will have to somehow quantify it. For example: "Rub palms and fingers together ten times, back of right hand ten times, back of left hand ten times, between fingers ten times." If your child is good at hitting all the areas he needs to scrub, suggest singing (to himself or silently) "Happy Birthday" or another song for a total of twenty seconds.

6. Rinse hands.

Once again, what is your criterion for "success" here? Try "Rub palms, backs of hands, and fingers under running water until all soap is gone." Or "Hold hands under running water for twenty seconds."

7. Turn off hot water first.
8. Turn off cold water last.
9. Dry hands.

Easier said than done. It's not unusual to see kids touch a towel or pat their palms with it and consider the job complete. Try "Press

> *towel between both open palms. Holding towel in your left hand,*
> *twist your right hand to dry the back of your hand and fingers.*
> *Press towel between both open palms again. Holding towel in*
> *your right hand, twist your left hand to dry the back of your hand*
> *and fingers."*
>
> 10. Replace towel on rack. (This may be a different skill.)

FOR GIRLS ONLY

According to the American Academy of Pediatrics, the average age of onset of menstruation ranges between nine and sixteen. So how do you know when to start talking to your daughter about menstruation?

For parents of a girl with an ASD, who will need more preparation, it is important to plan ahead—way ahead. You do not want the onset of menses to come as a surprise for any girl. Plan on introducing the subject in smaller units of information and be prepared to revisit it several or many times before she fully understands what it's all about. Typical young girls share a lot of information and provide one another with a lot of support through this special time. You may be the sole source for all of that. Long before the big day arrives, your daughter should be comfortable with her knowledge of how her body is changing, what to expect, and how to handle her period. There are a couple of very good books about girls with Asperger syndrome and other forms of autism, which you may wish to refer to for a broader discussion of social and emotional concerns. My favorites are *Asperger's and Girls* (Tony Attwood, Temple Grandin, and others) and *Girls Growing Up on the Autism Spectrum* (Shana Nichols, et al.).

Here we are focusing on teaching the mechanics of menstrual self-care. Ideally, your daughter should be a pro at knowing what to do with the paraphernalia of that time of the month long before she has to put it into practice. All women remember that first day, which is nothing if not a big surprise. Given that you can't plan when your daughter will have her first period, at least be sure she is confident and fluent in the basics.

The arrival of menstruation is an exciting, bewildering, and mildly stressful rite of passage for every young woman, and, as can be expected, having an ASD only complicates matters. By the time your daughter's period arrives, she should know and understand, to the extent that she can, the following:

- What having her period means.
- How long it might last and how often it might recur.
- The names and locations of the parts of her body that are involved.
- What girls do to manage their period.
- The importance of staying clean.
- What panty liners, maxipads, and tampons are and how to use them, including when to change them and how to dispose of them correctly.*

Purchase different brands, styles (wings, no wings), and absorbencies of pads. There is a surprisingly wide variation in texture and fit. Consider having your daughter wear a pad for a few minutes regularly to get used to how it feels. Practice placing and removing the pad and folding or rolling and wrapping it for proper disposal. (And remind her never to flush them!) Again, this is something we each do a bit differently, so you will have your own preferences when you teach your daughter.

When the big day arrives, some mothers and daughters make it a special personal time; others throw "red" or "period" parties. Obviously,

---

*Some writers on the subject advise starting off using pads instead of tampons. Even though pads may be somewhat messier, using them gives your daughter a chance to learn how to monitor her flow, how often she needs to change her pads, how her flow varies from day to day, and so on. Further, some young women have problems with using tampons for a variety of reasons, such as forgetting to remove them regularly and not having the fine-motor skill to insert them properly or comfortably.

this is a personal decision. You may, however, want to alert teachers, the school nurse, or anyone else your daughter might turn to if she needs assistance or reassurance. Put the basics of menstrual care on a structured teaching plan, and cover everything from when to change pads to remembering to check that extra supplies and perhaps even a fresh pair of panties are in the backpack or purse.

Chapter 13

AROUND THE HOUSE:
WHAT'S SO GREAT ABOUT CHORES?

There are many valid reasons why parents let kids with AS off the hook when it comes to pitching in around the house. Problems with motor skills, sensory issues, inattention issues, and difficulties with planning, organizing, and following through can make teaching these skills a challenge. As a result, our kids are often relieved of and excused from perhaps their only opportunity to really learn skills they will need in order to become independent.

We all realize that chores are necessary for instilling valuable lessons and for building both practical skills and self-esteem. However, the prospect of including our children in day-to-day home maintenance can be daunting. We have come to accept as a rule that kids don't like chores and that getting them to do them demands patience, oversight, and sometimes even conflict. Maybe you are convinced that there are many better ways for your child to spend his time. As some parents say, "He'll have enough to do when he grows up. Let him be a kid." This is a logical argument only if you are okay with having a twenty-year-old who has the household daily living skills of a ten-year-old.

Yes, getting your child to perform chores does require time and effort. But the benefits for all children—and for kids with AS especially—are indisputable. You would be hard pressed to find many other activities with such a rich payoff for everyone.

The immediate benefits of learning to perform age-appropriate household chores are obvious: acquiring real-world skills not only in the task at hand but also in related areas such as executive function, time management, organization, and the increased independence that comes with all of that. Experts also point to some longer-range benefits of even greater importance. Doing chores at home provides a safe environment for learning how to ask for help, how to recognize and fix a mistake, how to problem-solve, how to persevere, and how to be part of a team—all essential skills for success in school and on the job. Chores also provide opportunities to learn and practice basic social skills: negotiating; accepting correction appropriately; recognizing when others need help, offering it, and following through; and noticing what others are doing and offering them praise and compliments. Volunteer work and service activities provide excellent entry points into the larger community; for some people with AS, they are stepping-stones to employment and social relationships. According to a study conducted at the University of Massachusetts, a major predictor of adults' participation in volunteer work or community involvement was their having handled chores at home during childhood.

For our purposes, chores provide the individual component skills your child will be working on in a real-life context. Learning and practicing skills as part of the daily routine establishes them and also increases your child's ability to maintain the skill and to generalize it to other situations. And last but probably most important, your child has another opportunity for praise and encouragement.

TEACHING THE SKILLS

By now, you know the drill, but here's the list of steps again:

- Analyze and break down the steps; write them all down.
- Test-drive your task analysis; be on the lookout for activities that might be difficult for your child.
- Ask your child to perform the task without advance notice or preparation, just to see what comes easily to him and what does not. Note where it goes smoothly and where it breaks

down. Write down on your list what type of prompt might be needed at each step. Don't forget to note where no prompt will be needed.

• Pay attention to where a visual prompt or modification to the material might be helpful. For example, a photo that highlights the relative positions of the flatware and the plate will be more helpful than a wide shot of the whole table.

• Present the skill by modeling it for your child as you do it in the course of your day, not only during teaching times.

• Demonstrate for your child how to use any visual prompts or modified materials.

• Ask your child to perform the task with you at his side or behind him, offering whatever prompts are necessary.

• Write down how it went: which steps were independent, which were prompted, what type of prompt was used.

• Praise your child's effort and offer whatever reinforcement you have determined beforehand. Emphasize what he did well and ignore what still needs practice. Remember, however, to watch for the rough spots in your next trial and try to prevent the same errors.

• Depending on the skill, repeat. Obviously, you can't feed the cat five times in a row, but there's no reason you cannot unfold and refold a few towels if more practice is indicated.

• Run the last trial of the day without any prompts to get an idea of your child's progress and how productive the prompting has been. Ideally, prompt-free execution at the end of the teaching session should be at least a bit better than the first trial.

• Look at your data: in which direction are they headed? Even if your child is learning, the changes may be so incremental that you don't really notice them (which is why written data are so important). Don't throw in the towel if you do not see significant improvements right away, but if the data flatline or start to head south, reassess what you are doing.

CHOOSING CHORES

Where to begin? Start with the chart on page 62. As with any other skill, the earlier the better, provided that your child can handle the task safely. If your child has not had to do chores before, start with short tasks that need to be done often rather than a big job that he'll have few opportunities to practice. For example, better to assign your child a task that gets done at least once (and preferably several times) a day, such as putting away dishes, setting the table, or sweeping the kitchen floor. Focus on a chore that works naturally into a more elaborate routine. In this case, task by task, putting away dishes, setting the table, and cleaning the kitchen floor might all be steps in a larger housekeeping chain known as serving and cleaning up after dinner.

Start with tasks that do not require a lot of steps or supplies and that do not have the potential to go horribly wrong. Keep them modest and manageable—for example, learning to wipe down the kitchen counter or dust the bookshelves in the living room. The first thing you want to teach is how to do the task well. Then you want to teach your child to remember to perform the task when it is needed and, ideally, without your presence or prompting.

You probably have very clear ideas about how your home should run and how you prefer housekeeping chores to be done. Before choosing chores for your child, think carefully about what you would like him to do and, realistically, how well you believe he will be able to do it. What's more, how much latitude are you willing to allow in terms of your current housekeeping standards? For instance, if you decide that your child should be learning to completely clean his own room, what are the absolute minimum standards you can live with? Chances are your child will not leave any surface she dusts spotless from day one, and dish towels might not boast sharply creased folds right away. At the same time, carrying out a chore should not simply be busywork. After all, the point is for your child to learn skills for independence. Depending on the task, you might wish to base reinforcement on improved performance over time (see "Shaping" on page 162), or you might add steps to the chore gradually. An example would be starting out a youngster with putting away dishes that stack flat before tackling nested bowls or more fragile items.

Remember that we are looking at chores for the benefits that doing them can bring to your child and your family. Setting unrealistic expectations, not teaching a skill thoroughly, or presenting chores that your child finds overwhelmingly difficult will undermine the sense of competence and self-esteem we're trying to foster.

TRY TO WORK AND TEACH EFFICIENCY

When picking a chore to teach, it is helpful to consider in advance which aspects your child may have trouble with and plan ahead. You might also want to think of ways to make the job run more efficiently. Take dusting, for instance. Given the difficulties that some of our kids have with executive function and motor planning, you might not only teach the act of dusting but also set out the order in which a room should be dusted: start at the door and go around the room clockwise, dusting upper surfaces first, then working your way down. Or, if your child will be vacuuming, think of start and stop points in every room and the route you wish him to take. As with many other things, our kids easily fall into patterns of inefficiency that not only make their tasks more time-consuming but also demand excess energy and focus.

Even if you have been doing chores for decades, I highly recommend Jeff Campbell's brilliant little book *Speed Cleaning* and his website, www.speedcleaning.com. Campbell, owner of a successful San Francisco–based housecleaning service for more than thirty years, approaches housework logically, with clear explanations of the most efficient ways to tackle common household chores. A big believer in routine, teamwork, and efficiency, Campbell has come up with an approach that could have been custom-made for our kids. (Why should you dust from top to bottom? Because dust follows the laws of gravity, science fans!) Special instructions and reminders about using both hands will be useful to those who often forget to engage their nondominant hand when working. There is also a special chapter devoted to how to clean as a team, which may appeal to you, since it allows you to get some things done while monitoring your young apprentice.

CLEANING UP

Start as early as you can with simple cleanup routines. After all, your child is probably cleaning up after himself in school, so there's no excuse for him to be leaving a trail of stuff behind him at home. Make basic rules: for example, if you take it out, you put it back. And prompt your child to follow through each and every time. Try to have a place for everything to go, and use whatever organization or prompting tools your child may need. Examples:

- Label drawers, cabinets, file cabinets, closets, and so on with words or pictures depicting what is inside or what goes where.
- If there is an item that your child cannot put away, have a special basket or other designated spot to serve as its temporary home.
- If your child has developed his own unique system of storing things in his room, consider leaving it alone. Remember, the important thing is that the clutter gets picked up and items go where your child will be able to find them. Imposing a new system based on your personal preference or a scheme you read about in a book may be too confusing.
- When cleaning up involves using solutions or special equipment, some things you may wish to consider include:
  - Possible sensory reactions to cleaning products.
  - Difficulty using cleaning products safely; for example, can your child discriminate when a spray bottle nozzle is open or closed and remember to point any container of cleaning product away from his clothing, skin, and especially his face?
  - Can your child discriminate between one cleaning

product and another? There's not a lot of difference in overall appearance between a bottle of organic, nonirritating multipurpose cleaner and a bottle of truly dangerous stuff, like diluted sulfuric acid solutions used to eliminate rust and mineral deposits. Separate the supplies that your child can use safely from those you don't want to chance.

• Make a special tray or bucket containing the products your child can use. Explain that he is not to use any product not in his tray or bucket.

• Teach your child to read labels if he's old enough. Consider writing warnings on containers with a permanent marker: "OK," "NEVER USE," or "Ask before using," etc.

• Review safety precautions, such as wearing rubber gloves and how to rinse off cleaning product that may get on her face or in her eyes.

• Teach your child never to mix two cleaning products together. If it ever happens, teach her to leave the area immediately and notify an adult.

• Can your child handle equipment and supplies safely?

• Motor planning problems can result in broom and mop handles hitting the walls and furniture (and people!) behind your child, vacuum cords and hoses forming a dangerous pile on the floor (and getting damaged when they're run over by the vacuum), or your child accidentally mopping himself into a corner.

• Executive function and attention problems can make your child more likely to forget that there's a bucket of water in front of him or that the floor is not a good place to set Mom's prized collection of ceramic frogs when you're dusting. Teach your child the logistics of cleaning chores. Where do items go when you're dusting a shelf? Where do you put the toothbrushes while you're cleaning the holder? Where do you start and where do you finish? Again, Jeff Campbell's *Speed Cleaning* is invaluable.

- Address any problems your child has in terms of ascertaining what's "just right." Too much cleanser in the sink? Too little pressure when wiping mirrors? Water that's too cold to wash dishes?

TEACHING A SKILL: FOLDING

There isn't a book large enough to contain all of the skills you would probably like to teach. We'll walk through teaching folding, a basic skill with countless applications, because it's the type of everyday activity on which a multitude of problems with coordination, fine- and gross-motor skills, and other executive function intrude. It calls on eye-hand coordination, sound visual-spatial perception, motor planning, and the ability to make adjustments in the direction, force, and speed of actions based on the feel or appearance of what you're folding.

As you watch your child do the dry run of executing a skill without any help from you, pay close attention to a couple of things:

- **The grasp.** Most folding tasks begin with picking up the item by two adjacent corners, grasping them between the thumb (turned out, facing away from you) and the index finger or index and other fingers (turned in, facing you).
- **The positioning.** Faulty hand and finger positioning can make folding frustrating. Before you begin, model just picking up a square of cloth, such as a washcloth, and check your child's grasp and positioning. Correct and practice to fluency before teaching the whole task chain.
- **The pressure.** How hard/soft or quickly/slowly to do something may be difficult for a child to gauge accurately. One result is that she may not flick the cloth with sufficient force to straighten it or make it fall out flat on the folding surface. Simple observation and modeling may not convey the invisible dimensions of the task. Here hand-over-hand prompting through several motions might help.

To teach how to fold small square or rectangular items (napkins, washcloths, dish towels, hand towels, face towels, et cetera), choose a small item, preferably square, to begin. Stand beside your child at a flat surface, like a counter or table. You'll be working side by side with you prepared to provide physical prompts as needed. Have unfolded items in a basket or pile, not lying flat—"unfurling" an item is one of the steps in the chain.

1. Pick up a square by two adjacent corners; be sure your thumbs are facing away from you.
2. Place the square on the surface so that the bottom of the square "leads" and comes to rest first, followed by the top side (you are holding).
3. Using both hands, grasp top and bottom corners of the right-hand side and fold to the left, just as you would turn the pages of a book, until the edges meet.
4. Using both hands again, grasp the two bottom corners and fold upward, matching edges, to make a square.

If your child has trouble placing the square down so that it's smooth, try prompting the step hand-over-hand. It may be that your child is applying the wrong amount of pressure to guide how the material falls.

As for any steps where the edges should meet, don't let sloppy matches go. While a mismatch might seem a small thing, matching edges are the key to a neatly folded item. The task will be much more reinforcing if your child begins getting great (not necessarily perfect) results.

Work up gradually to larger items. As you do, your child will need to "unfurl" with progressively more force and control.

As you work with lighter items, your child will need to pay attention to straightening before folding.

As you move to less regularly shaped items, your child will have to do more problem solving and motor planning.

Work with a variety of materials. Here are some other things to practice folding:

- Money
- Paper (light, medium, and heavy)
- Play-Doh, rolled or pressed thin and flat to form a "sheet"
- Aluminum foil
- Felt
- Items that come prefolded: paper bags, newspapers, maps, that round plastic rain poncho that's supposed to fit back in a small square plastic pouch. As your child folds these, non-verbally draw her attention to the salient cues: the existing fold lines.

Folding Clothes

Here's a skill with almost daily opportunity for practice. Different clothing items have their own rules, and you may be particular about how you like things done in your house. Feel free to modify the steps described here to work for you. These are instructions for a short- or long-sleeved T-shirt, the best garment to start teaching with.

Make sure you start with everything right side out. Depending on how much material there is to wrestle, some kids get very distracted when they have to turn things right side out. Try teaching this:

- To right a sleeve or leg:
    1. Place your hand inside the sleeve or leg all the way to the end.
    2. Grasp the end firmly.
    3. Pull it toward you until it's completely extended, right side out, with no remaining bunches or folds.
- To right a whole sleeveless or short-sleeved shirt:
    1. Place the item on a flat surface.
    2. Place one hand in each sleeve or armhold as if about to put it on.
    3. Grasp the sleeve ends firmly.

4. Pull both hands toward you until the item is completely extended, right side out, with no remaining bunches or folds.

Generally, most clothing gets folded facedown. Teach your child to identify the front from the back (hint: teach her to spot the tag) and place the item facedown.

1. Smooth the shirt.
2. Grasp the two bottom corners at the hem and fold up toward the shoulders so that the bottom collar seam and the bottom hem meet.
3. Fold the left sleeve rightward, back over the back, to make a straight left edge.
4. Fold the right sleeve leftward, back over the back, to make a straight right edge.
5. Flip the shirt over so it's faceup.

Chapter 14

ALL ABOUT SCHOOL

GETTING READY FOR SCHOOL

For many families, school-day mornings are mildly stressful and rushed, even on good days. Somehow everyone gets out the door ready for the day. And while it may not always feel like the most organized hour or two, when you consider what actually gets done, it may be easier to appreciate the numerous hurdles that the school-day morning can present to our kids.

Four simple words—"Get ready for school!"—encompass a universe of skills, activities, judgment calls, distractions, temptations, and behaviors. Add the pressure of a limited amount of time, and there you have it: perhaps the least fun time of day (outside of homework; see page 304).

For some kids, morning difficulties are rooted in the night before, as a significant percentage of boys and girls with ASDs have to cope with sleep disorders. Naturally this sets the stage for trouble. None of us is at his or her best when sleep is wanting, and kids—particularly adolescents—are notoriously poor judges of how much sleep they need. In fact, we know that as kids grow older, they may need more sleep. So step one might be to look at ways to improve the quality and quantity of your child's sleep, especially on school nights.

The night before is also a perfect opportunity for finishing, organizing, picking out, arranging, and in other ways getting set for tomorrow. Don't let these tasks wait for the morning. Those last ten math problems that got postponed, the shirt that needs ironing, the permission slip that still requires your signature—they all look innocent enough around seven in the evening. But at seven in the morning, they will hijack your routine, in the process ratcheting up anxiety and possibly precipitating somebody's meltdown.

It's not just the time burden that you've added to the morning routine; by not preparing the night before, you've spiced the atmosphere with unpredictability. Rushing, looking for things, and all the discussion that goes with it make mornings anything but routine. We use routine to provide safe, predictable, structured practice for skill acquisition. When the morning routine has to be interrupted to find the missing book or printout that's due for today's assignment, all that structure flies out the window. Of course, we're working to embed routine skills so strongly that the occasional surprise should not derail things. But until your child has reached that point, seriously consider clearing the field: get everything from the night before done and get whatever you can ready for the morning.

What If the Problem Is School Itself?

Crabby, uncooperative, whiny, defiant, weepy, angry—if any of these descriptions fits your child on school mornings, the problem may not be so much getting ready to go as it is where she is going. For kids who so often enjoy learning (granted, perhaps only about specific topics), it's a cruel irony that for too many, school is the least enjoyable time of their day.

Simply having an autism spectrum disorder predisposes a child to difficulties in school for reasons that are well and amply documented in both professional literature and parent experience, yet these are still poorly understood and even less effectively addressed. The school bus, the lunchroom, the playground, the gym, the hallways, the bathrooms— these are just the most popular offenders of a child's need for predictability, order, and sensory comfort. As much as advocates of inclusion or mainstreaming don't like to hear it, some youngsters with ASD simply cannot tolerate more than a certain number of bodies in a space because of the movement, noise, social interaction, and unpredictability they bring. School can be stressful for an infinite number of other reasons particular to a child: the scent of places (gym, lunchroom) and substances (school supplies, cleaning products, other materials), visual overstimulation (bulletin boards, the way the sun hits the window around two in the afternoon), auditory sensitivity (the voices of children, the school public address system, the sounds that chairs make scraping against the floor, the squeak of swings on chains)—again, the list goes on. There may be social issues as well, ranging from a teacher or a classmate your child feels could be nicer all the way to the full-blown bully.

To find out what may be going on, first ask your child. Direct questions—such as "What did you do in school today?" "Is something bothering you?"—are typically so unproductive that many of us eventually give up asking. You can try asking another way. Engage your child in a more general discussion that is not specifically about him; read a book together or watch a video with a related theme; or encourage writing, drawing, building, singing, playing, or any other form of self-expression that might yield some clues.

Next, check with your child's teacher and other staff. Have they noticed anything different about your child's behavior? If the possible resistance to school is recent, you may discover that there has been some change that your child may not notice or may not mention but that is having an effect nonetheless: a substitute teacher, a new classmate, a change in schedule, a rearrangement in the classroom, a new assigned seat, a different type of work, a change in the relationship with a classmate. If you discover a change, you can discuss it with your child, or your child's teacher and other support staff may develop an organized approach to helping her cope with the change, perhaps by discussing it, using a Social Story, or implementing a behavior plan.

If the problem persists, arrange a meeting with your child's teacher and related services staff to discuss your concerns, then keep in touch frequently. Sometimes, especially in typical classrooms, a lot goes on that teachers do not see unless a problem demands notice and cannot be ignored. A child with an ASD whose behavior is otherwise deemed "good" (she is quiet, follows directions, and does her work) sometimes glides under the radar. Just because she is good does not mean that there isn't a problem.

If the problem continues and/or your child's reluctance to go to school becomes more serious, consult a professional. A psychologist, social worker, or psychiatrist with experience working with ASDs can help you get a clearer picture of what's happening and recommend treatment. School avoidance can become a serious a problem and may be related to or signal the beginnings of anxiety disorder, which is very common in Asperger syndrome and related ASDs. School avoidance and anxiety both can have detrimental long-term effects on social, emotional, behavioral, and academic functioning and should be addressed.

Typically, when we teach a behavior chain or routine such as getting ready for school, the first tool considered is the list. Consisting of words, pictures, symbols, or any combination of these, the list is ubiquitous through special education and teaching strategies for people with ASDs. The big secret is that it is not always successful. Though lists can be very important, even essential, to a learner's success, remember that a list is a *tool*, not a skill unto itself. Sometimes kids fail working with lists because no one has taught them how to use them. Try to think of lists as a scaffolding to support the development of the ability to create, maintain, and follow the invisible "inner list" that will be written through the establishment of routines and the growth of executive function skills.

Spend several days simply observing what goes on in your house on school mornings. Sure, you no doubt could describe vividly an average morning *chez vous*. But this requires direct, here-and-now observation, not recall. If you can, jot down your current morning routine from the moment you get out of bed to the moment you get out the door. What does your child do? What do you do? How long does each task take?

How often do you provide—at your child's request or otherwise—reminders, assistance, and other forms of help? How often do you decide to do something yourself instead of allowing your child to do it for herself? You may be surprised to find that you do more of one thing than you thought and less of another.

Next, identify which areas are the most problematic and which are the least. Within each of these categories, also describe how predictable problems or success are for each item. In other words, does Tommy need reminders about face washing every day? Can Sally get everything in her backpack most days? Chances are that when you look at the types of tasks that are consistently problems or consistently not problems, the items on the list will have something in common. You may find that Tommy also needs more reminders about most tasks related to grooming or that Sally tends to be pretty consistent when it comes to anything to do with her backpack. Zoe may do great with the self-care skills that form behavior chains but fall apart when it's time to look for something, substitute an item of clothing or juice flavor, or wait five extra minutes for a late bus. In contrast, Zac might have learned to be surprisingly flexible in response to change, but he may not be able to leave the house unless he engages in some routine related to his special interest, whether or not time allows for it. Every child is different, and your child's strength-versus-deficit profile will probably be unique.

INCREASING INDEPENDENCE AT SCHOOL

Even though you are not at school with your child, you can increase his independence there, too. It is not unusual for a child with an ASD such as Asperger's to need some extra help and support. Your child may also have an IEP or 504 plan. It is important that you revisit any modifications or supports in place and ask teachers and other professionals to monitor your child's progress. Someone should be tracking not only the acquisition of skills and learning but also your child's ability to work independently. If special supports, such as a one-on-one aide or paraprofessional, have been instituted, there should also be plans for fading that support (though this goal may not be fully realized for years). Ask that plans and goals for increasing independence be included in your child's IEP goals or incorporated into her program.

Arrange to meet with your child's teacher and let her know about the areas in which he is independent at home. For example, if he is putting on his own coat at home, he should be doing it at school. If you are addressing a skill at home, let the teacher know about that, too. Ideally, the skill can also be addressed there, or at the very least, unnecessary prompts and supports will not be offered. Despite the increasing number of students with ASDs and the wide availability of information, not every classroom is fully ASD-ready. In the best of all worlds, your child's teachers and therapists will be receptive to your sharing what you have learned about how your child learns. For example, oral verbal prompting is very commonly used in schools; you might wish to share your experiences with teaching without talking.

Keep the lines of communication with your child's teacher wide open. Developing independence will be easier for your child if there is some degree of consistency between school and home. For example, if the teacher uses a special color-coded system for organizing homework by subject, find out what it is and duplicate it at home. Most kids with ASDs have enough trouble mastering one system, let alone two.

To support independence at school:

- Keep a calendar on which to mark school days, holidays, special events, quiz and test dates, and dates when assignments are due. Though you will make sure that it's up-to-date and accurate, the job of writing on it and checking it daily belongs to your child.
- Have your child use an agenda or other book in which to record homework assignments. More tech-savvy kids may want to record assignments on their smartphone, iPad, or personal digital assistant. Encourage your child to create his own lists and reminders.

- Send your child to school ready to learn, with sufficient sleep, a good breakfast, and a morning free of unnecessary stress.

HOMEWORK

Love it or hate it, homework is a fact of life for most kids. For years now, some experts, particularly Dr. Tony Attwood, have presented a convincing case against homework for students with ASDs who may be overwhelmed by the dual curricula (academic and social) school requires and may need a clear division between school and home. While there are some kids who enjoy doing homework, for others it marks the least pleasant time of the day, the time when all their deficits seem to come home to roost. Here are some tips for reducing homework stress:

- **Plan for and protect a transition time from school to home.** Make the half hour (or whatever your child seems to need) between walking in the door and starting homework a low-demand, low-stress time. Some kids like to spend time alone; others want to chat excitedly about everything that happened at school. Some enjoy sharing a snack; others need to run around the house or the yard with the dog. Different kids have different styles of unwinding, and it's important for your child to learn when he needs his downtime and what works for him. If, on the other hand, your child is the type who wants to walk in the door, hit the homework, and get it done, you should respect that, too.
- **Look at the amount of homework.** If homework results in reactions beyond a typical level of complaining—arguments, meltdowns, major task avoidance—do not be afraid to question the amount and the type of homework your child is receiving. Some homework is essential, but some of it is practice.
  - If it's mostly practice or review, ask your child's teacher if your child can do fewer problems or exercises if he gets the first five or ten correct.

- If the day's homework includes subjects that are especially challenging, see if it's possible to reduce or eliminate work in areas where your child generally does well. Every youngster is different, but it is not unusual for children with AS and similar disorders to struggle with schoolwork that requires using abstract language or perspective taking, calls upon a high level of executive function (for example, report writing, special projects), or demands extended periods of concentration.

- See if it's possible to redistribute some of the home-work to the weekends. Teachers typically plan lessons months in advance. You could lighten the weekday home-work load by getting your child's spelling words, reading assignments, or other homework on Fridays to do over the weekend. (Some teachers think this is "cheating." It's not. Your child is not deriving any competitive advantage, merely keeping up to speed. This is simply another form of academic support, and you might consider having it written into the IEP as an accommodation.)

- **Discuss with the teacher how you will proceed if your child is confused about homework and/or you do not feel confident to help.** From my own experience, I know the only thing worse than having a child who doesn't clearly understand a quadratic equation is being the parent who doesn't get it, either. In this situation, your child should be allowed to stop work—without penalty—until he talks to his teacher. Also ask your child's teacher to send home any specific instructions or direct you to websites that she trusts. For example, today most textbook series have accompanying websites where you can find helpful information that is consistent with what your child is learning in class.

- **Find out from the teacher how much work needs to be shown in math and science.** While some kids with ASDs score high in math on assessments such as IQ tests, they sometimes solve problems using methods that come to them naturally but may not be the accepted approaches. Increasingly, standard-ized tests as well as those given by teachers score not only the correct answer but how you arrived at it. Many kids with ASDs lose points because they cannot show their work on paper or in a form that is considered correct—even when their answer is right. Parents who offer the strategies they were taught back in the day risk confusing their kids even further.

• **If homework continues to be a source of stress, discuss with your child's team the possibility of having resource room time added to his schedule or staying after or coming in early for extra help.** This will allow him to complete some homework at school with the assistance of a teacher familiar with the work.

HOMEWORK THAT WORKS

Make homework time one of the most predictable, reliable, consistent parts of your child's day. This is especially important if he or she is taking medications that wear off as the day wears on, such as Ritalin or Adderall, to control ADHD. In our house, I always felt like Cin-derella, racing to get through homework before the golden carriage of medication-supported focus turned back into a pumpkin of distrac-tion. Kids who do not take medication may experience the same atten-tion crash simply because they are exhausted from juggling the dual curricula of academic information and social information. Either way, some kids have a very small window in which good, productive work is even possible. Consider doing the easiest homework in the evening and getting up an hour earlier in the morning to tackle the hard stuff. This may also mean a slight schedule change in dosing for medications that support attention and focus, so check with your child's doctor first.

If, like many parents, you cannot avoid starting dinner or doing other things during homework, set aside at least a quiet fifteen to twenty minutes to review the most difficult assignments first. Better yet, with your child's knowledge and permission, go through the evening's homework while he's taking his transition break and be ready to help him plan what to work on and in what order.

Homework time is a prime opportunity to teach and practice independence and executive function. You are there to help and assist with the academic aspects of homework; you should not be functioning as a secretary, gofer, or worksheet finder. Set up systems and routines that support your child's learning to manage his own responsibilities. Unless he has a particularly difficult task before him and really needs your help, try not to sit down beside him. And certainly stand up and move away when he does not need you—for example, when he's copying spelling words. Stay in the vicinity and go into hover mode. If your child calls for help, do not sit down next to him until you have asked him what he thinks the problem is and what he's tried so far on his own.

Manage the Space

Many homework problems are not about the actual work per se but about managing (or not) the materials, the scheduling, the level of adult assistance, and other details. There is only so much time each day that your child can devote to homework, and maybe only so much time he can work at his best, so setting up the environment to minimize distractions and maximize efficiency is time well spent.

There should be a place for everything and everything in its place. The backpack, office supplies, papers, books, calculator, et cetera should have a place where they can *always* be found. If the backpack's home is on the bench by the front door, that should be its base for the entire time it's in your house.

Reduce the number of "trips" that items take once they get inside the house. In other words, bring homework materials from the backpack on the bench to the homework area and from the homework area to the backpack on the bench—don't carry the backpack back and forth from the bench to the table, upstairs to the bedroom, and then back downstairs, where it accidentally gets left behind the door in the TV room because your son made a detour.

To reduce homework (and school day) crises due to supplies, papers, or books being left in one location or the other, keep a duplicate set of all basic supplies at home: the contents of the pencil box, scissors, glue, ruler, calculator, blank paper, and so on. This requires that your child focus only on getting books, agendas, folders, and worksheets from one place to the next.

If forgetting to bring home books is a problem, consider asking for a duplicate set of textbooks to keep at home. This is a valid accommodation for an IEP or 504 plan, but it's not a request many school districts receive often. If your district agrees to supply a home set of textbooks, be sure to follow up early and often so that you have your home set when school begins. In the meantime, of course, work with school about developing a plan to help your child remember to bring home everything he needs. Consider a second set of textbooks to be a temporary support.

Whenever possible, choose containers, envelopes, and bags that are semitransparent, so you can see what's inside—like the protractor that got mixed in with the gym clothes.

If your child will be working at a dedicated workspace with a desk, set it up so that everything has a place. If possible, devote one drawer of the desk or small file cabinet to notebooks and books, which you store vertically, spine up. Designate a drawer, hanging folder, or plastic box for anything not school-related that ends up on the desk. Prior to homework, these items should be cleared from the desk and put away, out of sight, until homework is complete.

Using a Portable Office

Sometimes, especially when kids are younger and may need more support during homework, it's impractical for you to spend a lot of time with them on the other side of the house, away from other children or responsibilities. For kids who need a lot of parent support, a homework office that is set up on the dining room table may make the most sense.

- Just about all the office supplies you need for homework can fit in a single 9-by-12-inch basket or plastic box. Add other, more specialized supplies such as Post-it notes, different sizes of paper clips, and rarely used items as needed.

• Office supply stores also have plastic minichests of three or four drawers that measure about 9 by 12 inches and stand no more than 12 inches tall. These hold just about everything, plus they are lightweight enough to be moved from the kitchen table workspace to a bookshelf for storage.

• Bag it. Large (gallon-size) and extra-large (such as Ziploc Big Bags) plastic zip-top bags keep things together and totally visible. Freezer bags are thicker and more durable. Teacher supply stores such as Education Warehouse and Lakeshore also sell resealable plastic bags that have strong plastic handles for hanging up.

• Donna Goldberg, author of the indispensable *The Organized Student*, recommends a plastic tackle box for storing supplies. You can find them in hardware, home improvement, sporting goods, and crafts stores.

When It's Homework Time

Do not add to the paper pile. Sometimes you or your child may need to write down something—a formula or an outline—that he will need to refer to several times later on. Other times, though, you may just sketch a triangle or write a word down to show the syllable breaks. When you don't need what you write to be permanent, use a small dry-erase board or chalkboard instead.

Use color to help you distinguish different types of papers. Within ten minutes of starting homework, our dining room table became a sea of white index cards, worksheets, notebook paper, and graph paper that we often got lost in. Add to your stock of homework supplies paper in other colors. For example, we wrote math examples, drafts, and outlines on neon yellow notebook paper. The evening's to-do list was written on large colored index cards. Rulers, erasers, and calculators were big and/or bright—nothing white, beige, putty, or gray.

Color-code by subject. Some school supply lists specify certain colors of notebooks and folders for each subject, so check to see if the teacher already has a system in place. If she does, you will want to coordinate yours to hers, to reduce confusion. If your child likes using the system, you might also consider matching book covers, so subject books and materials stay together. Note that while some kids thrive on having a different color of folder for each subject, others find having to remember that red means social studies and blue equals science more information than they can handle comfortably. Again, it's all about what works for your child.

Organize paperwork. Some kids do best with a two-pocket folder, with one pocket labeled "Home" and the other labeled "School." When homework is complete, it goes into the school pocket, and from there can be filed in subject-specific notebooks, folders, or other holders.

Instructions and forms that your child may be referring to over time—the directions and rubric for the big research project, or the format for all book reports—should be photocopied and one copy kept in a permanent place, like in a binder that does not leave the house or posted on a bulletin board.

Papers that stay home should be hole-punched and filed in binders. Whether you keep one big, fat binder with several subject tab dividers or a skinny binder for each subject depends on the number of pieces that your child (notice I did not say *you*) can handle. Let your child decide whether to file the most recent papers first or last, then stick to the system. Again, find out and follow teacher preference whenever possible.

Don't forget the computer! Be sure your child has a filing system in place. Some suggestions:

- A folder labeled with your child's name and the school year
- Within that, subfolders for each subject
- Depending on your child's grade, subject folders can be further broken down by unit/topic (for instance, in American history, you might include subfolders for "World War I," "Stock Market Crash," "The Depression") or by quarter or month.

- If necessary, each subject folder should also have subfolders for:
  - Syllabus, general instructions (for example, how papers should be prepared, rubrics for grading, accepted bibliography form)
  - Homework
  - Class notes, long-term assignments
- Filenames for written work should include the date ("Lincoln report 03.15.11") and preferably the draft version ("Lincoln report A 03.15.11").
- When working on a file that will have several versions over time, get into the habit of opening it and then immediately renaming it with the day's date or the next draft number. This way the previous version is safely stored, and it's easy to identify the latest one. This is especially critical if your child will be working on more than one computer.
- If the more recent version somehow goes astray or did not get renamed, click the "Date Modified" tab in the document folder. Click it again to reverse the chronological order of documents so that the newest one comes out on top.
- Never get up from schoolwork without backing up. Have a dedicated flash drive or rewritable CD that is labeled and used only for school documents. These should never leave the house. If your child needs to carry files back and forth to school, have a second "traveling" flash drive or CD for that. (This sounds like overkill only to those of you who have eluded a big crash or malware attack—trust me.)

Keep Your Eye on Executive Function

Homework time provides countless opportunities for your child to practice her executive function skills. Unlike some other skills, using executive function is not a matter of learning what to do but more about learning what strategies she needs to make things happen. I think of kids' brains as being like cars: each model is different, but even two seemingly identical cars will have little differences in how responsive the steering is or how long it takes to brake. One car can take curves easily at 60 mph, while another skids out. Learning to use executive function is a lot like learning how to drive your particular car. For your child, that means understanding her limitations and strengths and knowing that, for example, she will not be able to complete her math homework in the ten minutes before her favorite TV show starts, or that she does her best writing first thing in the morning.

When we try to help our children maneuver around executive function issues, we almost can't help offering a road map and instructions based on how we work—how we drive our own cars. When it comes to playing music and remembering dates, my son drives a BMW compared to my Yugo (okay, seriously, a bike—with training wheels). But when it comes to accurately sizing up my daily responsibilities and taking action to be sure I can meet them all independently, it's exactly the opposite. Just because I am better at executive function skills than my son does not mean that I can necessarily teach him to develop his own skills by encouraging him to do what I do. Rather, I have to learn to teach him to recognize his own strengths and weaknesses and practice strategies that work for him.

Whenever possible, step back and let your child take over figuring things out for himself. Natural consequences can be great teachers. I'm not advocating a hard-core "sink or swim" approach, but the fact is, natural consequences are often the best teachers. The real-life consequences of neglecting to study for a quiz that a student forgot to write in his daily agenda did more to improve performance going forward than months of teacher and paraprofessional prompting. Do not automatically assume that it is your job to protect your child from natural consequences. People do learn from their mistakes, and while some children might derive less useful information from mistakes than others, you can be sure that they learn absolutely nothing when you do everything for them.

If, for instance, your child misplaces an item, coach her through retracing her steps instead of joining the search party yourself. If she comes back to say that she looked "everywhere" and did not find it, conduct your own quick search. If you spot the item, do not pick it up, but do offer her clues for searching more efficiently. Learning to tolerate frustration is another important side lesson that most of our kids could use, too.

Here are some suggestions for helping your child practice EF skills during homework. He should be:

- **Reviewing his agenda or homework sheet** and then writing down what he will need to complete each assignment.
- **Prioritizing his work** in some fashion, then placing numbers on his assignment list indicating what he will tackle first, second, and so on. For most kids, doing the more difficult work earliest makes the most sense.
- **Estimating and noting how much time he expects each assignment might take.** He should write this down, too, and when he's finished compare how realistic his estimate was. This will help your child practice self-reflection and learn to judge which tasks may take more time or effort. Some students use countdown timers such as the Time Timer (see "Where to Find It," page 345) or a regular kitchen timer. For others, however, paying attention to the time increases stress and sometimes diminishes the quality of work, as they feel compelled to race against the clock. If you do try a timer, here are some tips for making it less stressful.
  - Set the timer for small increments of time and small units of work. For example, set 15 minutes for copying ten spelling words once instead of 2 hours for completing all the evening's assignments.
  - Have a reason for the times you choose. Take some baseline measurements: observe your child doing a week's worth of homework and note about how long each type of task requires.
  - Be specific. "Math: 25 minutes" tells you nothing. "Math: 5 minutes, 15 double-digit multiplication problems, then 20 minutes for four story problems" is much

more useful. The day she brings home ten story problems, you can help her allocate her time more realistically.

• **Managing his materials**: making sure he has everything,
that it all gets stored away correctly, and that papers, books,
and supplies end up where they belong before bedtime. Of
course, you can prompt and check where needed, but do not
carry out these tasks for him.

• **Making decisions about where things go,** how he will
store them and file them, and what color-coding system he
will use (if any). People are more likely to keep up with an organizational system that makes sense to them.

• **Making decisions about when he should take breaks.**
When you think about it, we naturally insert breaks into our
own work: we glance at a magazine, make a quick phone call,
check our Facebook or Twitter accounts. Kids are no different,
and especially at the end of the day, when they may not be performing at their peak, breaks should be regarded as essential.
For most kids, five minutes is long enough to recharge a bit
but not so long that they completely fall out of the groove. If
your child has break times, be sure he doesn't use them to start
something he can't finish within the designated period. Unfortunately, that rules out most video games and other online
or electronic options. Given the fact that, depending on how
the game goes or how the computer acts, kids can return from
these upset, it's better to cross them off the list of choices.
(Besides, you can use access as a reinforcer once the work is
all done.) Whatever you decide, use a timer—not your verbal/
oral reminder—to make the break period stick; do not venture
onto the slippery slope of "Just another minute, pleeeeease?"
and do not negotiate.

Remember that learning to manage time is experiential—something your child can learn only by actually doing. It is not a teaching
exercise for you.

What do I need for homework?	Date ___	Take home	In bag	Homework done	Homework turned in	Notes
Subject	textbook					
	workbook					
	worksheet					
	notebook					
	other					
Subject	textbook					
	workbook					
	worksheet					
	notebook					
	other					
Subject	textbook					
	workbook					
	worksheet					
	notebook					
	other					
Subject	textbook					
	workbook					
	worksheet					
	notebook					
	other					

Chapter 15

THE FIRST SOCIAL SKILL: PLAY

You may well ask, what does play have to do with independence? And how can play be a "skill"?

When a child cannot catch or hit a ball, ride a bike, shoot a basket, or jump rope, it's easy—and partially accurate—to attribute the trouble to having an ASD. There is a tendency to assume that those with AS and similar ASDs are not interested or that play and sports do not matter. That view, so common yet so shortsighted, misses the fact that play is the social stage of childhood and the ability to at least approach an impromptu game of catch without fear (and the word *fear* barely describes the nerve-wracking aversion many kids with ASD have to any physical activity that will expose their weaknesses) is a priceless bit of social currency. In fact, one might argue that for kids with ASD, basic play skills are more, not less, important.

By now, readers will be familiar with the importance of executive function. As discussed, we do not learn executive function so much as we develop and strengthen the innate, underlying neurological wiring for it through practice. Children as young as two practice executive function skills through play. Once you realize the value of play in developing virtually the entire range of social, emotional, and cognitive skills, it becomes clear how and why the perseverative, solitary, routinized early play of kids with ASDs is so detrimental. The good news: it's **never too late** to learn to play.

PLAY IS THE CURRENCY OF THE SOCIAL REALM

Play skills are the foundation skills of socialization for everyone. Unfortunately, many of us dealing with children on the spectrum get the impression early on that play with other children, particularly physical play, is something that our kids simply are not good at or choose not to do. Perhaps you or someone else has tried to teach your youngster physical play skills such as throwing and catching, riding a bike, or kicking a ball. When it doesn't work, it's easy to attribute the problem to the many common interfering issues and conditions—sensory problems, difficulties with fine- and gross-motor skills, and so on—and let it go. If your child's negative early experiences involved a team sport, such as Little League or soccer, you may have other reasons for not teaching these skills as avidly as you might. Too many unhappy memories start on the playing field in the futility of trying to convince your child to participate in or even just try something he knows he is not good at.

Childhood is full of experiences, rites of passage, and things that "everybody does" that our kids can choose to live without, sometimes quite happily. Alas, having a basic repertoire of physical play skills is not one of them. The problem is that not only are play skills the foundation skills of other social skills, play is the stage where a critical portion of childhood social practice occurs. Some types of play require a level of skill in performance, and I'm not talking about the skill level needed for someone to make a team or be the king of the four-square court. The playground, the softball field, the park, and your own backyard are the places where your child can learn and practice a range of skills that yield benefits far beyond just catching a ball.

Dr. Teresa Bolick, a psychologist who specializes in working with youngsters with ASDs, says it best: "Play is the child's work. It's an integral part of the toolkit for managing everyday life." Play helps children learn to understand the way the world works and how other people behave. Through play, kids explore cause and effect, practice joint attention (the ability to coordinate visual attention with that of another person), and learn to problem-solve—from figuring out how to dislodge a ball from a hedge to helping decide who goes first. Play with others requires attending to others: watching, looking, and responding to what they say and do. One aspect that may make it challenging for our kids—the plentiful use of nonverbal language to communicate among players—should not be a reason to rule out these types of activities. Rather, it's an indication that this is a skill that should probably be addressed, if not with a large group of other kids in a public or competitive situation, then certainly at home, in the yard, or in the park, one-on-one with you.

Our focus here is not the social skills of play but the physical skills that give the social skills a broader context for application. For instance, you're coaching him on how to catch and throw not necessarily so that he'll join Little League (though it's not a bad idea, if your child is interested) but so that he can play catch with his friends and family. As Dr. Tony Attwood points out, there are people with AS and ASDs for whom physical performance is a natural ability. In addition to the usual list of individual sports typically recommended for kids with AS (bowling, archery, martial arts, individual track and field events, swimming, diving, cycling, and so on), Dr. Attwood includes some other interesting suggestions: fencing (eye contact not required), marathon running (because some with AS can tolerate discomfort), and playing pool (the physics of the game can be intriguing).

HOW TO BE A GREAT COACH

Dr. Tony Attwood offers some helpful suggestions for making these teaching times low-stress and even fun:

> If you have problems when you take them to sports when you're with friends: my advice is, don't! Do it on your own, because the child doesn't want to make a mistake in a public forum. Often they need to learn the skills on their own to perfection before they can demonstrate them in a social context. Play with him, just the two of you, in the park, in a quiet area,

with no one around, so that your child can practice and have the supportive environment of a parent.

I also ask that when parents do these activities, please be functioning at the same level as your son or daughter. If you are brilliant at it and they are not, they don't want to do it. You should fake incompetence—fail to catch the ball, throw it inaccurately, trip over things—and still say, "Wow, I'm having fun."

While there are some very sports-minded moms out there, dads seem more likely to hold expectations and attitudes about what it means to teach sports skills. Generally speaking, these approaches are a poor fit for kids with ASDs. No one likes feeling that his efforts are unappreciated or ineffectual. Unfortunately, dads who attempt to engage their spectrum kids in sports and games are too often discouraged and frustrated. When his child doesn't respond as he had hoped, Dad's disappointment goes far beyond the prospect of little Joey never pitching for the Yankees. Playing catch or teaching your daughter to pass a football are important bonding times, too, and for some dads, these represent just one more of too many parenting experiences ASDs intrude upon. Here are a couple of thoughts from my husband, Phil Bashe, for whom sports played an important role throughout his life. After more than a decade of accompanying our son to various activities and talking to other dads, he offers these thoughts.

Kids on the spectrum lack theory of mind, so they may react more negatively to failure than other kids, because it doesn't occur to them that other kids miss the ball, too.

Keep your eye on the big picture. For example, baseball, by design, is a game of failure. Fail to get a hit 7 times out of 10, and you're a .300 hitter destined for the Hall of Fame. When your kid goes down after strike three, remind him that even the pros go through times when they can't hit or throw or catch or kick or pass the ball to save their lives.

Share stories about difficulties you faced with mastering certain sports or sports skills. If you don't remember any, feel free to borrow someone else's or make some up.

Before you throw that first ball, take a deep breath and a chill pill. Expect that your child may miss the throw/pitch/pass time after time. If you expect him not to give up, you have to be upbeat and encouraging and demonstrate saintly patience, even if—*especially* if—your inner jock is screaming, "Just keep your eye on the ball and hit it already!"

TEACHING THE SKILLS

The principles of teaching, as you know well by now, are always the same, no matter what the skill. Again, you will start with these:

- Analyze and break down the steps; write them all down.
- Test-drive your task analysis; be on the lookout for movements or manipulations of the materials that might be difficult for your child. This is especially the case with physical skills such as throwing or riding a bike. You probably really can't describe in words how you keep your balance, and we throw with our weight over our leading leg, which naturally is the leg opposite the hand that's throwing.
- Ask your child to perform the task without advance notice or preparation, just to see what comes easily to him and what does not. Note where it goes smoothly and where it breaks down. Write down on your list what type of prompt might be needed at each step. Don't forget to note where no prompt will be needed.
- Pay attention to where a visual prompt or modification to the material might be helpful. Generally, when it comes to physical play skills, you probably will not be using too many of these. However, some play skills lend themselves beautifully to video modeling.

• Present the skill by modeling it for your child slowly, even stopping the action in a living freeze-frame at important points.

• Demonstrate for your child how to use any visual prompts or modified materials. Again, these will probably be few.

• Ask your child to perform the task with you at his side or behind him, offering whatever prompts are necessary.

• Write down how it went: which steps were independent, which were prompted, what type of prompt was used.

• Praise your child's effort and offer whatever reinforcement you have determined beforehand. Emphasize what he did well and ignore what still needs practice. Remember, however, to watch for the rough spots in your next trial and try to prevent the same errors.

• Depending on the skill, repeat it. Physical play skills are learned almost entirely through practice. Make it engaging and fun, and you will have completed twenty or thirty trials of catching before you know it.

• Run the last trial of the day without any prompts to get an idea of your child's progress and how productive the prompting has been. Ideally, prompt-free execution at the end of the teaching session should be at least a bit better than the first trial.

• Look at your data: in which direction are they headed? Even if your child is learning, the changes may be so incremental that you don't really notice them (which is why written data are so important). Don't throw in the towel if you do not see significant improvements right away, but if the data flatline or start to head south, reassess what you are doing.

SAFETY FIRST

Some kids with ASDs give the appearance of being generally clumsy. Others, however, have problems with motor planning, coordination, and balance that could make some types of physical play riskier for them than they should be. If your child works with an occupational therapist or physical therapist, talk to her before you begin. No matter how much you may wish your child could hit a baseball, if a professional treating your child or his pediatrician indicates that some skills are beyond him at this time, move on to something else. The point of learning play skills is to play and to enjoy doing it. If a child feels nauseated by the smell of basketballs or is so anxious about falling off a bicycle that he tries to pedal with his eyes squeezed shut, obviously you should stop. Consider outside professional help, such as a coach or trainer who is certified in working with people with disabilities, or a BCBA. That said, don't give up! Commit to revisiting it in the future.

For most of our kids, however, repeated, gradual exposure to the equipment, the environment, and the skills can overcome a lot. Again, we are talking about training for the casual social game of softball, hoops, or soccer, as well as to encourage physical activity. If you are not reasonably accomplished in any of these activities, don't worry. This is about teaching basics. Once your child has acquired the fundamentals, if he wants to move on to playing with friends in the neighborhood or on a more structured team, go for it.

CATCHING AND THROWING

In addition to practicing a basic physical play skill, playing catch also offers countless opportunities to work on nonverbal communication, eye contact, turn taking, theory of mind, and attention. It's easy to schedule, doesn't call for much in the way of equipment, and there's no keeping score. When you teach throwing and catching, look carefully at where either skill breaks down for your child.

Teach catching first. You may need to work with a second teaching person if your youngster requires hand-over-hand or other physical prompting from behind to get started. You can and should always fade this as soon as you can, but use it where necessary. After all, your goal is for your child to feel competent right out of the box. Here are some recommendations for fun, instructional play:

- **Start with the right equipment.** Begin with balls that are large, on the softish side, and easy to handle comfortably. (Hey, dads, that means not a football, not a hard ball, not a basketball.) Relax; you'll get there.
- **Start low and slow.** Many kids have difficulty keeping their eye on the ball while coordinating the rest of their bodies to get into position to catch and then capture the ball with their hands. No matter what age your child is, sit down across from him on the floor and practice rolling the ball back and forth.
- **Stick to one dimension for now.** Your child will become more adept at predicting the ball's rate of movement and trajectory this way, plus it's easier to capture an object that is moving over one plane in space—horizontally only—rather than horizontally and vertically at the same time. Vary the speed and the direction. As your child's skill improves, introduce a surprise bounce and practice rolling the ball against the wall and then catching it.
- **Get comfortable.** For some kids, the first contact experience with a ball is having it zoom toward them as they put up their hands defensively to slap it away. As a child who did not learn to catch successfully until I was about nine or ten, I can relate. A ball careening toward me was horrifying, and my responses kept classmates in stitches. An unpredictable object you don't feel confident to stop or control can provoke anxiety, even if it's supposed to be fun. If your child is coming to this with a history of bad experiences behind him, be patient and make sure that you plan for early success and frequent, lavish reinforcement.
- **Use physical boundaries.** When instructing your youngster on how to catch any type of ball, set him up with either a backstop or a fence fifteen to twenty feet behind him. It can be discouraging enough to miss a ball, and having to chase after it can make things worse.
- **Learn how to handle the ball.** Some kids simply do not

know how to handle a ball so that it stays where it's supposed to stay or goes where it's supposed to go. Sit for a while and let your child simply hold the ball and get used to the feel, the smell, the weight, and the texture of it. Thanks to our motor neurons and lots of practice, this is a skill that most of us never think twice about. That's not to say you have the pitching form of a C. C. Sabathia, but you know—feeling almost instinctively—where your fingers go, how you grip the ball, how to move your arm, when to let go, and so on. Look at how close the hands are and how the fingers are positioned: spread out for holding a basketball, or close together for gripping a baseball. Before you start, use hand-over-hand prompts to show your child how to hold the ball correctly. You may get some resistance; he may be accustomed to doing it some way that is inefficient or awkward. Chances are, what he is doing may also make the movement less fluent and less enjoyable to execute.

• **Learn to watch a partner and predict what's coming next.** What you are doing with your face will be as important as what you're doing with your arms and legs. Do not let the ball go until your child has made eye contact with you and then shifts his gaze to the ball. If you sit there for five, ten, even fifteen seconds, that's fine. Just try not to talk it through. Remember how difficult verbal prompts are to fade and how few opportunities for verbal prompting there will be out in the real world. Your goal is for your child to attend, expect, and respond without being told what to do. One benefit is that he will be better able to avoid some of the verbal prompting that playmates and others may offer not so kindly if he is not focused and engaged.

• **Vary the speed and direction.** You might start by moving the ball toward the child and having him grab it without your letting go of it. This also offers a good chance for you to evaluate your child's grip.

• **Reduce defensive reactions to the approaching ball.** Be sure that when your child captures the ball—whether you are rolling it or throwing it—he's really got it in a firm, steady grip. Elbows should be bent to absorb the force of the ball, and his hands should have caught the ball long before it reaches his body. Little things mean a lot. Correct bad habits like pulling the ball close to the body (really only useful for football receivers and baseball players who don't want to lose that fly ball), closing the hands before the ball arrives, and holding the fingers improperly.

• **Teach in a logical progression.** Start slow, low, and close, and only then move to quicker, higher, and farther away. Start by rolling the ball on the floor from a distance of two feet and gradually increase it; when you start tossing the ball, begin with a low, level, underhand throw or with a long, slow bounce that provides extra time for positioning. Roll the ball with both of you seated, then roll it while you are both standing.

• **Slow the motion.** In the amazingly detailed and practical guide *Fundamental Motor Skills and Movement Activities for Young Children*, authors Joanne M. Landy and Keith R. Burridge suggest teaching kids first to catch objects that naturally float and move with extra "hang time" to aid in developing visual tracking and coordination. Play catch with scarves and balloons. (With the latter, the more you inflate them, the less predictable their courses.)

• **Invite your pets to play.** Dogs and sometimes cats like to chase balls, and they won't say anything about your form.

• **When you teach throwing, teach underhand first, then overhand.** Follow the same strategies in terms of progressing from slow, low, and close to quicker, higher, and farther.

• **When your child throws, watch for body positioning.** His weight should shift to his forward leg, which should be opposite his throwing arm. In other words, left leg in front when throwing with the right hand, and vice versa for lefties.

• **Practice throwing at targets,** moving from larger and closer to smaller and farther away. Have him throw into a box, a chalk circle, a hula hoop placed on the ground, a garbage can, and so on.

• **Teach your child when to let go.** How do you tell? Too much height and too little distance indicates that she's letting go too soon; throws that come in too low or too long mean that she's letting go too late.

KICKING

Soccer, one of the most popular childhood games, is one of the most challenging for kids on the spectrum. Unlike softball or football, where everyone on the field has a position (at least for a while), a soccer game in progress looks like a free-for-all. With so many bodies moving so unpredictably, it's easy to understand why our kids might shy away. That said, soccer is also one of the last great pickup games that kids can organize on their own if they have a ball and some space. It is also a popular recess activity.

First, work on balance. Practice standing on one leg, then standing on one leg and gently swinging the other forward. Encourage your child to also use his arms. They will be critical for balance once he starts kicking from a moving position.

Following the sequence outlined under "Catching and Throwing," start slow, low, and close, with your child kicking a stationary ball and then graduating to a ball that is moving toward him. Check the position of the kicking foot to be sure that your child is contacting the ball with the instep of the foot, not the top or the toes. Again, you can slow the action by having your child kick a balloon. Practice kicking at gradually increasing distances and also kicking for targets.

RIDING A BICYCLE

Learning to ride a bicycle is one of the few rites of passage that most kids are as excited about as their parents are. You probably remember the first time you pedaled away into what felt like a bigger world, even if it was just the sidewalk in front of your house. Given the nearly universal nature of this experience, it's easy to overlook just how complex a skill set it requires. Mix in motor skill problems, difficulties with balance and coordination, and a dollop of anxiety about falling, and it's not surprising that our kids often fall behind the curve here. According to a recent information poll on About.com:Pediatrics, more than 40 percent of neurotypical kids can ride a bike without training wheels by age five, while another third have it down by age seven.

Forget Everything You Think You Know About Riding a Bike

First, if your child either has struggled to learn this or is held back by anxiety at the prospect of even trying to ride a bike, accept that whatever approach has been used before is not going to work, and give it up. We want to keep bike riding a comfortable experience, so do not send your kid off down the driveway and try to analyze what's going on. Here we suspend some of our teaching steps in the interest of making this a positive experience—in other words, light on falls and scrapes.

There are some mechanical aids you can use that may help in teaching the skill, but each has its drawbacks. Training wheels are an old standby and do keep riders from falling, but they do not really teach kids how to balance. In fact, while riding a bike with training wheels, the rider can learn to pedal or turn corners faster than she could safely after the training wheels have come off. However, using training wheels can help your child learn to brake efficiently. Experts also caution against training with a single training wheel, because the rider will be unbalanced. If you do opt to use training wheels, they should be raised a little higher off the ground as your child's skills improve.

Running alongside your child and then letting go is another traditional approach. While this age-old method is popular and effective, kids who are anxious, have trouble with balance, or are likely to panic when they realize you're not there are not good candidates. If you decide to go this route, remember to support the child from his shoulders and run along behind. Do not hold the handlebars under any circumstances, and do not hold on to the back of the seat. You can buy special handles that attach to the seat area and harness-and-handle combinations that allow you to help your child balance without having to be so hands-on. Whether the introduction of extra paraphernalia will be effective and whether you can use it safely are questions to consider.

Building Some Basic Skills

Most kids rode a tricycle, which teaches pedaling and steering but not much in the way of balancing and nothing about braking (beyond the Fred Flintstone foot friction system). A scooter is a good intermediary step between a trike and a bike, since it combines balancing with steering, though without pedaling. Many scooters come equipped with hand brakes, which some authorities believe should also be on the learner's bicycle, especially if you believe that your child is likely to take his feet off the pedals when he panics. With the coaster brakes usually found on kids' bikes (the ones that you pedal backward to brake), removing your feet from the pedals eliminates your ability to brake and almost guarantees a fall. You can get a bike with both braking systems, though it may be a little more expensive.

Break down the skills needed to ride and address them individually as needed.

- **Gear up.** *Every rider should be wearing a helmet and any other appropriate safety gear every time.* Of course, a well-fitting helmet is obvious, but cyclist Sheldon Brown mentions the immediate and long-term value of kneepads and gloves. The reason? One painful fall may put off a reluctant or anxious learner forever (or, as we say in the behavior world, make bike riding aversive). Long before your child mounts that bike, teach him to put on his helmet and other gear correctly so that it does the job it was designed for.
- **Be sure that your child's bike is the right size.** He should be able to place his feet on the ground easily when seated. For learning, you might also consider using a slightly smaller bike. Do not try to teach your child to ride a bike that is too big for him or purchase a larger bike thinking he will grow into it. If your child's feet cannot reach the ground comfortably (if, for

instance, when stopped, he's holding the bike still by standing on tiptoes), it is not safe for him now.

• **Focus on balance.** Much has been written about so-called no-pedal bikes. The idea is that a rider learns to balance a moving bike without pedaling, so that his feet are always comfortingly close enough to the ground. For many kids with balance and coordination issues, learning to balance without pedals is essential. However, you do not need to purchase, rent, or borrow a special bike for that purpose. Bicycle pedals can be removed quickly, easily, and safely, and you can reattach them when the time is right.

• **Teach pedaling.** Some kids have trouble getting the pedal positioned so that when they press down and forward to take off, the pedal rotates forward. Take time to show your child what position the pedal should be in to start. Poor pedal position results in wobbly takeoffs from which your child then has to pedal extra hard to sustain momentum and keep the bike up.

• **Teach braking.** If you're using a bike with hand brakes, it should be easy enough. Be sure that your child knows to squeeze the brakes firmly, gently, and with equal pressure on both the front and back brakes.

• **Teach mounting and dismounting.** There are safe ways to mount and dismount; make sure your child knows them.

• **Consider teaching pedaling as a separate skill.** Some children with ASDs who do not get a lot of exercise might find that pedaling takes more concentration and physical effort than it should. Maybe they did not ride a tricycle, or if they did, it's been years since they've done it. If your child cannot pedal fluently and smoothly for a reasonable distance, consider separating this skill out. If you can, have him practice pedaling on a stationary bike until the motions go on autopilot and he can pedal without thinking. Once again, be prepared for the skill not to generalize with the same degree of fluency to a real bike. Take this detour, though, if your child's struggle with pedaling is enough to make learning aversive or if he is so distracted by it that he cannot ride safely.

• **Head up, eyes forward.** Learning to look—and keep on looking—can be a challenge for some of our kids. They may turn to see if you're still running behind, glance down at their feet, or become easily distracted. You might consider having your child practice pedaling on a Wii-type interactive cycling game.

Putting It All Together

Learning to Bicycle Without Pain, Teaching Bicycling Without Strain, a short, charmingly homemade video produced by the International Bicycle Fund, outlines an approach that teaches individual skills separately—balancing, stopping, steering, pedaling—instead of all at once. This is helpful for kids on the spectrum who may have problems with physical multitasking. You can find this video at www.ibike.org/education/teaching-kids.htm.

While most kids learn to ride a bike in a matter of days, be prepared to go a lot slower. One study that used positive behavior support (another term for ABA) to teach a nine-year-old boy with Asperger syndrome and an unhappy history of learning this skill gave it sixty-four teaching sessions over about three months.

If That Doesn't Work . . .

Consider attending a bicycle riding program. Some are offered by local organizations. The best known is Lose the Training Wheels, a nonprofit organization that runs a five-day program with about an hour's worth of instruction by specially trained professionals and volunteers. About 85 percent of participants learn to ride by the end of the five-day camp, during which special rollers are attached to the back of the bike and gradually changed to shift more of the balancing work to the child. Check its schedule to see if the program will be coming to your area: www.losethetrainingwheels.org.

A FINAL WORD

When you have that rough day or your child walks away from your teaching time frustrated, angry, or defeated, please don't give up. Yes, you and your child are in this thing together for the long haul. But never forget that you know things about what he will need to get where he wants—and deserves—to go in life that he may not yet fully appreciate. Certainly, there are things about having an ASD we can never change, nor should we want to. But think carefully and critically before giving in to the idea that whatever your child cannot do today is "because he has [fill in the blanks]" or "she just can't learn."

Though we've reached the end of the book, I hope this is only the beginning for you to continue teaching your child essential skills for independence. As I said before, adaptive behavior skills encompass the universe of our daily activities and every intellectual, emotional, and social resource we rely on to lead independent successful lives. At www.pattyrbashe.com, you will find more tips, forms, and helpful information. Teaching your child to negotiate the daily demands of living is the first step to building the emotional and social competence that will carry him through life.

PART III

The

Toolbox

Quick Tip: Using Velcro

There are two parts to any Velcro project: a surface on which an item (a picture, a check mark, and so forth) will be placed and removed repeatedly, and the item that gets moved.

There are two different Velcro textures: one is hard and loopy, the other is soft and cottony-looking.

Always affix the hard, loopy piece to the surface on which items will be attached. (If you have the hard, loopy stuff on pieces that are moved about, you will find them stuck to clothing, carpets, and furniture. They also pick up a lot of dust, hair, and other debris in their travels—yuck.)

Always affix the soft, cottony piece to the item that will be attached and removed repeatedly; we'll call this the moving piece.

To position Velcro so that your moving item aligns perfectly with the sticky surface, join a hard loopy piece to a soft cottony piece. Keep the plastic backing that covers the adhesive on both sides in place. If the pieces are not precut, cut them together now, so they are exactly the same size.

With the two pieces joined facing each other, position the soft cottony piece where you wish to place it on the moving item. If necessary, mark the position lightly. Carefully remove the plastic that covers the sticky adhesive backing the soft cottony side and press it into place.

At this point, the adhesive backing of the hard, loopy side is still protected by the plastic sheet. Carefully remove the plastic sheet backing and, with the two Velcro pieces still joined, position the moving item exactly where you would like it. Press firmly so that the adhesive on the hard, loopy side takes. Separate the pieces.

Scissors alert: the adhesive used on Velcro dries quickly to a sticky, gummy little blob. Designate a special pair of scissors that you will not use for anything else but cutting Velcro. Even these often get gummed up over time. You can wipe them down after each use with rubbing alcohol, which breaks up some of the gunk. Or you can cut your Velcro with an X-Acto knife instead.

Blank Forms and Templates

TASK ANALYSIS

Skill	
Goal	
Teaching Plan	

Step	Description
1	
2	
3	
4	
5	
6	
7	
8	
9	
10	
11	
12	

Notes

Start here, writing down a clear description of every step.

Task Components	Task Breakdown

Use this form to determine how much further you should break down the steps.

Task Components	Date	Date	Date	Date	Date	Date	Date
Task Breakdown/Analysis							
Independent (no prompts) Yes/No							
Percentage of steps independent (divide number of independent yeses by total)							

Independent, no assistance	Ind	Tactile prompt, shoulder	P Sh	Hand-over-hand	P HOH
Visual prompt	Visual	Tactile prompt, elbow	P El	Verbal, oral prompt	V/OR
Gestural prompt, nonverbal	Gest	Tactile prompt, wrist	P Wr	Verbal, oral with other prompt	V/OR +
Shadow	Shadow				

Step	Nontactile Prompts				Tactile Prompts				Verbal/Oral	
1	Ind	Visual	Gest	Shadow	P Sh	P EI	P Wr	P HOH	V/OR	V/OR +
2	Ind	Visual	Gest	Shadow	P Sh	P EI	P Wr	P HOH	V?OR	V/OR +
3	Ind	Visual	Gest	Shadow	P Sh	P EI	P Wr	P HOH	V/OR	V/OR +
4	Ind	Visual	Gest	Shadow	P Sh	P EI	P Wr	P HOH	V/OR	V/OR +·
5	Ind	Visual	Gest	Shadow	P Sh	P EI	P Wr	P HOH	V/OR	V/OR +
6	Ind	Visual	Gest	Shadow	P Sh	P EI	P Wr	P HOH	V/OR	V/OR +
7	Ind	Visual	Gest	Shadow	P Sh	P EI	P Wr	P HOH	V/OR	V/OR +
8	Ind	Visual	Gest	Shadow	P Sh	P EI	P Wr	P HOH	V/OR	V/OR +
9	Ind	Visual	Gest	Shadow	P Sh	P EI	P Wr	P HOH	V/OR	V/OR +
10	Ind	Visual	Gest	Shadow	P Sh	P EI	P Wr	P HOH	V/OR	V/OR +
11	Ind	Visual	Gest	Shadow	P Sh	P EI	P Wr	P HOH	V/OR	V/OR +
12	Ind	Visual	Gest	Shadow	P Sh	P EI	P Wr	P HOH	V/OR	V/OR +
13	Ind	Visual	Gest	Shadow	P Sh	P EI	P Wr	P HOH	V/OR	V/OR +
14	Ind	Visual	Gest	Shadow	P Sh	P EI	P Wr	P HOH	V/OR	V/OR +
15	Ind	Visual	Gest	Shadow	P Sh	P EI	P Wr	P HOH	V/OR	V/OR +
Number of steps at level										
Percentage of steps at level										

BASIC ONE STEP, OR A FEW STEPS

Task or Skill

Day	Date	Yes/No	Prompt	Notes
Monday				
Tuesday				
Wednesday				
Thursday				
Friday				
Saturday				
Sunday				
Percentage yes (divide yeses by total days)				
Percentage yes + independent (divide yeses that are independent by total days)				

BASIC ONE STEP, OR A FEW STEPS

Task or Skill										
Weekly Summary	Date	% Yes	% Independent	Notes						

BASIC TASK WITH MULTIPLE STEPS

Task or Skill				Notes
Day/Date	Yes/No	Prompt		
1.				
2.				
3.				
4.				
5.				
6.				
7.				
8.				
9.				
10.				
Percentage yes (divide yeses by total steps)				
Percentage yes + independent (divide yeses that are independent by total steps)				

Use one sheet per day to track progress.

Supplies for Running Teaching Programs

You can find the individual components of your teaching kit in office supply, crafts, and other stores. However, for one-stop shopping and a product line designed specifically to meet the needs of people using behaviorally based teaching programs, Different Roads to Learning is the place. Established and run by parents of a child on the spectrum, Different Roads to Learning has done the work of weeding through numerous products to offer not the widest selection but, in my opinion, the best.

Different Roads to Learning
www.difflearn.com
37 East 18th Street, 10th floor
New York, NY 10003

There are hundreds of teachers' supply stores out there, and they vary widely in terms of quality and service. Two of the best are Lakeshore, which serves teachers of both general and special education, and Super Duper, which focuses on supplies for teachers of children with special needs.

Lakeshore Learning Store
www.lakeshorelearning.com
2695 E. Dominguez St.
Carson, CA 90895

Super Duper Publications
www.superduperinc.com

The MotivAider is my personal favorite of my many teaching gadgets; I couldn't live without it. A square timer that vibrates silently and automatically resets for the desired interval, it's great for teaching self-monitoring and self-management, reminding, and helping kids develop a sense of time. True: it costs more than a regular kitchen timer, but it also does so much more. It also comes with a helpful booklet on using to help with self-management. The manufacturer's website has a great video demonstrating its use.

The MotivAider
http://habitchange.com
Behavioral Dynamics, Inc.
202 LaBree Avenue North
P.O. Box 66
Thief River Falls, MN 56701

The VibraLite is like a MotivAider except that it is a wristwatch that comes in a variety of styles and colors. Though the VibraLite is slightly more expensive and a bit more complicated to program, it has the advantage of serving as a watch and being more discreet than a timer. It can also be set to run multiple programs and sound at different times without resetting.

VibraLite
http://www.vibralite.com/
Global Assistive Devices, Inc.
1121 East Commercial Boulevard #39
Oakland Park, FL 33334

The Time Timer is widely available through suppliers listed above. Available in several different sizes, the classic Time Timer is like a countdown timer that uses a potent visual—the dial features a red section representing the time left that shrinks as the minute hand moves forward. While it may be effective to helping kids who have difficulty managing their time or are working at something where speed of completion is an important dimension of the task (for instance, getting ready for school), some kids just can't keep their eyes off the spectacle of the ever-shrinking red space. Great news, though: the company also makes the Time Timer available on watches, iPhone and iPod apps, and as software you can load onto a computer so that the countdown is always visible.

Time Timer
http://timetimer.com/
Time Timer LLC
7707 Camargo Road
Cincinnati, OH 45243

Timers in general are very useful. If you are only keeping straight time and do not need to worry about automatic reset, there are a number of timers available from outlets such as Amazon.com. A few tips on choosing the right timer:

- The timer must be able to count by seconds.
- Avoid the bulky, dial-style kitchen timer; not only is it usually pretty clunky, it counts only in minutes and often with an unnecessarily noisy ring.
- If possible, get a timer that can be clipped to clothing or a clipboard, or that has a magnet that can be attached to a metal surface.
- They are not easy to find, but well worth the hunt: small timers that can ring, vibrate, flash a light, do all three, or do any combination of them.
- Don't waste your money on gimmicks. When I got a timer that changed colors to signify "countdown status," from green through yellow to red when time was up, my son could not stop looking at it. Obviously, this interfered with him staying on task. After a few weeks, some little circuit in this overpriced timer must have blown, and now all the numbers on the screen look like they're in Klingon (and what self-respecting *Star Trek* fan could part with that?).

Basic Supplies
For Data Collection
    Pens, pencils, marker
    Forms (make your own or see Blank Forms and Templates)
    Clipboard or notebook
    Timer
    Handheld counter
    Graph paper

For Lists, Checklists, Instructions Posted

Prelaminated poster board sheets (available in different sizes from
Michael's and other crafts or office supply stores)

Permanent and dry-erase markers

Small laminated board

Velcro for lists with changing elements or instructions

For Activity Schedule Books

Small (7-by-9-inch) three-ring binder, preferably with "view" cover,
so you can change the cover

Small (approximately 6-by-8½-inch) top-loading plastic sheet
protectors with holes to fit small three-ring binder

Card-weight paper cut either to fit inside the plastic sheet
protectors or large enough to be hole-punched and bound
inside the book separately

Velcro to affix photos, tokens, and other objects to either the plastic
sheet protectors or the card stock pages

Note: you can use a piece of card stock to make a plastic sheet
protector stiff enough to support a picture or token affixed to it
with Velcro.

Acknowledgments

Thank you to everyone who supported, encouraged, taught, corrected, redirected, prompted, and guided me in the writing of this book.

First, I'd like to thank the families who participated in the "You're So Smart" surveys and offered their suggestions and questions, which helped shape the book. Further back, thanks to the OASIS (Online Asperger Syndrome Information and Support) website community, particularly the parents who responded to the first surveys. Thanks especially and always to OASIS website owner, founder, and my writing partner for *The OASIS Guide to Asperger Syndrome*, my friend Barbara Kirby.

Thank you to the experts who took the time to answer my questions and share their thoughts: Dr. Peter Gerhardt, Dr. Tony Attwood, Dr. Ami Klin, Dr. Jed Baker, Dr. James Snyder, and Dennis Debbaudt. In my training in applied behavior analysis, I could not imagine having had better teachers. At the Cody Center for Autism and Developmental Disabilities/Stony Brook University BCBA program, I thank Dr. Rene Chituk, Dr. Susan Milla, and Dr. Bobby Newman, all great teachers, mentors, and friends.

Although they were not directly involved, a number of colleagues offered me professional opportunities and support that made this project easier than it might have been. Thank you to my new family at the Cody Center: Dr. John Pomeroy, Dr. David Makowski, and most of all Dr. Ellen Woodward, who has been the right person at the right time more times than I can count.

My agent and friend Sarah Lazin still amazes me. I cannot imagine having this part of my career without her wisdom, guidance, and honesty. Thank you, Sarah!

When Crown first published *The OASIS Guide to Asperger Syndrome* in 2001, I knew the book had found a good home. All these years later, I am grateful for the house's ongoing support of that book and their enthusiasm for this one. Thanks to my current editor, Kate Kennedy, and her predecessors

Lindsay Orman and Jo Rodgers. As always, thanks to my first editor there, Betsy Rapaport, who took a chance.

Special thanks closer to home to our family for being there: my fabulous in-laws Robert and Rochelle Bashe, and sibs-in-law Danielle and Patrick Dill, Tasha and Ivan Karmel, and Michelle Assoian. Extra-extra-special thanks to my best friend, my sister Mary Kay Romanowski Vitro, and my nephew, Douglas Vitro. Shout outs to my other sis, Johnetta Romanowski, Jeff Bender, and Rick, Donna, and Dmitriy Romanowski, too.

Finally, to my husband, Phil, who makes everything—literally—possible: thank you, thank you, thank you. I love you. And to Justin, who every day both dazzles and humbles me with his strength, courage, humor, tolerance, intelligence, and determination: thank you for being who you are.

Notes

5   *"There is an enormous discrepancy"* Author interview with Dr. Ami Klin, June 2, 2010.

16 *"For me, a new chapter started"* Jerry Newport and Mary Newport, with Johnny Dodd, *Mozart and the Whale: An Asperger's Love Story* (New York: Touchstone, 2007), 58–59.

20 *Table: OASIS Preliminary Survey Results* and *Graph: Preliminary Survey* Based on informal survey conducted by the author. Participants were members of the OASIS (Online Asperger Syndrome Information and Support) website message board, 2007–08.

19 *"It becomes conspicuous to the peer group"* Author interview with Dr. Tony Attwood, July 18, 2010.

25 *While current statistics suggest 1 in 110 children* Centers for Disease Control and Prevention, Catherine Rice (corresponding author), "Prevalence of Autism Spectrum Disorders—Autism and Developmental Disabilities Monitoring Network, United States, 2006," *Morbidity and Mortality Weekly Report*, December 18, 2009, 1–20.

25 *One 2005 study estimated a prevalence of 9.5 per 10,000* S. Chakrabarti and Eric Fombonne, "Pervasive Developmental Disorders in Preschool Children: Confirmation of High Prevalence," *American Journal of Psychiatry* 162, no. 6 (2005): 1133–41.

25 *Asperger syndrome affects as many as 1 in 250* Ehlers and Gillberg estimated a prevalence between 1 in 210 and 1 and 280. S. Ehlers and Christopher Gillberg, "The Epidemiology of Asperger Syndrome: A Total Population Study," *Journal of Child Psychology and Psychiatry* 34 (1993): 1327–50.

25 *four times more common in boys than in girls* Tony Attwood, *The Complete Guide to Asperger's Syndrome* (London: Jessica Kingsley, 2007), 46.

27 *sometimes referred to as "atypical autism"* Peter Tanguay, "Pervasive Developmental Disorders: A Ten-Year Review," *Journal of the American Academy of Child and Adolescent Psychiatry* 39, no. 9 (Sept. 2000), 1079–95.

29 *"the drive to analyze and construct systems"* Simon Baron-Cohen, *Autism*

and Asperger Syndrome: The Facts (Oxford: Oxford University Press, 2008), 63.

30 *Motor clumsiness* Brenda Smith Myles, Jill Hudson, Jung Hyo Lee, Sheila M. Smith, Yu-Chi Chou, and Terri Cooper Swanson, "A Large-Scale Study of the Characteristics of Asperger Syndrome," *Education and Training in Developmental Disabilities* 42, no. 4 (2007): 448–59.

36 *"It is only natural and right to count"* Patricia Romanowski Bashe and Barbara L. Kirby, *The OASIS Guide to Asperger Syndrome* (New York: Crown, 2005), 58–59.

38 *"Quite often, standardized instruments testing cognitive and language functioning"* Ami Klin, Celine A. Saulnier, Sara S. Sparrow, Domenic V. Cicchetti, Fred R. Volkmar, and Catherine Lord, "Social and Communication Abilities and Disabilities in Higher Functioning Individuals with Autism Spectrum Disorders: The Vineland and the ADOS," *Journal of Autism and Developmental Disorders* 37 (2007): 748–59.

39 *One of the first studies, by Digby Tantam, in 1991* Digby Tantam, "Asperger Syndrome in Adulthood," in *Autism and Asperger Syndrome*, in Uta Frith ed. and trans., (Cambridge: Cambridge University Press, 1991), 147–83.

39 *In a well-regarded 2008 study, Mats Cederlund and colleagues followed* Mats Cederlund, Bibbi Hagberg, Eva Billstedt, I. Carina Gillberg, and Christopher Gillberg, "Asperger Syndrome and Autism: A Comparative Longitudinal Follow-Up Study More than 5 Years After Original Diagnosis," *Journal of Autism and Developmental Disorders* 38 (2008): 72–85.

39 *In fact, while IQ is usually associated with greater adaptive skills* Miriam Liss et al., "Predictors and Correlates of Adaptive Functioning in Children with Developmental Disorders," *Journal of Autism and Developmental Disorders* 31, no. 2 (2001): 219–30.

40 *"Placement in regular education may inadvertently widen the gap"* S. Williams White, L. Scahill, A. Klin, K. Koenig, and F. Volkmar, "Educational Placements and Service Use Patterns of Individuals with Autism Spectrum Disorders," *Journal of Autism and Developmental Disorders* 37 (2007): 1410.

40 *"Instruction in adaptive skills should in fact be intensified"* Ami Klin, Celine A. Saulnier, Sara S. Sparrow, Domenic V. Cicchetti, Fred R. Volkmar, and Catherine Lord, "Social and Communication Abilities and Disabilities in Higher Functioning Individuals with Autism Spectrum Disorders: The Vineland and the ADOS," 758.

40 *a finding Klin and colleagues describe as "worrisome"* Ibid., 759.

40 *"the need to prioritize adaptive skill instruction as its own goal"* Ibid.

40 *"only significant if they fail to exist"* Rick Lavoie, *It's So Hard to Be Your Friend* (New York: Simon and Schuster, 2005), 13.

41 *"Zero Order Skills are generally performed automatically"* Ibid., 16.

44 *"personal and social self-sufficiency in real-life situations"* Ami Klin, Sara S. Sparrow, Wendy D. Marans, Alice Carter, and Fred R. Volkmar, "Assessment Issues in Children and Adolescents with Asperger Syndrome," in Ami Klin, Fred Volkmar, and Sara Sparrow, eds., *Asperger Syndrome* (New York: Guilford Press, 2000), 316.

44 *Other considerations in determining what is adequate or appropriate* Heward, 2005 (via Gerhardt); E. Amanda Boutot and Brenda Smith Myles, *Autism Spectrum Disorders: Foundations, Characteristics, and Effective Strategies* (Upper Saddle River, NJ: Pearson, 2010), 6.

44 *"[the] ability to translate cognitive potential into real-life skills"* Klin, Saulnier, Sparrow, Cicchetti, Volkmar, and Lord, 748.

46 *A search of a major online professional database revealed* Gerhardt, "Bridges to Adulthood for Learners with Autism Spectrum Disorders," presentation, 2009, PowerPoint, slides 33–6.

47 *"learning by action"* Author interview with Dr. Ami Klin, June 2, 2010.

49 *"It pays to have one's eyes on the future"* Author interview with Dr. Ami Klin, June 2, 2010.

50 *they do not always recognize the true factors that brought about their success* G. P. Barnhill and B. Smith Myles (2001), "Attributional Style and Depression in Adolescents with Asperger Syndrome," *Journal of Positive Behavior Intervention* 3, no. 3: 175–82.

52 *Several studies have demonstrated some of the factors* E. Amanda Boutot, "Fitting In: Tips for Promoting Acceptance and Friendships for Students with Autism Spectrum Disorders in Inclusive Classrooms," *Intervention in School and Clinic* 42, no. 3 (2007): 156–61.

53 *"These children often show a surprising sensitivity"* Hans Asperger, "'Autistic Psychopathy' in Children," in Uta Frith, ed. and trans., *Autism and Asperger Syndrome* (Cambridge: Cambridge University Press, 1991), 48.

54 *Parents we polled for* The OASIS Guide Raw data from Zoomerang parent surveys completed in 1999–2000.

56 *One study found that* Ozonoff, Rogers, and Pennington (1991), cited in Sally Ozonoff and Elizabeth McMahon Griffith, "Neuropsychological Function and the External Validity of Asperger Syndrome," in Ami Klin, Sara Sparrow, and Fred Volkmar, eds., *Asperger Syndrome* (New York: Guilford Press, 2000), 86–87.

67 *"Structure is crucial"* Author interview with Dr. Tony Attwood, July 18, 2010.

70 *According to a recent study, children between the ages of six and twelve* Sue Shellenberger, "On the Virtues of Making Your Children Do the Dishes," *Wall Street Journal*, August 27, 2008, D1.

71 *"destroying their laundry"* Ibid.

83 *these findings are not accepted everywhere* Author interview with Dr. Ami Klin, June 2, 2010.

84 *"Imagine what your world would be like"* Simon Baron-Cohen, *Mindblindness: An Essay on Autism and Theory of Mind* (Cambridge, MA: MIT Press, 1995), 1.

88 *"the everyday tendency to process incoming information"* Francesca Happé, "The Weak Central Coherence Account of Autism," in Fred Volkmar, Rhea Paul, Ami Klin, and Donald Cohen, eds., *Handbook of Autism and Pervasive Developmental Disorders* (New York: John Wiley and Sons, 2005), 1:640.

89 *"People may fail to do something"* Author interview with Dr. Ami Klin, June 2, 2010.

94 *Performance in daily activities that require motor coordination* "Developmental Coordination Disorder," in *The Diagnostic and Statistical Manual of Mental Disorders*, 4th ed., text revision (Washington, DC: American Psychiatric Association, 2000), 58.

94 All *participants with AS also met the DSM diagnostic criteria* Dido Green, Anna L. Barnett, Leslie Henderson, Jorg Huber, and Sheila Henderson, "The Severity and Nature of Motor Impairment in Asperger's Syndrome: A Comparison with Specific Developmental Disorder of Motor Function," *Journal of Child Psychology and Psychiatry* 43, no. 5 (2002): 665–68.

95 *Both have poor gestural abilities, odd or mannered speech* Dido Green and Gillian Baird, "DCD and Overlapping Conditions," in David Sugden and March Chambers, eds., *Children with Developmental Coordination Disorder* (London and Philadelphia: Whurr Publishers, 2005), 114.

98 *"Imitation may be a core cognitive process"* Justin H. G. Williams, Gordon D. Waiter, Anne Gilchrist, David I. Perrett, Alison D. Murray, and Andrew Whiten, "Neural Mechanisms of Imitation and 'Mirror Neuron' Functioning in Autism Spectrum Disorder," *Neuropsychologia* 44 (2006): 610–21.

99 *"They mimic the movement but not the goals"* Author interview with Dr. Ami Klin, June 2, 2010.

102 *A 2006 study that compared* Adam Winsler, Beau Abar, Michael A. Feder, Christian D. Schunn, and David Alarcón Rubio, "Private Speech and Executive Functioning Among High-Functioning Children with Autism

Spectrum Disorders," *Journal of Autism and Developmental Disabilities* 37 (2007): 1617–35.

111 *According to Dr. Wilens, about 70 percent* Timothy E. Wilens, *Straight Talk About Psychiatric Medications for Kids*, 3rd ed. (New York: Guilford Press, 2009), 145.

112 *There are three types of ADHD* CHADD Facts, "The Disability Named AD/HD: An Overview of Attention-Deficit/Hyperactivity Disorder," online at www.chadd.org/facts/add_facts01.htm.

112 *anxiety disorders . . . affecting more than 19 million individuals yearly* National Institute of Mental Health, online at www.nimh.nih.gov/anxiety/anxiety/index.htm.

112 *Dr. Ami Klin describes children who* Author interview with Dr. Ami Klin, June 2, 2010.

113 *"that they feel they must complete"* Wilens, 180.

113 *up to one in four subjects with AS also had OCD* Ailsa J. Russell, David Mataix-Cols, Martin Anslon, and Declan G. M. Murphy, "Obsessions and Compulsions in Asperger Syndrome and High-functioning Autism," *British Journal of Psychiatry* 186 (2005): 527.

113 *OCD may involve behaviors . . . how one looks or feels physically* Ibid., 527.

114 *seizures occur in about one in four of those diagnosed with autism* Fred R. Volkmar and Ami Klin, "Issues in the Classification of Autism and Related Conditions," in Fred Volkmar, Rhea Paul, Ami Klin, and Donald Cohen, eds., *Handbook of Autism and Pervasive Developmental Disorders* (New York: John Wiley and Sons, 2005), 1:640, 7.

114 *Major depression—described as depression lasting more than two weeks* Wilens, 163.

115 *the prevalence of depression among individuals with AS is at least 50 percent* Simon Baron-Cohen, *Autism and Asperger Syndrome: The Facts* (Oxford: Oxford University Press, 2008), 98.

115 *"despondency, lack of motivation, and negativity"* Author interview with Dr. Ami Klin, June 2, 2010.

116 *"usually have an ongoing, continuous mood disturbance that is a mix"* Child and Adolescent Bipolar Foundation, online at www.bpkids.org; also see "About Pediatric Bipolar Disorder" (2010), also from the Child and Adolescent Bipolar Foundation.

116 *"very depressed but at the same time very agitated and out of control"* Wilens, 168.

117 *(coprolalia) is among the rarest of TS symptoms* Tourette Syndrome Association, online at www.tsa.org.

117 *About 15 percent of all children under eighteen experience tics* Wilens, 186.

118 *Between 5 percent and 15 percent of school-age children* Ibid.

119 *first documented in the* British Medical Journal *in 1896* Sally Shaywitz, *Overcoming Dyslexia* (New York: Alfred A. Knopf, 2003), 13.

119 *reading, writing, and spelling difficulties* Various fact sheets available from the International Dyslexia Association, online at www.interdys.org.

119 *responding appropriately to spoken language* Learning Disabilities Association of America (LDA) fact sheet "Dyslexia," available online at www.learning.com.

120 *Between 6 percent and 7 percent* David C. Geary, "Mathematical Difficulties: What We Know and Don't Know," online at www.ldonline.org/article/5881.

123 *"Although we are only talking about"* Caroline Cassels, "RSNA 2008: Imaging Study May Explain Language Delays in Autism," Medscape Medical News, online at www.medscape.com.

133 *"Parents have reached their use-by date"* Author interview with Dr. Tony Attwood, July 18, 2010.

133 *"What is it worth to them?"* Author interview with Dr. Peter Gerhardt, July 16, 2010.

149 *researchers helped a highly prompt-dependent nineteen-year-old man with Asperger syndrome* Kelly J. Bouxsein, Jeffrey H. Tiger, and Wayne W. Fisher, "A Comparison of General and Specific Instructions to Promote Task Engagement and Completion by a Young Man with Asperger Syndrome," *Journal of Applied Behavior Analysis* 41 (2008): 113–16.

154 *A seventeen-year-old young man with Asperger syndrome* Brenda Smith Myles, Heather Ferguson, and Taku Hagiwara, "Using a Personal Digital Assistant to Improve the Recording of Homework Assignments by an Adolescent with Asperger Syndrome," *Focus on Autism and Developmental Disabilities* 22, no. 2 (2007): 96–99.

154 *from a teacher standing some distance away* Gerhardt, "Bridges to Adulthood for Learners with Autism Spectrum Disorders," presentation, 2009, PowerPoint, slides 54–61.

168 *visual supports can be especially helpful for students who teachers and others assume* Linda Hodgdon, *Visual Strategies for Improving Communication: Practical Supports for School and Home* (Troy, MI: QuirkRoberts Publishing, 1995), 11.

176 *"share accurate information meaningfully and safely"* Carol Gray, *The Social Stories 10.0* (Jenison, MI: Jenison Public Schools, 2004); see also

Gray's *New Social Story Book, Revised and Expanded 10th Anniversary Edition* (Arlington, TX: Future Horizons, 2010).

188 *"The bulk of the work that needs to happen with our children"* Author interview with Dr. Ami Klin, June 2, 2010.

188 *"leveling the playing field"* James S. Rosenfeld, "Section 504 and IDEA: Basic Similarities and Differences," Wrightslaw, online at www.wrightslaw.com/advoc/articles/504_IDEA_Rosenfeld.html (accessed November 17, 2010).

192 *Certainly that is the view* Author interview with Dr. Ami Klin, June 2, 2010.

243 *"are often very good at criticism"* Author interview with Dr. Tony Attwood, July 18, 2010.

245 *"'It's easier to succeed by not trying than to try and keep failing'"* Author interview with Dr. Peter Gerhardt, July 16, 2010.

245 *tendency to overreact, to "catastrophize"* Author interview with Dr. Tony Attwood, July 18, 2010.

317 *"Play is the child's work"* Teresa Bolick, *Asperger Syndrome and Young Children* (Gloucester, MA: Fair Winds Press, 2004), 85.

318 *Dr. Tony Attwood offers some helpful suggestions* Tony Attwood, *The Complete Guide to Asperger's Syndrome* (London: Jessica Kingsley, 2007), 269.

318 *"If you have problems when you take them to sports"*: Author interview with Dr. Tony Attwood, July 18, 2010.

328 *One painful fall may put off a reluctant or anxious learner* Sheldon Brown, "Teaching Kids to Ride," online at www.sheldonbrown.com/teachride.com.

330 *One study that used positive behavior support* (another term for ABA) Michael J. Cameron, Robert L. Shapiro, and Susan A. Ainsleigh, "Bicycle Riding: Pedaling Made Possible Through Positive Behavioral Interventions," *Journal of Positive Behavior Interventions* 7, no. 3 (summer 2005): 153–58.

Aguirre, Sarah. "Age Appropriate Chore Charts." About.com. http://hous keeping.about.com (accessed July 20, 2010).

Alberto, Paul A., and Anne Troutman. *Applied Behavior Analysis for Teachers*. 6th edition. Upper Saddle River, NJ: Merrill Prentice Hall, 2003.

Allik, Hiie, Jan-Olov Larsson, and Hans Smedje. "Sleep Patterns of School-Age Children with Asperger Syndrome and High-Functioning Autism." *Journal of Autism and Developmental Disabilities* 36 (2006): 585–95.

American Academy of Pediatrics. *Caring for Your Baby and Young Child: Birth to Age 5*. Revised edition. Edited by Steven P. Shelov and Robert E. Hannemann. New York: Bantam, 1998.

American Psychiatric Association. *Diagnostic and Statistical Manual of Mental Disorders—Text Revision*. 4th edition. Washington, DC: American Psychiatric Association, 2000.

Anderson, Stephen R., Amy L. Jablonski, Marcus L. Thomeer, and Vicki Madaus Knapp. *Self-Help Skills for People with Autism: A Systematic Teaching Approach*. Bethesda, MD: Woodbine House, 2007.

Asperger, Hans. "'Autistic Psychopathy' in Childhood." In *Autism and Asperger Syndrome*, 37–92. Edited and translated by Uta Frith. Cambridge: Cambridge University Press, 1991.

Attwood, Tony. *Asperger's Syndrome: A Guide for Parents and Professionals*. London: Jessica Kingsley, 1998.

———. *The Complete Guide to Asperger's Syndrome*. London: Jessica Kingsley, 2007.

Attwood, Tony, and Temple Grandin. *Asperger's and Girls*. Arlington, TX: Future Horizons, 2006.

Avikainen, Sari, Andreas Wohlschlager, Sasu Liuhanen, Ritva Hanninen, and Riitta Hari. "Impaired Mirror-Image Imitation in Asperger and High-Functioning Autistic Subjects." *Current Biology* 13 (February 2003): 339–41.

Bailey, Jon, and Mary Burch. *How to Think Like a Behavior Analyst*. Mahwah, NJ: Lawrence Erlbaum, 2006.

Barnhill, Gena P. "Outcomes in Adults with Asperger Syndrome." *Focus on Autism and Other Developmental Disabilities* 22, no. 2 (2007): 116–26.

Barnhill, Gena, and Brenda Smith Myles. "Attributional Style and Depression in Adolescents with Asperger Syndrome." *Journal of Positive Behavior Interventions* 3, no. 3 (2001): 175–82.

Baron-Cohen, Simon. *Mindblindness: An Essay on Autism and Theory of Mind.* Cambridge, MA: MIT Press, 1995.

———. *Autism and Asperger Syndrome: The Facts.* Oxford: Oxford University Press, 2008.

Binder, Carl. "Everybody Needs Fluency (PowerPoint)." Working Together Conference on Autism, New York, 2004.

Blakeslee, Sandra. "Cells That Read Minds." *New York Times*, January 10, 2006.

Bolick, Teresa. *Asperger Syndrome and Adolescence.* Gloucester, MA: Fair Winds Press, 2001, 2004.

———. *Asperger Syndrome and Young Children: Building Skills for the Real World.* Gloucester, MA: Fair Winds Press, 2004.

Boutot, E. Amanda. "Fitting In: Tips for Promoting Acceptance and Friendships for Students with Autism Spectrum Disorders in Inclusive Classrooms." *Intervention in School and Clinic* 42, no. 3 (2007): 156–61.

Boutot, E. Amanda, and Brenda Smith Myles. *Autism Spectrum Disorders: Foundations, Characteristics, and Effective Strategies.* Upper Saddle River, NJ: Pearson, 2011.

Bouxsein, Kelly J., Jeffrey H. Tiger, and Wayne W. Fisher. "A Comparison of General and Specific Instructions to Promote Task Engagement and Completion by a Young Man with Asperger Syndrome." *Journal of Applied Behavior Analysis* 41 (2008): 113–16.

Brobst, Jennifer B., James R. Clopton, and Susan S. Hendrick. "Parenting Children with Autism: The Couple's Relationship." *Focus on Autism and Other Developmental Disabilities* 24, no. 1 (March 2009): 38–49.

Brown, Sheldon, and John Allen. "Teaching Kids to Ride." 2010. www.sheldon brown.com/teachride.html (accessed September 25, 2010).

Cameron, Michael J., Robert L. Shapiro, and Susan A. Ainsleigh. "Bicycle Riding: Pedaling Made Possible Through Positive Behavioral Interventions." *Journal of Positive Behavior Interventions* 7, no. 3 (summer 2005): 153–58.

Campbell, Jeff. *Speed Cleaning.* New York: Dell, 1991.

Carey, Benedict. "Childhood: Autism Diagnoses Rising, US Reports." *New York Times*, October 6, 2009.

Cassels, Caroline. "Medscape Medical News: RSNA 2008: Imaging Study

May Explain Language Delays in Autism." www.medscape.com. December 2, 2008 (accessed September 5, 2010).

Cederlund, Mats, Bibbi Hagberg, Eva Billstedt, I. Carina Gillberg, and Christopher Gillberg. "Asperger Syndrome and Autism: A Comparative Longitudinal Follow-Up Study More than 5 Years After Original Diagnosis." *Journal of Autism and Developmental Disorders* 38 (2008): 72–85.

Centers for Disease Control and Prevention, Catherine Rice (corresponding author). "Prevalence of Autism Spectrum Disorders—Autism and Developmental Disabilities Monitoring Network, United States, 2006." *Morbidity and Mortality Weekly Report* (Dec. 18, 2009): 1–20.

Chakrabarti, S., and Eric Fombonne. "Pervasive Developmental Disorders in Preschool Children: Confirmation of High Prevalence." *American Journal of Psychiatry* 162, no. 6 (2005): 1133–41.

"Child Development Chart." The Parent Guru. 2008. http:/www.ask-nanny .com/child-development.html (accessed September 9, 2009).

Chores-Help-Kids.com. 2005–6. http://www.chore-help-kids.com (accessed July 20, 2010).

Cohen, Marlene J., and Donna L. Sloan. *Visual Supports for People with Autism*. Edited by Sandra L. Harris. Bethesda, MD: Woodbine House, 2007.

Council for Exceptional Children. "Improving Executive Function Skills— An Innovative Strategy That May Enhance Learning for All Children." Council for Exceptional Children. http://www.cec.sped.org (accessed January 5, 2009).

Dawson, Peg, and Richard Guare. *Executive Skills in Children and Adolescents*. New York: Guilford Press, 2004.

de Boer, Sonja R. *Successful Inclusion for Students with Autism: Grades PreK– 6*. San Francisco: Jossey-Bass, 2009.

Dingfelder, Sadie F. "Autism's Smoking Gun?" APA (American Psychological Association) Online. October 2005. http://www.apa.org/monitor/oct05/ autism.html (accessed July 15, 2009).

Ehlers, S., and Christopher Gillberg. "The Epidemiology of Asperger Syndrome: A Total Population Study." *Journal of Child Psychology and Psychiatry* 34 (1993): 1327–50.

Faherty, Catherine. *What Does It Mean to Me?: Structured Teaching Ideas for Home and School*. Arlington, TX: Future Horizons, 2000.

Fein, Deborah, and Michelle A. Dunn. *Autism in Your Classroom: A General Educator's Guide to Students with Autism Spectrum Disorders*. Bethesda, MD: Woodbine House, 2007.

Feinstein, Adam. *A History of Autism: Conversations with the Pioneers*. Chichester, UK: Wiley-Blackwell, 2010.

Fombonne, Eric. "Epidemiological Surveys of Autism and Other Pervasive Developmental Disorders: An Update." *Journal of Autism and Developmental Disorders* 33, no. 4 (2003): 365–82.

Freitag, Christine M., Christina Kleser, Marc Schneider, and Alexander von Gontard. "Quantitative Assessment of Neuromotor Function in Adolescents with High Functioning Autism and Asperger Syndrome." *Journal of Autism and Developmental Disorders* 37 (2007): 948–59.

Frith, Uta. *Autism and Asperger Syndrome*. Cambridge: Cambridge University Press, 1991.

———. "Emanuel Miller Lecture: Confusions and Controversies About Asperger Syndrome." *Journal of Child Psychology and Psychiatry* 45, no. 4 (2004): 672–86.

Ganz, Jennifer. "Self-Monitoring Across Age and Ability Levels: Teaching Students to Implement Their Own Positive Behavioral Interventions." *Preventing School Failure* 53, no. 1 (2008): 39–48.

Geary, David C. "Mathematical Difficulties: What We Know and Don't Know." Online at www.ldonline.org/article/5881.

Goldberg, Donna, and Jennifer Zwiebel. *The Organized Student: Teaching Children the Skills for Success in School and Beyond*. New York: Fireside, 2005.

Grandin, Temple, and Kate Duffy. *Developing Talents: Careers for Individuals with Asperger Syndrome and High-Functioning Autism*. Shawnee Mission, KS: Autism Asperger Publishing, 2004.

Gray, Carol. *Social Stories 10.0*. Jenison, MI: Jenison Public Schools, 2004.

———. *The New Social Story Book*. Arlington, TX: Future Horizons, 2010.

Green, Dido, and Gillian Baird. "DCD and Overlapping Conditions." In David Sugden and Mary Chambers, eds., *Children with Developmental Coordination Disorder*, 93–118. London and Philadelphia: Whurr Publishers, 2005.

Green, Dido, Anna L. Barnett, Leslie Henderson, Jorg Huber, and Sheila E. Henderson. "The Severity and Nature of Motor Impairment in Asperger's Syndrome: A Comparison with Specific Developmental Disorder of Motor Function." *Journal of Child Psychology and Psychiatry* 43, no. 5 (2002): 665–68.

Greydanus, Donald E., and Philip Bashe. *Caring for Your Teenager*. New York: Bantam, 2003.

Hamilton, Jon. "Writing Study Ties Autism to Motor-Skill Problems." National Public Radio. November 11, 2009. www.npr.org/templates/story/story.php?storyId=120275194 (accessed November 13, 2009).

Happé, Francesca. "The Weak Central Coherence Account of Autism." In

Handbook of Autism and Pervasive Developmental Disorders, edited by Fred R. Volkmar, Rhea Paul, Ami Klin, and Donald Cohen, 1:640–49. New York: John Wiley and Sons, 2005.

Hippler, Kathrin, and Christian Klicpera. "A Retrospective Analysis of the Clinical Case Records of 'Autistic Psychopaths' Diagnosed by Hans Asperger and His Team at the University Children's Hospital, Vienna." *Philosophical Transactions of the Royal Society Series B* 358 (2003): 291–301.

Hodgdon, Linda. *Visual Strategies for Improving Communication: Practical Supports for School and Home*. Troy, MI: QuirkRoberts, 1995.

Howlin, Patricia. *Autism: Preparing for Adulthood*. London: Routledge, 1997.

————. "Outcomes in Autism Spectrum Disorders." In *Handbook of Autism and Pervasive Developmental Disorders*, edited by Fred R. Volkmar, Rhea Paul, Ami Klin, and Donald Cohen, 1:201–20. New York: John Wiley and Sons, 2005.

Iacoboni, Marco. *Mirroring People: The Science of Empathy and How We Connect with Others*. New York: Picador, 2009.

Iacoboni, Marco, and Mirella Dapretto. "The Mirror Neuron System and the Consequences of Its Dysfunction." *Nature* 7 (December 2006): 942–51.

Jansiewicz, Eva M., Melissa G. Goldberg, Craig J. Newshaffer, Martha B. Denckla, Rebecca Landa, and Stewart H. Mostofsky. "Motor Signs Distinguish Children with High Functioning Autism and Asperger's Syndrome from Controls." *Journal of Autism and Developmental Disorders* 36 (2006): 613–21.

Kalb, Claudia. "When Does Autism Start?" Newsweek.com. February 28, 2005. http://www.newsweek.com/id/48872 (accessed July 11, 2009).

Klin, Ami, James McPartland, and Fred R. Volkmar. "Asperger Syndrome." In *Handbook of Autism and Pervasive Developmental Disorders*, edited by Fred R. Volkmar, Rhea Paul, Ami Klin, and Donald Cohen, 1:88–125. New York: John Wiley and Sons, 2005.

Klin, Ami, David Pauls, Robert Schultz, and Fred Volkmar. "Three Diagnostic Approaches to Asperger Syndrome: Implications for Research." *Journal of Autism and Developmental Disorders* 35, no. 2 (April 2005): 221–34.

Klin, Ami, Celine A. Saulnier, Sara S. Sparrow, Domenic V. Cicchetti, Fred R. Volkmar, and Catherine Lord. "Social and Communication Abilities and Disabilities in Higher Functioning Individuals with Autism Spectrum Disorders: The Vineland and the ADOS." *Journal of Autism and Developmental Disorders* 37 (2007): 748–59.

Klin, Ami, Sara S. Sparrow, Wendy D. Marans, Alice Carter, and Fred R. Volkmar. "Assessment Issues in Children and Adolescents with Asperger

Syndrome." In *Asperger Syndrome,* edited by Ami Klin, Fred Volkmar, and Sara Sparrow, 309–39. New York: Guilford Press, 2000.

Klin, Ami, Fred R. Volkmar, and Sara S. Sparrow. *Asperger Syndrome.* New York: Guilford Press, 2000.

Kogan, Michael D., et al. "Prevalence of Parent-Reported Diagnosis of Autism Spectrum Disorders Among Children in the US, 2007." *Pediatrics: Official Journal of the American Academy of Pediatrics.* October 5, 2009. doi: 10.1542/peds.2009-1552 (accessed October 7, 2009).

Kubina, Richard M., and Pamela Wolfe. "Potential Applications of Behavioral Fluency for Students with Autism." *Exceptionality* 13, no. 1 (2005): 35–44.

Kurtz, Lisa A. *Understanding Motor Skills in Children with Dyspraxia, ADHD, Autism, and Other Learning Disabilties.* London: Jessica Kingsley, 2008.

Landy, Joanne M., and Keith R. Burridge. *Fundamental Motor Skills and Movement Activities for Young Children.* West Nyack, NY: Center for Applied Research in Education, 1999.

Lavoie, Rick. *It's So Much Work to Be Your Friend: Helping the Child with Learning Disabilities Find Social Success.* New York: Simon & Schuster, 2005.

Lee, Gloria K., et al. "Health-Related Quality of Life of Parents of Children with High-Functioning Autism Spectrum Disorders." *Focus on Autism and Other Developmental Disabilities* 24, no. 4 (December 2009): 227–39.

Lee, Hyo Jung, and Hye Ran Park. "An Integrated Literature Review on the Adaptive Behavior of Individuals with Asperger Syndrome." *Remedial and Special Education* 28, no. 3 (May/June 2997): 132–39.

Lee, Katherine. "Giving Kids Chores That Are Right for Their Age." About. com School-Age Children. 2010. http://www.childparenting.about.com/ (accessed July 20, 2010).

Liss, Miriam, et al. "Predictors and Correlates of Adapative Functioning in Children with Developmental Disorders." *Journal of Autism and Developmental Disorders* 31, no. 2 (2001): 219–30.

Mahler, Kelly J. *Hygiene and Related Behaviors for Children and Adolescents with Autism Spectrum and Related Disorders.* Shawnee Mission, KS: Autism Asperger Publishing, 2009.

Mannix, Darlene. *Life Skills Activities for Special Children.* Paramus, NJ: Center for Applied Research in Education, 1992.

Maurice, Catherine. *Let Me Hear Your Voice: A Family's Triumph over Autism.* New York: Fawcett Columbine, 1994.

Mazefsky, C. A., D. L. Williams, and N. J. Minshew. "Variability in Adaptive Behavior in Autism: Evidence for the Importance of Family History." *Journal of Abnormal Child Psychology* 36, no. 4 (May 2008): 591–99.

McClanahan, Lynn E., and Patricia J. Krantz. *Activity Schedules for Children with Autism: Teaching Independent Behavior.* Bethesda, MD: Woodbine House, 1999.

Meadan, Hedda, James W. Halle, and Aaron T. Ebata. "Families with Children Who Have Autism Spectrum Disorders: Stress and Support." *Exceptional Children* 77, no. 1 (2010): 7–36.

Meltzer, Lynn. *Executive Function in Education: From Theory to Practice.* New York: Guilford Press, 2007.

Miller-Kuhaneck, Heather, ed. *Autism: A Comprehensive Occupational Therapy Approach.* 2nd edition. Bethesda, MD: American Occupational Therapy Association Press, 2004.

Minshew, Nancy J., John A. Sweeney, Margaret L. Bauman, and Sara Jane Webb. "Neurologic Aspects of Autism." In *Handbook of Autism and Pervasive Developmental Disorders,* edited by Fred R. Volkmar, Rhea Paul, Ami Klin, and Donald Cohen, 1:473–518. New York: John Wiley and Sons, 2005.

National Research Council. *How People Learn: Brain, Mind, Experience, and School.* Washington, DC: National Academy Press, 2000.

NCLD. "Executive Function Fact Sheet." National Council for Learning Disabilities. http://www.ncld.org/content/view/865/391/ (accessed January 5, 2009).

Newport, Jerry, and Mary Newport with Johnny Dodd. *Mozart and the Whale: An Asperger's Love Story.* New York: Touchstone, 2007.

NICHCY, National Dissemination Center for Children with Disabilities. "A Parent's Guide: Finding Help for Young Children with Disabilities (Birth to 5)." NICHCY, National Dissemination Center for Children with Disabilities. August 1994, updated 2005. www.nichcy.org (accessed 2010).

Nichols, Shana, Gina Marie Moravcik, Samara Pulver Tetenbaum, and Liane Holliday Willey. *Girls Growing Up on the Autism Spectrum.* London: Jessica Kingsley, 2009.

Ogden, Cynthia, and Margaret Carroll. "Prevalence of Obesity Among Children and Adolescents: United States, Trends 1963–1965 Through 2007–2008." CDC National Center for Health Statistics, NCHS Health and Stats. June 2010.

Ozonoff, Sally, and Elizabeth McMahon Griffith. "Neuropsychological Function and the External Validity of Asperger Syndrome." In *Asperger Syndrome,* edited by Ami Klin, Sara Sparrow, and Fred Volkmar, 72–96. New York: Guilford Press, 2000.

Ozonoff, Sally, Mikle South, and Sally Provencal. "Executive Functions." In *Handbook of Autism and Pervasive Developmental Disorders*, edited by Fred R. Volkmar, Rhea Paul, Ami Klin, and Donald Cohen, 1:606–27. New York: John Wiley and Sons, 2005.

Paavonen, E. Julia, Kimmo Vehkalahti, Raija Vanhala, Lennart von Wendt, Taina Nieminen-von Wendt, and Eeva T. Aronen. "Sleep in Children with Asperger Syndrome." *Journal of Autism and Developmental Disorders*, 38 (2008): 41–51.

Parks, Stephanie. *Inside HELP: Hawaii Early Learning Profile: Administration and Reference Manual*. Palo Alto, CA: VORT, 2004.

Paul, Rhea, et al. "Adapative Behavior in Autism and Pervasive Developmental Disorder–Not Otherwise Specified: Microanalysis of Scores on the Vineland Adaptive Behavior Scales." *Journal of Autism and Developmental Disorders* 34, no. 2 (April 2004): 223–28.

Pennsylvania State University. "All by Myself: Self-Help Skills in Child Care." Penn State Better Kid Care Program. http://betterkidcare.pse .ued/angelunits/onehour/allbymyself/all%20by%20myselflessona.html (accessed September 9, 2009).

Pitterman, Cara. "Time for Chores." Scholastic. 2010. http://www2.scholastic .com (accessed July 20, 2010).

"Poll Results: At What Age Did Your Child Start to Ride a Bike without Training Wheels?" 2010. http://pediatrics.about.com/gi/pages/poll.htm? (accessed September 25, 2010).

Public Broadcasting System. "Social and Emotional Development." The Whole Child, ABCs of Child Care, Social. http://www.pbs.org/wholechild/abc/social (accessed September 9, 2009).

Rinehart, Nicole J., John L. Bradshaw, Avril V. Brereton, and Bruce J. Tonge. "Movement Preparation in High-Functioning Autism and Asperger Disorder: A Serial Choice Reaction Time Task Involving Motor Reprogramming." *Journal of Autism and Developmental Disorders*, 2001: 79–88.

Rinehart, Nicole J., Mark M. Bellgrove, Bruce J. Tonge, Avril V. Brereton, Debra Howells-Rankin, and John L. Bradshaw. "An Examination of Movement Kinematics in Young People with High-functioning Autism and Asperger's Disorder: Further Evidence for a Motor-Planning Deficit." *Journal of Autism and Developmental Disorders* 36 (2006): 757–67.

Rogers, Sally J., and Geraldine Dawson. *Early Start Denver Model for Young Children with Autism*. New York: Guilford Press, 2010.

Romanowski Bashe, Patricia A., and Barbara Kirby. *The OASIS Guide to Asperger Syndrome*. Revised edition. New York: Crown, 2005.

Rosenfeld, S. James. "Section 504 and IDEA: Basic Similarities and Differences." Wrightslaw.com. www.wrightslaw.com/advoc/articles/504_IDEA (accessed November 17, 2010).

Russell, Ailsa J., David Mataix-Cols, Martin Anslon, and Declan G. M. Murphy. "Obsessions and Compulsions in Asperger Syndrome and High-Functioning Autism." *British Journal of Psychiatry* 186 (2005): 525–28.

Savner, Jennifer L., and Brenda Smith Myles. *Making Visual Supports Work in the Home and Community.* Shawnee Mission, KS: Autism Asperger Publishing, 2000.

Schopler, Eric, Gary B. Mesibov, and Linda J. Kunce. *Asperger Syndrome or High-Functioning Autism?* New York: Plenum Press, 1998.

Shaywitz, Sally. *Overcoming Dyslexia.* New York: Alfred A. Knopf, 2003.

Shea, Victoria, and Gary B. Mesibov. "Adolescents and Adults with Autism." In *Handbook of Autism and Pervasive Developmental Disorders*, edited by Fred R. Volkmar, Rhea Paul, Ami Klin, and Donald Cohen, 1:288–311. New York: John Wiley and Sons, 2005.

Shellenberger, Sue. "On the Virtues of Making Your Children Do the Dishes." *Wall Street Journal*, August 27, 2008.

Shore, Stephen, ed. *Ask and Tell: Self-Advocacy and Disclosure for People on the Autism Spectrum.* Shawnee Mission, KS: Autism Asperger Publishing, 2004.

Sicile-Kira, Chantal. *Autism Life Skills: From Communication and Safety to Self-Esteem and More—10 Essential Abilities Every Child Needs and Deserves to Learn.* New York: Perigee, 2008.

Smith Myles, Brenda, Diane Adreon, and Jennifer Stella. *Asperger Syndrome and Adolescence: Practical Solutions for School Success.* Shawnee Mission, KS: Autism Asperger Publishing, 2001.

Smith Myles, Brenda, Heather Ferguson, and Taku Hagiwara. "Using a Personal Digital Assistant to Improve the Recording of Homework Assignments by an Adolescent with Asperger Syndrome." *Focus on Autism and Developmental Disabilities* 22, no. 2 (Summer 2007): 96–99.

Smith Myles, Brenda, Jill Hudson, Jung Hyo Lee, Sheila M. Smith, Yu-Chi Chou, and Terri Cooper Swanson. "A Large-Scale Study of the Characteristics of Asperger Syndrome." *Education and Training in Developmental Disabilities* 42, no. 4 (2007): 448–59.

Smith Myles, Brenda, and Jack Southwick. *Asperger Syndrome and Difficult Moments: Practical Solutions for Tantrums, Rage, and Meltdowns.* Second edition. Shawnee Mission, KS: Autism Asperger Publishing, 2005.

Soorya, Latha V, Laura M. Arnstein, Jennifer Gillis, and Raymond G. Romanczyk. "An Overview of Imitation Skills in Autism: Implications for Practice." *The Behavior Analyst Today* 4, no. 2 (2003): 114–23.

South, Mikle, Sally Ozonoff, and William M. McMahon. "Repetitive Behavior Profiles in Asperger Syndrome and High-Functioning Autism." *Journal of Autism and Developmental Disorders* 35, no. 2 (April 2005): 145–58.

Spencer, Vicky G., and Cynthia G. Simpson. *Teaching Children with Autism in the General Education Classroom*. Waco, TX: Prufrock, 2009.

Stieglitz Ham, Heidi, Martin Corley, Rajendran Gnanathusharan, Jean Carletta, and Sara Swanson. "Brief Report: Imitation of Meaningless Gestures in Individuals with Asperger Syndrome and High-Functioning Autism." *Journal of Autism and Developmental Disorders* 28, no. 3, 2007.

Stoddart, Kevin P. *Children, Youth and Adults with Asperger Syndrome: Integrating Multiple Perspectives*. London: Jessica Kingsley, 2005.

Stuart, Annie. "Health and Parenting." WebMD. 2008. http://www.webmd.com/parenting/features/chores-for-children (accessed July 20, 2010).

Sutton, Nina. *Bettelheim: A Life and a Legacy*. Translated by David Sharp. New York: Westview Press, 1996.

Szatmari, P., S. E. Bryson, M. H. Boyle, D. L. Streiner, and E. Duku. "Predictors of Outcome Among High Functioning Children with Autism and Asperger Syndrome." *Journal of Child Psychology and Psychiatry* 44, no. 4 (2003): 520–28.

Tanguay, Peter. "Pervasive Developmental Disorders: A Ten-Year Review." *Journal of the American Academy of Child and Adolescent Psychiatry* 39, no. 9 (Sept. 2000): 1079–95.

Tantam, Digby. "Asperger Syndrome in Adulthood." In *Autism and Asperger Syndrome*, edited by Uta Frith, 147–83. Cambridge: Cambridge University Press, 1991.

Thede, Linda L., and Frederick L. Coolidge. "Psychological and Neurobehavioral Comparisons of Children with Asperger's Disorder versus High-Functioning Autism." *Journal of Autism and Developmental Disorders* 37 (2007): 847–54.

Thorwarth Bruey, Carolyn, and Mary Beth Urban. *The Autism Transition Guide*. Bethesda, MD: Woodbine Press, 2009.

Towbin, Kenneth E. "Pervasive Developmental Disorder Not Otherwise Specified." In *Handbook of Autism and Pervasive Developmental Disorders*, edited by Fred R. Volkmar, Rhea Paul, Ami Klin, and Donald Cohen, 1:165–200. New York: John Wiley and Sons, 2005.

Vargas, Julie S. *Behavior Analysis for Effective Teaching*. New York: Routledge, 2009.

Verte, Sylvie, Hilde M. Geurts, Herbert Roeyers, Jaap Oosterlaan, and Joseph A. Sergeant. "Executive Functioning in Children with an Autism Spectrum Disorder: Can We Differentiate Within the Spectrum?" *Journal of Autism and Developmental Disorders* 36, no. 3 (April 2006): 351–72.

Volkmar, Fred R., Rhea Paul, Ami Klin, and Donald Cohen, eds. *Handbook of Autism and Pervasive Developmental Disorders.* 2 vols. Hoboken, NJ: John Wiley and Sons, 2005.

Volkmar, Fred R., and Ami Klin, "Issues in the Classification of Autism and Related Conditions" In Fred Volkmar, Rhea Paul, Ami Klin, and Donald Cohen, eds. *Handbook of Autism and Pervasive Developmental Disorders.* Hoboken, NJ: John Wiley and Sons, 2005. 1:5–41.

Wallis, Claudia. "A Powerful Identity, a Vanishing Diagnosis." *New York Times,* November 3, 2009.

Wiggins, Lisa D., Jon Baio, and Catherine Rice. "Examination of the Time Between First Evaluation and First Autism Spectrum Diagnosis in a Population-Based Sample." *Developmental and Behavioral Pediatrics* 27, no. 2 (April 2006): S79–S87.

Wilens, Timothy E. *Straight Talk About Psychiatric Medications for Kids.* Third edition. New York: Guilford Press, 2009.

Williams, Justin H. G., Gordon D. Waiter, Anne Gilchrist, David I. Perrett, Alison D. Murray, and Andrew Whiten. "Neural Mechanisms of Imitation and 'Mirror Neuron' Functioning in Autistic Spectrum Disorder." *Neuropsychologia* 44 (2006): 610–21.

Willliams White, Susan, Lawrence Scahill, Ami Klin, Kathleen Koenig, and Fred R. Volkmar. "Educational Placements and Service Use Patterns of Individuals with Autism Spectrum Disorders." *Journal of Autism and Developmental Disorders* 37 (2007): 1403–12.

Winerman, Lea. "The Mind's Mirror." APA (American Psychological Association) Online. October 2005. http://www.apa.org/monitor/oct05/mirror .html (accessed July 15, 2009).

Wing, Lorna. "Asperger's Syndrome: A Clinical Account." *Psychological Medicine* 11 (1981): 115–29.

———. "Reflections on Opening Pandora's Box." *Journal of Autism and Developmental Disorders,* April 2005: 197–203.

Winsler, Adam, Beau Abar, Michael A. Feder, Christian D. Schunn, and David Alarcón Rubio. "Private Speech and Executive Functioning Among High-Functioning Children with Autistic Spectrum Disorders." *Journal of Autism and Developmental Disorders* 37 (2007): 1617–35.

Wolman, David. "The Truth About Autism: Scientists Reconsider What They Think They Know." *Wired.* February 25, 2008. http://www.wired

.com/print/medtech/health/magazine/16-03/ff_autism (accessed July 11, 2009).

Wrobel, Mary. *Taking Care of Myself: A Healthy Hygiene, Puberty and Personal Curriculum for Young People with Autism*. Arlington, TX: Future Horizons, 2003.

Index

About the Author

Patricia Romanowski Bashe, MSEd., BCBA, is a Board Certified Behavior Analyst, certified special education teacher, and senior education specialist at the Cody Center for Autism and Developmental Disabilities at Stony Brook University, New York. She has taught individuals with ASD from early intervention through high school, and is a popular presenter on autism and related subjects. Mother of a wonderful young man with Asperger syndrome, she is also coauthor of the popular *OASIS Guide to Asperger Syndrome*, with Barbara Kirby (2001, revised 2005), which was recognized in 2007 by the New York State Association for Behavior Analysis (NYSABA) for its effective portrayal of ABA in the mass media. Before pursuing her career in education, she was an award-winning editor and writer of another twenty-three books that have nothing to do with autism but do include four national bestselling celebrity autobiographies, including *The Rolling Stone Encyclopedia of Rock & Roll* and *Temptations* (with Otis Williams), on which the Emmy-winning miniseries was based. She lives happily on Long Island with her husband, the author Philip Bashe, their son, Justin, and three cats who challenge her science-based approach to managing behavior daily. For more information, tips, and forms, visit her website: www.pattyrbashe.com.

COMPLETELY REVISED AND UPDATED

the OASIS GUIDE *to*
ASPERGER
SYNDROME

Advice, Support, Insight, *and* Inspiration

Including new information on:
• Diagnosis and evaluation
• Medication and therapies
• Social skills development

PATRICIA ROMANOWSKI BASHE, M.S.Ed.,
and BARBARA L. KIRBY,
founder of the OASIS Asperger Web site

FOREWORDS BY SIMON BARON-COHEN, Ph.D.,
and TONY ATTWOOD, Ph.D.

The Oasis Guide to Asperger Syndrome is a comprehensive resource for anyone guiding a child with AS through the challenges of growing up. Filled with practical information and emotional support, this is the most complete and authoritative guide available, written by authors who know firsthand the joys and challenges of raising a child with AS.

The OASIS Guide to Asperger Syndrome
$27.50, hardcover (Canada $39.95)
ISBN 978-1-4000-8152-3

Available wherever books are sold